Timeless Recipes
for All Occasions

Family Favourites by Jean Paré

Second Printing June 2006
Content originally published in *Millennium Edition*, 1999

Library and Archives Canada Cataloguing in Publication
Paré, Jean, date
Timeless recipes for all occasions: family favourites/by Jean Paré; foreword by Judy Schultz. – Rev. ed.
(Special occasion series)
(Company's Coming)
Includes bibliographical references and index.
ISBN 1-897069-05-7
1. Cookery. I. Title. II. Series: Paré, Jean, date- . Company's Coming series.
III. Series: Paré, Jean, date- . Special occasion series.
TX714.P358 2006   641.5   C2005-905772-6

Published by
Company's Coming Publishing Limited
2311 – 96 Street
Edmonton, Alberta, Canada T6N 1G3
Tel: 780-450-6223   Fax: 780-450-1857
www.companyscoming.com

Company's Coming is a registered trademark owned by Company's Coming Publishing Limited

Colour separations by Friesens, Altona, Manitoba, Canada
Printed in China

Front Cover

1. Berry Spectacular, page 100
2. Broccoli Salad, page 137
3. Bran Buns, page 45
4. Springtime Salad, page 141
5. Margo's Rosemary Chicken, page 85
6. Caramel Chocolate Squares, page 158
7. Chinese Chews, page 157
8. Parsley Pesto Pasta, page 113

We gratefully acknowledge the following suppliers for their generous support of our Test and Photography Kitchens:

Broil King Barbecues
Corelle®
Hamilton Beach® Canada
Lagostina®
Proctor Silex® Canada
Tupperware®

Our special thanks to the following businesses for providing props for photography:

Anchor Hocking Canada
Bombay Company
Call The Kettle Black
Cherison Enterprises Inc.
Chintz & Company
Dansk Gifts
Emile Henry
From Times Past Ltd. - Antiques & Interiors
La Cache
Le Gnome
Scona Clayworks
Stokes
The Basket House
The Bay
The Royal Doulton Store
Tile Town Ltd.

Special thanks to all staff who provided family heirloom pieces.

"Here's to the tastes and trends of today.
May they become our traditions of tomorrow."

"I would like to say a special thank you to my long-time friends in Vermilion
and area who shared their memories, recipes and old cookbooks
when I was doing the research for this book. These ladies are near and dear to me
and have been a source of support and inspiration for many years."

Jean Paré

Table of Contents

Foreword by Judy Schultz...............................6

Culinary Journey...8

Recipes

Appetizers..18

Beef 30

Bean Salad, page 137

Beverages...41

Breads & Quick Breads..................................45

Brunches & Lunches 52

Cakes...61

Candy & Snacks..75

Chicken..81

Condiments 91

Cookies..93

Fruit Shake, page 43

Peach Shake, page 42

Desserts 99

Fish & Seafood.................................108

Pasta 113

Pies 121

Pork 130

Salads 135

Soups......................................146

Squares 152

Vegetables 161

Garlic Dip, page 26

Final Thoughts by Jean Paré..........................166

Bibliography 167

Measurement Tables 168

Index 169

Chocolate Crisps, page 76

Foreword

The first time I saw a Jean Paré cookbook, it was over a cup of coffee in a friend's kitchen. We'd polished off a pineapple dessert that tasted like heaven, and she volunteered the recipe.

"Page 59," she said, handing me a blue, coil-bound cookbook: *150 Delicious Squares*. It was dog-eared, splashed and stained. Several pages hung at half-mast, including the memorable page 59, with Jean's recipe for pineapple-filled bars.

For the past quarter century, Jean's cookbooks have been standard equipment in thousands of kitchens. They've come to represent a slice of Canadian history that is tangible, pleasurable and edible. A huge chunk of our population can now identify Jean and her Company's Coming cookbooks on name recognition alone.

Fifty years from now, the name of any current politician or celebrity will be a distant memory, but Jean's recipe for hermits will still be relied upon to stock any well-filled cookie jar. Her career has been built upon the simple virtues of good food, prepared with love, for the people we care about most.

Hermits, page 97

As her biographer, I've spent considerable time with her over the past year, drinking an ocean of coffee and researching her fascinating history for *Jean Paré: An Appetite for Life*. During our many hours together, I've been struck by how the food we eat reflects our lives.

For instance, where were you in '62? If we knew what you were eating that year, we could probably figure out where you were geographically, socially and economically. Did your mother favour tuna casserole or lobster Newburg for her bridge club luncheon? When, if ever, did she serve smoked salmon?

Lobster Newburg, page 112

Your family's grocery list could even tell us something about how you worshipped. Did you eat fish on Friday? Was bacon on or off the menu? And when your cupboards began to feature rotini and radiatore pasta next to the elbow macaroni, did Italy seem a little closer, and your view of the world a little larger?

A flip through the pages of *Timeless Recipes for All Occasions* prompts questions like these even as it evokes heartwarming memories of the consoling taste of a warm cookie or the welcoming aroma of a chicken casserole. This book also speaks volumes about what was once seen as "women's work." The smell of fresh bread or the evocative scent of pickle relish cooking in the fall were clues to the life skills of those women who fed their families with food made from scratch.

As Jean talked about the evolution of her 100-plus cookbooks, it was like listening to a short course in Canadian history. The presence of certain dishes on the table, such as Shipwreck, for example, once revealed both the day of the week and something about the life and times of the cook. It was called a washday dinner, requiring only one dish that could look after itself while the cook was attending to more pressing matters. Considering the name, it may have had Maritime roots, but it was popular everywhere for its simple, always available ingredients: sliced potatoes, ground beef and a tin of tomato soup.

As I leaf through this book, my own prairie childhood tumbles off the pages. It fascinates me that Jean's recipe for hermit cookies is so familiar. They were our favourite drop cookie, but they belonged to the larger world of Ladies' Aid community cookbooks. Check out any church, in any small town in Canada, and you'll find a batch of hermit cookies.

The recipe for Jean's mother's cooked salad dressing was familiar too, but it had a different name in my family. Aunt Roma's boiled dressing, we called it. A jar of this mustard-flavoured, vinegar-spiked dressing was a staple in our fridge, and every cook in my family lived by the eleventh commandment: Thou shalt not make a potato salad or devil an egg unless you give it a spoonful of Roma's boiled dressing.

"It's an old recipe," Jean says thoughtfully. "Kind of tangy. I never make potato salad without it."

Neither do I—and legions of women are certain to have made their potato salads with that same dressing, long before it was published in any cookbook.

Canadians are bound together by a common heritage of food. While reflecting the past, Jean's ongoing series of

Jean Paré, Canada's most popular cookbook author

cookbooks also describes the present and future of food across this nation. As her cookbooks continue to roll off the presses, they frequently reveal a trend or identify a need. From the microwave oven to the slow cooker, from low-fat to reduced carbohydrates, they just keep coming. Today's trends, tomorrow's traditions—captured forever in one woman's legacy of good, ordinary food. It's Jean's gift for future generations.

Judy Schultz
author and food writer

Do You Remember?

*Here are some moments from the past 100 years
that will bring back memories for some
and give insight to others.*

1900–1909

Barrels of molasses and wheels of cheddar at the general store

First Canadian-produced milk powder

Baking powder made by the local druggist

Victor "talking machines"

Homemade yeast from hops

Machine-made ice cream cones

Jell-O becomes popular

Horseless carriages produced in Windsor (Ford) and Oshawa (McLaughlin)

Calories, protein, fat, carbohydrates and minerals identified and, along with water, considered the five basics for essential health. (Note: vitamins were still unknown)

Proper food and nutrition seen as treatment or cure, not as disease prevention

Turn of the Century

1900 Meatpacking, butter and cheese processing, bread baking and sugar refining among Canada's top 10 industries (all related to agriculture, whether cattle, dairy or crop)

Sugar spun into cotton candy

1901 Canada Fruit Marks Act—first Canadian food grading

1903 Canned tuna

1904 Burgers on a bun, ice cream cones, iced tea, popcorn, peanut butter and puffed rice all introduced at St. Louis World's Fair

Campbell's cans pork and beans; "Campbell's Kids" debut

Tea bag

America's first pizzeria in New York's "Little Italy"

1906 Kellogg's Corn Flakes

First graduates in nutrition and dietetics at University of Toronto

1907 Meat Inspection and Canned Food Act implemented for factories

Hershey's Kisses

1908 Dixie Cups

1909 Canada's first airplane flight at Baddeck, Nova Scotia

Culinary Journey

From the dawn of time, humans have sought to fulfill their basic need for food in ingenious ways. Prehistoric hunters designed spears and traps to capture their prey. Gatherers quickly learned to observe the experiences of other creatures before swallowing a bright berry or wriggling snail. Before long, farmers began to produce crops and raise livestock for themselves and the growing communities around them. Our quest for food has shaped not just what we put on our tables, but the way in which our societies have developed.

What food we eat, how we eat it, and with whom is a fascinating look back in history. Come with us as we journey through time, looking at the evolution of cooking methods, appliances and utensils. When did nutrition come into vogue? How has our increased knowledge of what foods do to our minds and bodies impacted our day-to-day food choices? And be sure to spend some time reading the "Do You Remember?" timelines. Did you realize that the Oreo cookie has been around since 1912? Do you remember when Neil Armstrong stepped foot on the moon? Enjoy these historical moments, social and culinary, as you leaf through *Timeless Recipes for All Occasions*.

The History of Nutrition and Food Guides

In Canada

Canada has had some form of nutrition guidelines for more than 50 years.

As you might expect, the guide we use today is a result of an evolutionary process, reflecting changes we have made to our eating habits and lifestyles over the years. It has also been influenced by the findings and implementations of food guides in the United States, which were written earlier. In addition, newer methods of food processing, storage and transportation, advances in knowledge of dietary requirements and nutrition education techniques, have meant constant updates to our nutrition guidelines.

1942

Wartime food rations and an economic recession, coupled with a physically active Canadian lifestyle, led to a country of people with relatively poor eating habits. It seemed necessary to develop a practical, easy-to-follow food guide, and so Canada's first nutrition guidelines were introduced, named *Canada's Official Food Rules*. In 1944, the name was changed to *Canada's Food Rules*.

1949

After the war, living standards began to rise in North America and western Europe. The public found themselves exercising less and eating more. Alarmingly, incidence of chronic degenerative diseases such as diabetes, heart disease and cancer began to rise. Although only a few years old, changes already had to be made to *Canada's Food Rules* to reflect the new dietary needs of a country in the midst of growth. This change, made in 1949, was just the first of many to come.

1910–1919

In Flanders Fields by Canadian poet John McCrae

First World War: 1914 – 1918

Jam made for the war effort

Oven temperature determined by how long piece of white paper took to turn brown

Canada's first commercial radio station broadcast—Montreal

First boxes of granulated sugar

Dietitians upset that toast and coffee considered a good breakfast by most people

Preserving with glass jars, rubber rings and metal screw-ring lids

Copper boiler used for boiling water bath container as well as for bathing

Cookies become firmer during the First World War so that they can be sent overseas

Tango and fox trot are popular dances

Band concerts, social debuts and fancy dinners in cities

Church picnics, baseball games and sleigh rides in rural communities

Pound cake—pound of sugar, pound of butter, pound of eggs and pound of flour

Wartime cake—eggless, milkless, butterless; kept well and transported well; used in both world wars

1910 5-cent chocolate bar

Heinz begins ketchup production in Leamington, Ontario

1911 Procter & Gamble develops hydrogenated vegetable shortening—Crisco

Electric skillets, grills, toasters and waffle irons introduced at New York Electric Exhibition

1912 Oreo cookie

Morton's free-flowing table salt introduced

Vitamins identified and added to list of dietary essentials

1915 Corning Pyrex

1918 Armistice ends First World War at the 11th hour of the 11th day of the 11th month

Canned Fruit and Vegetable Act introduces grading to commercial food-canning processes

1919 Canadian painters form the Group of Seven

The Great War

1920–1929

Honey and dried fruits, such as dates and raisins, were staple ingredients

Lemon curd popular for use in tarts, pies, as cake filling or for spreading on toast, scones or biscuits

Penny candy at the general store

Cream pies, molded desserts using gelatin or the new flavoured jelly powders, and rice, tapioca and sago basis for many desserts

Motion picture "talkies"

Chicken á la king in patty shells, Boston cream pie and Washington pie

The Edmonton Grads basketball team wins the first of 18 consecutive Underwood International Trophies

Oysters popular, especially at Christmas (for example, oyster stew)

Kraft processed cheese, and Rice Krispies

Refrigerators, wringer-washers, water heaters, toasters, vacuum cleaners available

More women working outside the home, particularly in journalism and politics

1920 League of Nations

Food and Drug Act to protect Canadians against health hazards and fraud from sale of food, drugs, cosmetics and medical devices

1921 Quaker Oats Company quick-cooking oatmeal (one of first "convenience" foods)

Betty Crocker "born"

Schooner Bluenose launched in Nova Scotia

1921 to 1926—Four more vitamins identified; cod liver oil recommended for children as vitamin D supplement

1922 Insulin discovered by Banting and Best

1923 Kellogg's develops "test kitchen"

1924 Popsicles

1925 Green Giant character appears

1928 Fleming discovers penicillin

1929 Canadian women legally declared "persons"

Wall Street stock market crash

1959

At this point the name of the guide was changed to *Canada's Food Guide*, to reflect the flexibility with which Canadians could apply the advice.

1977

By 1977, clear evidence showed a link between food habits and the risk of developing certain diseases. To combat this problem, scientists and health professionals wanted a guideline which would allow people to choose a diet that provided adequate protein, vitamins and minerals, and to control body weight and reduce the risk of developing nutrition-related problems. For the first time, the food groups were arranged around an image of a cheerful sun.

1982

In 1982, Health and Welfare Canada again made revisions to *Canada's Food Guide* and three major principles emerged:

1. variety in food choices and eating patterns;
2. moderation in the use of fat, sugar, salt and alcohol; and
3. balance between energy intake and energy expenditure.

1992

With more research on the Canadian diet, Health Canada released *Canada's Food Guide to Healthy Eating* in 1992. The look was new: instead of a ring of food groups around a sun, it was presented as a rainbow. The change was designed to encourage Canadians to recognize that they needed fewer portions from food groups such as meats and alternatives, and more from fruits, vegetables and grains. The guide's clear, simple messages promoted healthy eating in a general way. As this book goes to press, Health Canada is working on new guidelines to incorporate the diets of the many different cultures that now call Canada home.

The Roaring Twenties

In the United States

An official nutrition standard based on scientific information in the United States has existed for the past 100 years. Much of the nutrition of the first 50 years was impacted by the World Wars and the lack of food products, or the lack of money to purchase food wisely.

1941

The first *Recommended Dietary Allowances* was released, listing specific recommendations for calories and nine essential nutrients.

1943

The *Basic Seven* food guide was issued in 1943. It gave alternative food choices rather than recommending number of servings because of limited supplies of certain food during the war.

1946

The *Basic Seven* was revised to the *National Food Guide* and recommended number of servings. The complexity of determining serving sizes confused the public and led to revisions 10 years later.

1956

A new food guide was published that contained only four food groups. Its recommended number of servings was easier to understand. This more simplistic guide was the basis for American nutrition for over 20 years.

1977

Dietary Goals for the United States was issued, setting quantitative goals for intake of essential nutrients. It attempted to establish limits to avoid excessive food comsumption. However, its feasibility and accuracy were questioned and the new goals did not receive general support.

1980

It wasn't until 1980 that a set of guidelines was published, aimed at healthy Americans. *Dietary Guidelines for Americans* was based on up-to-date information and has been revised several times since then. Today's guidelines address the issues of body weight and fat intake. To help implement an education program in schools, the pyramid graphic was designed.

1930 – 1939

The Great Depression—frugal foods (macaroni, chipped beef, salmon loaf, meatloaf, casseroles)

Pasteurized milk available only in larger communities

Synthetics available—nylon, rayon and imitation rubber

Eggs highly valued; available to people on relief only if sick

Nutritionists advocate use of whole grain or lightly milled flours rather than refined (sound familiar?)

Lemons, bananas and oranges were luxury items, especially in the Prairies and Midwest

Shirley Temple sings "On the Good Ship Lollipop"

In the early 1930s, a reasonable and adequate diet for a family of five in Toronto was $7.65 per week

Horse-drawn delivery wagons for ice, bread and milk; milk bottles by back door with frozen "top hats"

The "boarding house reach"

Elbow macaroni, spaghetti and alphabet shapes for soup

Fèves au lard (pork and beans) often made with maple syrup in Quebec, otherwise made with molasses. Often baked overnight for Friday breakfast in Quebec, or soaked overnight in preparation for Saturday Night Special elsewhere

Yeast cakes (fresh or dry) used to make bread

1931 *Joy of Cooking* cookbook

1934 Alberta first province to grade creamy butter

Ritz crackers

Campbell's Chicken Noodle Soup and Cream of Mushroom Soup

Girl Scout Troop 129 in Philadelphia bake and sell first Girl Scout cookies to raise funds

1937 Kraft Dinner

1939 Start of Second World War

Banana bread recipes common in church cookbooks

Angel food cake, daffodil cake, sunshine cake

Dates Squares in the East, matrimonial cake in the West

Pressure cookers developed for military use but are soon used in homes

The Dirty Thirties

1940–1949

Proper diet helps keep men healthy for war service, and industrial production up, by preventing time lost through illness

Nutrition and health education introduced to schools

War Savings Stamps and Bonds

Prime rib roast—$1

Ganong's ribbon candy and chicken bones; Coke Floats

"Don't say bread, say McGavin's"

Spanish Rice, "creole" everything, tube steaks, canned salmon

Apple juice fortified with vitamin C; vitamin D added to evaporated milk to prevent rickets in children

Shipwreck one of first all-in-one casserole meals

Pressure cookers start cook-in-a-hurry pattern; pressure canners used for canning vegetables, meat and fish

Cabbage rolls bring Polish and Ukrainian influence into Canadian homes

Victory gardens help offset food shortages; pickling and preserving becomes even more popular

Jams and jellies produced for overseas as well as home; sugar rations increased for those who make jams and jellies

1940 Pre-cut, pre-packaged meats in cellophane

1942 Food rationing begins

Alaska Highway opens

1947 Oil strike at Leduc, Alberta

End of food rationing

1948 Vitamin B12 discovered

1949 Adding iodine to table salt becomes mandatory

Pillsbury's Grand National Recipe and Baking Contest, forerunner to its biennial Bake-off cooking and baking contest

Fast-rising granulated yeast replaces yeast cakes; faster straight dough method replaced sponge method

Fruit cakes keep well and travel well, so are used for overseas and weddings

Chiffon cakes from California

Icings made with corn syrup rather than rationed sugar

Second World War

The History of Cooking Appliances

Blender: The invention of the blender goes back to 1922. At the time, blenders were only used for bartending or for blending malts. In 1936, the blender was redesigned for domestic use. By 1955, they were produced in designer colours to get the attention of the housewife and to increase sales.

Bread Machine: The electric bread machine, which turned raw ingredients into hot cooked loaves, was invented in 1990.

Can Opener: The tin can was first introduced in 1810 in England. Unfortunately, there was no simple way to open it, so British soldiers resorted to using pocket knives, bayonets or their guns to open them. It wasn't until 1858 that the first can opener was invented and it did not gain widespread use because it was not yet safe. In 1925, a serrated rotation wheel was added. The electric can opener appeared in 1931.

Coffee Pot: It wasn't until 1800 that coffee preparation was made simpler by boiling ground beans in water until it smelled good, and then pouring the water through a filter. This was done in a French invention called a "biggin," which consisted of two slender metal containers separated by a plate containing holes, acting as a filter. The biggin was patented in America in 1873. In 1939, a heat-tempered glass chemistry pot was modified to include a top with a filter.

Dishwasher: In 1880, Josephine Cochrane was determined to invent a dishwasher because she was tired of her servants breaking expensive dishes. She came up with a design that worked best for hotels and restaurants, and patented it in 1886. By 1914, her company was offered smaller machines for the average American home. But at the time, hot water and electricity were not abundant, making the machines inefficient and impractical. In 1949, the first home electric dishwasher was introduced.

Food Processor: The first food processor was marketed in 1947. It was equipped with a juice squeezer, pasta wheel, flour mill, can opener, slicer, shredder, mixer, mincer, and centrifuge. In 1963, a model with a cylindrical tank and an inner knife revolving close to the bottom and walls quickly became popular with chefs. By 1973, food processors had better slicing and shredding discs and were safer. In 1977, half a million food processors were bought for Mother's Day in New York City alone.

Garbage Disposal: The garbage disposal arrived in home sinks in 1941.

Microwave Oven: In 1946, an engineer was testing a magnetron tube when he discovered that the chocolate bar in his pocket had melted. He was so intrigued that he placed a bag of popcorn kernels near the tube and, within minutes, the kernels were popping. He realized that microwaves created enough vibration within food that friction heat was produced and the food cooked, melted or heated. The first microwave oven was made for commercial use only. The first home model was introduced in 1955.

Outdoor Barbecue: It's almost impossible to accurately trace the history of outdoor cooking. The Louisiana Acadians and the Texans both claim to have introduced barbecuing into the American cuisine. According to the Acadians, the word barbecue comes from the French "barbe queue," meaning "from whiskers to tail" (meaning to cook the entire animal). The Texans give credit to the Spaniards who were the first to learn about barbecue cookery from the Carib Indians. The Indians smoke-dried fish, fowl and game on a green wood lattice over open fire or heated stones. The Spaniards named this lattice "barbacoa," which was later translated to "barbecue."

Oven: Until the late 1700s, a turnspit (the forerunner of the rotisserie) was the most valued tool in the kitchen. The spit was hand-cranked over the fire until the meat was done. A rope-and-pulley mechanism was added, which led to a drum-shaped wooden cage mounted on the wall. A small dog was locked in the cage and as the dog ran, the cage revolved and cranked the spit. Leonardo da Vinci invented a more humane, mechanical self-turning spit, powered by heat rising through the chimney. The first electric stove (a combination of oven and range) was invented in 1890. Heat control was a definite problem, making the unit unreliable. It wasn't until the 1920s that a heat-controlled range became a popular appliance in the kitchen. The first self-cleaning oven arrived in homes in 1963.

1950–1959

Second World War veterans' appetite for sushi, sukiyaki, pizza and beef Bourguignon heightens interest in foreign food

Chickens sold in "parts," but not a big market

Ottawa teenager Paul Anka sings "Diana"

Food stamps—Lucky Green, Pinky, Domino and Gold Bond

Polio epidemic

Weight control rather than weight reduction stressed; recognition that heart disease relates to diet

Jellied salads—chicken, ham, tuna, salmon, vegetables, fruit

Kraft Television Theatre

Fast and easy mixes for cakes and puddings

Rice Krispies squares; Nanaimo bars; Lipton onion soup dip; nuts and bolts, canned luncheon meats

Saddle shoes and circle skirts

Cream cheese indispensable for appetizers and cheese balls

North American version of Chinese food popular

Dr. Benjamin Spock

Outdoor barbecuing in summer; "oven barbecuing" in winter

1952 Dow produces Saran Wrap

Colonel Sanders franchises Kentucky Fried Chicken

1953 Vitamin A added to margarine; vitamin D added to milk

1954 Butterball self-basting turkeys

General Electric offers appliances in decorator colours

Swanson's frozen TV dinners

1955 Domestic microwave ovens produced

1956 U.S. Department of Agriculture reduces the Basic Seven food groups to four

1957 Saccharin arrives on tables in little pink packets

Soviet Union launches first satellite, Sputnik I

1959 St. Lawrence Seaway opens

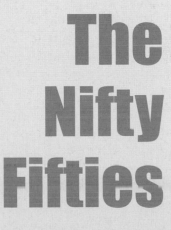

The Nifty Fifties

1960–1969

Uncooked freezer jam a popular recipe

Corning ware casseroles with cornflower pattern; Teflon

Obesity control even stronger; fad diets popular

The Twist; listening to the hi-fi

Back-to-nature movement— organic and health foods flourish; vegetarian and macrobiotic diets

Deluge of snack and nibbler recipes, including pâtés

Teased hair, beehives and white lipstick

Cheese fondue; spinach salad; brownies; frozen, ready-made pizzas

Italian-style main dishes (chicken cacciatore, lasagne)

"Gourmet" more common (stroganoff, sherry in sauces, wine in cooking)

No-knead or casserole breads a big hit

Cake mixes and pudding mixes only part of the recipe (dump cake, friendship cake, sex-in-a-pan)

Flaming desserts the rage (cherries jubilee, crêpes Suzette)

Cheesecake in many variations; parfait pies using jelly powder

Sweetened condensed milk popular ingredient in desserts

1960 Native women given right to vote in Canada

1963 Assassination of U.S. President John F. Kennedy

1964 Nachos introduced at Dallas State Fair

Chicken parts sales soar

Buffalo Chicken Wings created at bar in Buffalo, New York

Northern Dancer wins Kentucky Derby

1965 Canada adopts the red-and-white maple leaf flag

General Foods launches Tang

Pillsbury's "Poppin' Fresh" Dough Boy

1969 Neil Armstrong first man on the moon

Canada bans use of DDT

22% of food dollar spent away from home; concern by nutritionists about quality of fast food

the psychedelic years

Pressure Cooker: In 1679, a French inventor developed the steam digester, a machine consisting of a metal container with a safety valve and tightly fitting lid. Its function was to increase internal steam pressure, in turn raising the cooking liquid's boiling point. Although the idea was sound, the steam digester caused many accidents because of an unreliable safety valve. A safer pressure cooker was designed in 1810 on orders of French emperor Napoleon Bonaparte, who wanted preserved food available for his army troops.

Range (Stovetop): The concept of using a stovetop cooking method came in 1630 with the development of a large, metal, closed-top, coal-powered range. This unusual concept of cooking above an enclosed fire was slow to catch on because cooking time was slower than that of the turnspit. In 1802, a cast-iron, even-heating range with a modern flue was patented, as well as the gas range.

Refrigerator: Ice caves and ice chests were commonly used in the 1800s to keep food cold, but only for short periods of time because of the continual need to add more ice as it melted. The first refrigerator for domestic use was designed in 1882. It wasn't until the 1920s and '30s that a practical model became available.

Toaster: Toasting bread dates back to around 2600 B.C., when Egyptians used the method to slow the molding process. For over 4000 years, people throughout the world toasted their bread, like the Egyptians, over an open fire. In 1910, the first electric toaster was invented, but the bread had to be watched carefully and flipped manually from side to side. In 1919, springs and a variable timer were incorporated. The first pop-up toasters for use in the home were sold in 1926.

Slow Cooker: The electric slow cooker made its way into North American kitchens in 1971. Off to a good start, it declined in popularity until a huge resurgence in the 1990s.

Whistling Tea Kettle: A retired cookware executive from New York invented a tea kettle in 1921 that whistled when the water came to a boil.

The History of Cutlery and Other Kitchen Items

Aluminum Foil: R.S. Reynolds worked for his uncle's tobacco company in Kentucky. Loose tobacco needed to be tightly wrapped in thin sheets of tin and lead to keep out moisture. He started his own company in 1919, supplying tin-lead wraps to tobacco and candy manufacturers. In 1947, Reynolds developed paper-thin aluminum foil.

Bundt Pan: In 1950, a group of Minneapolis women asked the owner of Nordic Products if he could make an aluminum version of the cast-iron kugelhupf pan, common in Europe. Ten years later the *Good Housekeeping Cookbook* showed a pound cake that had been made in that pan, and a demand was suddenly created. The bundt pan became very popular after a bundt cake made the finals in the 1966 Pillsbury Bake-Off Contest.

Chopsticks: For centuries, the Chinese thought it was quite uncouth and barbaric to serve a large piece of meat that in any way resembled the original animal. Their philosophy was that food had to be diced, not at the table, but in the kitchen before it was served, which hints at the eating utensils required—chopsticks.

Fork: Prior to the invention of the fork, people ate with their hands. In the 1530s it was proper to use only three fingers of the hand to eat; using all five fingers was considered indecent. The word "fork" comes from the Latin word "furka," which is a farmer's pitch fork. Small examples of these ancient tools date back to the fourth millennium B.C., but were probably not used for tableware. Small dining forks date back to the eleventh century. It was not until the eighteenth century that the fork became fashionable.

1970–1979

One-half of adult Canadians overweight; new wave of health-conscious eating

Pocket calculators, tape cassettes, digital watches

Spicy cuisine abounds

Canadians discover yogurt

Microwave ovens in more and more households; cooking fish particularly popular

UPCs and scanners in stores

Tupperware parties

Roasting bags and cooking film; self-basting turkeys

Formulated foods (instant breakfasts, meal replacements)

Food presentation more important, and plates more colourful with larger borders

Quiche a luncheon favourite

PCBs, PVCs, mercury, asbestos, fluorocarbons —all big health issues

Sit-down dinner parties; influx of make-ahead recipes such as layered salads

Fancy drinks and liqueurs a part of home entertaining (Harvey Wallbanger cake, Brandy Alexander pie, grasshopper pie)

Carrot cake thought to be a healthy alternative to other desserts

1970 Canadian Metric Commission

1971 Salad bars arrive in restaurants

1972 Paul Henderson's series-winning "shot heard 'round the world" in Canada-Russia hockey tournament

1973 Cuisinart food processor unveiled at Chicago housewares show

1974 Recognition of impact of diet on cardiovascular disease

International Women's Year

French Quebec's official language

Per-serving calorie counts in cookbooks

1976 T. Eaton Co. ends mail-order catalogue

1977 Revised *Canada's Food Guide* has some 30 changes, including four food groups instead of five

1978 International Association of Culinary Professionals (IACP)

1979 Baby food manufacturers stop adding sugar and salt

The Diet Decade

The Yuppie Years

1980 – 1989

Fast-food chains sell 200 hamburgers per second in the U.S.

Garnishing an art form

Cabbage Patch Kids dolls

Array of international breads gain popularity (focaccia, crostini, pita, flatbreads, tortillas)

International appetizers take off—tapas, dips, hummus, nachos, caponata

Creative crêpes lead to new "wrappers"—tortillas, egg rolls, rice papers, pitas, frozen puff pastry, phyllo

Italian cooking continues with fresh basil, homemade pasta, pasta-making machines, pasta salads

Microwave cooking finally finds acceptance

Rice appears in more varieties (arborio, basmati, brown, wild)

Salad greens more varied—radicchio, Belgian endive, arugula, fresh herbs, edible flowers

Vinaigrette salad dressings use flavoured oils or olive oil; topping salad off with hot meat—chicken, shrimp

Salsas common chip dip; pesto shows up in pasta sauces, vinaigrettes

Stir-fry appeals to healthy eating trend—fast, flexible too

Mega-muffins

Zucchini garden overflow—recipes for every possible use

1980 "O Canada" replaces "God Save The Queen" as national anthem

1981 Jean Paré publishes first cookbook, Company's Coming *150 Delicious Squares*

U.S. Food and Drug Administration approves aspartame as artificial sweetener

1982 *Canada's Food Guide* revised again to stress variety, balance and moderation

Canada "brings home" the Constitution

1984 "Blackened" cooking has its beginnings

1988 Free Trade Agreement between Canada and U.S.

1989 U.S. pasta consumption soars to 18 lbs. per person annually

"Decadent" desserts (but served in smaller portions); designer desserts in upscale restaurants

Popular food and nutrition issues: reducing fat intake, cholesterol, oat bran, calcium, osteoporosis

Knife: The first stone knives were invented 1.5 million years ago in Africa and Asia, and were used for butchering prey. Knives have been an important part of our weaponry and cutlery. The word "knife" is from the Anglo-Saxon word "cnif." For many centuries a person owned just one knife. Only the nobility could afford separate knives for weapons and eating. Knives had pointed tips up until 1630 when the table knife became rounded for polite table practice. Only steak knives retained their pointed tips.

Non-Stick Coating: The world's first non-stick frying pan was invented in France in 1954, and had captured the American market by 1961.

Place Setting: Full place settings that included the fork, knife and spoon took ages to come together at the table. Around 200 years ago, most inns throughout North America and Europe served the meal with one or two of the utensils but never all three. Wealthy people often brought their own utensils when dining out. With the advent of the place setting came all the rules of table etiquette, such as which utensil to use for which food, how to set the table and where to place each utensil before, during and after eating.

Plastic Containers: In the 1930s, Earl Tupper had a dream of shaping plastics into various bowls and containers. His first invention, a 7-ounce (200 mL) plastic water glass, appeared in 1945. His next development was polyethylene bowls with snug-fitting lids. Tupperware Home Parties Inc. was formed in 1951 and the operation went on to become a multimillion-dollar business.

Pots and Pans: Cast-iron pots, invented in 1642, had a 1-quart (1 L) capacity, a coarse exterior, three legs and a lid. The first enamelled cast-iron pot, with the now-familiar shimmering white finish, appeared in 1778. In 1886, lightweight, durable and easy-to-clean cookware made of aluminum was produced. But it wasn't until 1903 when aluminum cookware became all the rage.

Spoon: The spoon was invented 20,000 years ago in Asia. Spoons of wood, ivory, stone and gold have been found in ancient Egyptian tombs. The name comes from the Anglo-Saxon word "spon." It grew to be a popular utensil for liquids. In Italy during the fifteenth century, spoons with a figure of an apostle on the handle were treasured, especially as a baptismal gift. But they were also expensive. Thus the saying, "a privileged child is born with a silver spoon in its mouth."

Stainless Steel Cutlery: Before the invention of stainless steel, forks, knives and spoons were made of a compound of carbon and steel which made them durable but incredibly hard to keep clean. They discoloured extremely quickly and required constant work to keep them shiny. The first stainless steel cutlery was produced in 1920.

Steel Wool Scouring Pads: In 1917, a San Francisco man sold aluminum cookware door to door, but found it hard to get into kitchens to demonstrate his product. He decided to offer a gift for every in-home demonstration. Knowing that the biggest frustration with cookware was when food stuck to pans, he developed square steel-wool pads which had been dipped into a soapy solution. They became such a success, he stopped selling pots and pans and spent all his time manufacturing soap pads. His wife named them SOS pads, which meant "save our saucepans."

1990 – 1999

North Americans obsess about amount of fat in food; learn to count fat grams and compute percentage of calories it provides

Electric bread machines a must-have

Food companies produce "low-fat" and "no-fat" dairy and dairy-type products

Fresh and organically grown foods are stressed

Cross-cultural cooking takes off; East-meets-West cuisine (spring rolls, noodle salads, curries, peanut dipping sauce, hot-and-sour soup)

Renewed interest in classic "comfort" foods—but streamlined

Mediterranean flavours more popular than ever (olive oils, Greek salads)

Fat-reduced baking products (often using honey in place of sugar, getting rid of added nuts, using part whole-grain flour)

1990 Blended fruit juices (fruit "smoothies") enriched with "healing" extracts debut in California

Health and Welfare Canada publishes *Canada's Guidelines for Healthy Eating*

1991 Canadians spend 31% of their food dollars in restaurants

1992 New guide called *Canada's Food Guide to Healthy Eating* places greater emphasis on grains, fruits and vegetables

1994 New Canadian food labelling laws go into effect

1995 Betty Crocker starts on-line hotline to answer cooks' questions

Pillsbury raises grand prize for Bake-Off cooking and baking contest to one million dollars

1996 A man wins the Pillsbury Bake-Off for first time

1997 100th anniversary of Jell-O

1999 Jean Paré publishes 50th cookbook title, Company's Coming *Low-Fat Pasta*

Baby Boomers Meet Generation X

Appetizers

Appetizers and finger foods became the fashion in the early twentieth century. Prior to then, they appeared more simply in the form of soup, seafood on the half shell and dainty, open-faced sandwiches. Cocktail appetizers evolved from free samples set out for patrons in public bars and from more people hosting home cocktail parties. In the late 1930s, the first catering shop opened, dedicated specifically to buffet and cocktail food. Today we wouldn't consider having a special get-together or party without a starter or two. Any of the hot and cold appetizers on the following pages will have friends and family gathering around for more.

Cheese Bites

Crispy on the outside—soft on the inside.
May be frozen untoasted. Bake an extra two minutes
from frozen state. Serve as is or with cocktail picks.

Hard margarine (or butter), softened	2 tbsp.	30 mL
Light salad dressing (or mayonnaise)	2 tbsp.	30 mL
Grated sharp Cheddar cheese	3/4 cup	175 mL
Finely grated onion	2 tbsp.	30 mL
Finely chopped pimiento	1 1/2 tsp.	7 mL
Cayenne pepper, sprinkle		
Sandwich loaf bread slices, crusts removed, flattened with rolling pin	8	8

Paprika, sprinkle (optional)

Mix first 6 ingredients in small bowl.

Spread each bread slice with about 1 tbsp. (15 mL) cheese mixture. Roll up like jelly roll.

Sprinkle with paprika. Place on ungreased baking sheet. Toast in 350°F (175°C) oven for about 10 minutes. Cuts into 4 pieces each. Makes 32 appetizers.

1 appetizer: 38 Calories; 1 g Protein; 2.1 g Total Fat; 3 g Carbohydrate; 65 mg Sodium; trace Dietary Fibre

Pictured on page 19.

Mushroom Turnovers, page 19

Top: Cheese Tarts, this page   Bottom: Cheese Bites, page 18

Mushroom Turnovers

Cute little duffers. A winner to be sure. These freeze well.

CREAM CHEESE PASTRY

Light cream cheese, softened	8 oz.	250 g
Hard margarine (or butter), softened	1/2 cup	125 mL
Milk	1/4 cup	60 mL
All-purpose flour	2 cups	500 mL
Salt	1/2 tsp.	2 mL

MUSHROOM FILLING

Canned sliced mushrooms, drained and chopped	10 oz.	284 mL
Finely chopped onion	1/2 cup	125 mL
Hard margarine (or butter)	2 tsp.	10 mL
Lemon juice	1 tsp.	5 mL
Seasoned salt	1/2 tsp.	2 mL
Salt	1/4 tsp.	1 mL
Pepper	1/4 tsp.	1 mL
Milk	1/2 cup	125 mL
All-purpose flour	4 tsp.	20 mL
Sherry (or alcohol-free sherry)	1 tbsp.	15 mL

Cream Cheese Pastry: Beat cream cheese and margarine well in medium bowl. Mix in milk, flour and salt. Shape into ball. Cover and chill for at least 1 hour.

Mushroom Filling: Sauté mushrooms and onion in margarine in non-stick frying pan until onion is soft.

Stir in lemon juice, seasoned salt, salt and pepper.

Gradually whisk milk into flour in small bowl until smooth. Add sherry. Stir into mushroom mixture until boiling and thickened. Cool thoroughly. Roll out dough about 1/8 inch (3 mm) thick. Cut into 3 inch (7.5 cm) rounds. Place 1 1/2 tsp. (7 mL) mushroom filling in centre of each. Moisten edge. Fold over. Press to seal. Arrange on ungreased baking sheet. Cut tiny slits in top of each. Bake in 425°F (220°C) oven for 11 to 13 minutes. Makes 48 turnovers.

1 turnover: 55 Calories; 1 g Protein; 3.2 g Total Fat; 5 g Carbohydrate; 147 mg Sodium; trace Dietary Fibre

Pictured on page 18.

Note: To freeze uncooked turnovers, place on baking sheet and freeze. Pack frozen turnovers in plastic containers. Bake from frozen state in 350°F (175°C) oven for 20 to 25 minutes until browned. If baked and frozen, heat in 325°F (160°C) oven for 15 to 20 minutes.

Cheese Tarts

Pastry appetizers always are the first to go. Make ahead, reheat and serve.

Grated medium Cheddar cheese (see Note)	1 cup	250 mL
Unbaked mini tart shells	24	24
Large egg, fork-beaten	1	1
Skim evaporated milk	1/2 cup	125 mL
Dill weed	1/2 tsp.	2 mL
Onion powder	1/4 tsp.	1 mL
Pepper	1/8 tsp.	0.5 mL

Divide cheese among tart shells.

Combine egg, evaporated milk, dill weed, onion powder and pepper in small bowl. Spoon over cheese. Bake in 350°F (175°C) oven for 20 to 25 minutes until set. Makes 24 tarts.

1 tart: 63 Calories; 2 g Protein; 4.2 g Total Fat; 4 g Carbohydrate; 83 mg Sodium; trace Dietary Fibre

Pictured on this page.

Note: Cheese and last 5 ingredients can be processed in blender and poured into each tart shell. Much faster.

> *"The whole family watched Bonanza on TV every Sunday evening and had hot chocolate and cinnamon toast."*
>
> Jean Paré

Mushroom Toasties

These hot appetizers go fast.

Hard margarine (or butter), softened	1/2 cup	125 mL
Light cream cheese, softened	4 oz.	125 g
Onion powder	1/4 tsp.	1 mL
Garlic salt	1/4 tsp.	1 mL
Canned sliced mushrooms, drained and chopped	10 oz.	284 mL
Chopped fresh chives (or 1 tsp., 5 mL, dried)	1 tbsp.	15 mL
White (or brown) bread slices, crusts removed, cut into 4 squares each	10	10

Beat margarine, cream cheese, onion powder and garlic salt together in medium bowl.

Add mushrooms and chives. Stir.

Arrange bread on broiler tray. Broil 1 side on top rack in oven until toasted. Turn bread over. Spread each square with 2 tsp. (10 mL) mushroom mixture. Broil on centre rack until bubbly hot. Makes 40 appetizers.

1 appetizer: 46 Calories; 1 g Protein; 3.2 g Total Fat; 4 g Carbohydrate; 114 mg Sodium; trace Dietary Fibre

Pictured on page 21.

Mushroom Canapés

Both creamy and cheesy. Serve hot.

Sausage meat	1/2 lb.	225 g
Chopped green onion	1/4 cup	60 mL
Light salad dressing (or mayonnaise)	3/4 cup	175 mL
Baguette slices	24	24
Fresh mushrooms, sliced	24	24
Grated medium Cheddar cheese	2 cups	500 mL
Paprika, sprinkle		

Scramble-fry sausage meat in non-stick frying pan. Drain well.

Add green onion and salad dressing. Stir.

Spread 1 tbsp. (15 mL) sausage mixture on each slice of baguette. Divide mushroom slices evenly over sausage mixture. Sprinkle generous 1 tbsp. (15 mL) cheese over mushroom slices. Sprinkle each canapé with paprika. Arrange on ungreased baking sheet. Bake in 350°F (175°C) oven for 20 minutes. Cool slightly. Makes 24 canapés.

1 canapé: 140 Calories; 5 g Protein; 7.5 g Total Fat; 13 g Carbohydrate; 268 mg Sodium; 1 g Dietary Fibre

Pictured on page 21.

> *"During the Second World War, if you had a wedding coming up in your family, you had to start saving your ration coupons in order to be able to feed a large group of 50 or so."*
>
> Jean Paré

Mushroom Surprise

There's a mushroom hiding in that biscuit! Then again, it might be an onion.

Refrigerator country-style biscuits (10 per tube)	12 oz.	340 g
Canned whole mushrooms, drained and liquid reserved	2 × 10 oz.	2 × 284 mL
Reserved mushroom liquid		
Grated Parmesan cheese	3/4 cup	175 mL

Cut each biscuit into quarters. Press and shape each piece into flat circle large enough to cover mushroom.

Pat mushrooms dry with paper towel. Wrap in biscuit rounds. Press around mushroom, pinching together to seal.

Place reserved mushroom liquid in small bowl. Place Parmesan cheese in separate small bowl. Dip 1 at a time into mushroom liquid then into cheese to coat. Arrange on greased baking sheet. Bake in 400°F (205°C) oven for about 10 minutes until browned. Makes 40 appetizers.

1 appetizer: 4 Calories; 2 g Protein; 1.2 g Total Fat; 4 g Carbohydrate; 141 mg Sodium; trace Dietary Fibre

Pictured on page 21.

Variation: For a different flavour, substitute finely grated commercial Cheddar cheese product for Parmesan cheese.

PICKLED ONION SURPRISE: Substitute pickled onions for mushrooms.

Top: Mushroom Toasties, this page
Centre: Mushroom Canapés, this page
Bottom: Mushroom Surprise, above

Guacamole Mold,
below

Guacamole Mold

Double duty. Use as a salad or as a spread for tortilla chips.

Envelopes unflavoured gelatin	2 x 1/4 oz.	2 x 7 g
Water	1/2 cup	125 mL
Lime juice	2 tbsp.	30 mL
Small ripe avocados, mashed smooth	3	3
Light sour cream	3/4 cup	175 mL
Light salad dressing (or mayonnaise)	1/3 cup	75 mL
Spicy salsa, run through blender	1/2 cup	125 mL
Salt	1/2 tsp.	2 mL
Garlic powder	1/4 tsp.	1 mL
Hot pepper sauce (optional)	1/8 tsp.	0.5 mL
Small cherry tomatoes, halved (optional)		

Sprinkle gelatin over water in small saucepan. Let stand for 1 minute. Heat and stir until gelatin is dissolved.

Whisk next 8 ingredients together in medium bowl. Stir in gelatin mixture.

If you have a 4 cup (1 L) mold with round indentations, place a cherry tomato half in each. Pour gelatin mixture over top. Chill for at least 2 1/2 hours before unmolding. If you don't have a mold with indentations, decorate top and sides with tomatoes after unmolding. Makes 4 cups (1 L) guacamole.

2 tbsp. (30 mL) guacamole: 45 Calories; 1 g Protein; 3.8 g Total Fat; 3 g Carbohydrate; 123 mg Sodium; 1 Dietary Fibre

Pictured above.

Teriyaki Chicken Wings

A tasty marinade produces these delicious wings.

Commercial teriyaki sauce	1/2 cup	125 mL
Liquid honey	1/4 cup	60 mL
Fancy molasses	1 tbsp.	15 mL
Lemon juice	1 tbsp.	15 mL
Small onion, chopped	1	1
Garlic cloves, minced (or 1/2 tsp., 2 mL, powder)	2	2
Grated fresh gingerroot	2 tsp.	10 mL
Dry mustard	1/2 tsp.	2 mL
Salt	1/2 tsp.	2 mL
Chicken drumettes (or whole chicken wings)	4 lbs.	1.8 kg

Stir first 9 ingredients in large bowl.

Add drumettes. If using whole wings, discard wing tips and cut wings apart at joint. Stir well. Cover. Refrigerate for 5 hours or overnight, stirring occasionally.

Line large baking sheet with greased foil. Arrange drumettes on foil. Bake in 375°F (190°C) oven for 20 to 30 minutes, turning wings at halftime, until glazed and tender. Makes about 32 drumettes or 48 wing pieces.

1 drumette (with skin): 83 Calories; 6 g Protein; 4.9 g Total Fat; 4 g Carbohydrate; 247 mg Sodium; trace Dietary Fibre

Pictured on page 23.

Chili Con Queso

Pronounced CHIH-lee kon KAY-soh. No need to go south of the border to enjoy this Mexican favourite. Serve with tortilla chips or raw vegetables.

Canned stewed tomatoes, with juice, broken up	14 oz.	398 mL
Chopped onion	1 cup	250 mL
Garlic powder (or 1 clove, minced)	1/4 tsp.	1 mL
Canned chopped green chilies, with liquid	4 oz.	114 mL
Process cheese loaf (such as Velveeta), cubed	1 lb.	454 g

Put first 4 ingredients into medium saucepan. Cook, uncovered, over medium until liquid is evaporated.

Add cheese. Stir over low until melted. Makes 4 cups (1 L) dip.

2 tbsp. (30 mL) dip: 51 Calories; 3 g Protein; 3.4 g Total Fat; 2 g Carbohydrate; 273 mg Sodium; trace Dietary Fibre

Pictured on page 23.

Sesame Wings

A nutty, buttery coating makes these irresistible. Serve hot.

Sesame seeds	1/2 cup	125 mL
Fine dry bread crumbs	1/2 cup	125 mL
Paprika	1 tsp.	5 mL
Salt	1 tsp.	5 mL
Garlic powder	1/4 tsp.	1 mL
Hard margarine (or butter), melted	1/2 cup	125 mL
Prepared mustard	1 tbsp.	15 mL
Chicken drumettes (or whole wings)	2 lbs.	900 g

Measure first 5 ingredients into small bowl. Mix well.

Stir margarine and mustard together in small dish.

Dip each drumette into margarine mixture, then into seed mixture to coat completely. If using whole wings, discard wing tips and cut wings apart at joint. Place on foil-lined baking sheet with sides. Bake in 350°F (175°C) oven for about 45 minutes until tender. Makes about 16 drumettes or 24 wing pieces.

1 drumette (with skin): 167 Calories; 7 g Protein; 13.9 g Total Fat; 3 g Carbohydrate; 304 mg Sodium; trace Dietary Fibre

Pictured below.

Jalapeño Pie

This has a fair bit of heat to it. Use the whole can of jalapeños if you dare. Serve warm.

Hard margarine (or butter)	2 tsp.	10 mL
Finely chopped onion	1 cup	250 mL
Canned jalapeño peppers, drained, seeded and chopped	1/2 × 4 oz.	1/2 × 114 mL
Grated sharp Cheddar cheese	2 cups	500 mL
Large eggs, fork-beaten	4	4
Salt	1/2 tsp.	2 mL
Garlic powder	1/4 tsp.	1 mL

Melt margarine in non-stick frying pan. Add onion. Sauté until soft.

Scatter onion, jalapeño peppers and cheese in greased 8 × 8 inch (20 × 20 cm) pan.

Combine eggs, salt and garlic powder in small bowl. Beat. Pour over top. Bake in 350°F (175°C) oven for about 30 minutes. Cuts into 25 squares.

1 square: 56 Calories; 3 g Protein; 4.3 g Total Fat; 1 g Carbohydrate; 140 mg Sodium; trace Dietary Fibre

Pictured below.

Left: Sesame Wings, above   Centre: Teriyaki Chicken Wings, page 22   Top right: Jalapeño Pie, above   Bottom right: Chili Con Queso, page 22

Mustard Ham Balls, below
Ginger-Sauced Meatballs, below
Cranberry Meatballs, page 25

Mustard Ham Balls

Serve hot with picks. Soft and glazed.
Good choice for any get-together.

Lean ham, ground	1 1/2 lbs.	680 g
Ground chicken	1/2 lb.	225 g
Milk	1/2 cup	125 mL
Large egg, fork-beaten	1	1
Seasoned salt	1/2 tsp.	2 mL
Salt	1/2 tsp.	2 mL
Dry bread crumbs	1 1/2 cups	375 mL
Brown sugar, packed	1 cup	250 mL
All-purpose flour	2 tsp.	10 mL
Dry mustard	2 tsp.	10 mL
White vinegar	1/2 cup	125 mL
Water	1/2 cup	125 mL
Prepared mustard	2 tsp.	10 mL

Mix first 7 ingredients in large bowl. Shape into 1 inch (2.5 cm) balls. Arrange on greased baking sheet. Bake in 400°F (205°C) oven for 15 minutes until firmed a bit and browned. Turn into ungreased 3 quart (3 L) casserole.

Stir brown sugar, flour and dry mustard together in small bowl. Stir in vinegar, water and prepared mustard. Pour over ham balls. Bake, uncovered, in 350°F (175°C) oven, basting 2 or 3 times with sauce, for about 45 minutes. Makes about 80 ham balls.

4 ham balls (with sauce): 144 Calories; 11 g Protein; 2.7 g Total Fat; 19 g Carbohydrate; 676 mg Sodium; trace Dietary Fibre

Pictured above.

Ginger-Sauced Meatballs

Easy to double for a crowd.

Lean ground beef	1/2 lb.	225 g
Lean ground pork	1/2 lb.	225 g
Milk	1/4 cup	60 mL
Large egg, fork-beaten	1	1
Dry bread crumbs	1 cup	250 mL
Worcestershire sauce	1 tsp.	5 mL
Onion flakes	1 tbsp.	15 mL
Salt	3/4 tsp.	4 mL
Pepper	1/4 tsp.	1 mL
Chili sauce	1 cup	250 mL
Water	3/4 cup	175 mL
Gingersnap cookie crumbs (about 10 cookies)	1 cup	250 mL

Combine first 9 ingredients in large bowl. Mix well. Shape into 1 inch (2.5 cm) balls. Arrange on greased baking sheet. Bake in 375°F (190°C) oven for 15 minutes until cooked through. Makes 40 meatballs.

Stir chili sauce and water together in small saucepan. Add cookie crumbs. Heat, stirring often, until simmering. Simmer for about 1 minute. Makes 2 cups (500 mL) sauce. Serve over meatballs.

3 meatballs with sauce: 123 Calories; 9 g Protein; 4.5 g Total Fat; 11 g Carbohydrate; 381 mg Sodium; 1 g Dietary Fibre

Pictured above.

Zucchini Treats, below

Cranberry Meatballs

Meatballs dressed up with an exceptionally good sauce.

Large eggs, fork-beaten	2	2
Soy sauce	2 tbsp.	30 mL
Finely chopped onion	1/2 cup	125 mL
Parsley flakes	1 tbsp.	15 mL
Garlic powder (or 2 cloves, minced)	1/2 tsp.	2 mL
Corn flake crumbs	1 cup	250 mL
Salt	2 tsp.	10 mL
Pepper	1/2 tsp.	2 mL
Lean ground beef	2 lbs.	900 g
Canned cranberry sauce	14 oz.	398 mL
Chili sauce	1/2 cup	125 mL
Ketchup	1/2 cup	125 mL
Brown sugar, packed	2 tbsp.	30 mL
White vinegar	1 tbsp.	15 mL

Mix first 8 ingredients in large bowl.

Add ground beef. Mix well. Shape into 1 inch (2.5 cm) balls. Arrange in greased 3 quart (3 L) casserole.

Mix remaining 5 ingredients in small bowl. Pour over meatballs. Bake, uncovered, in 350°F (175°C) oven for 45 minutes. Makes 80 meatballs.

4 meatballs (with sauce): 182 Calories; 10 g Protein; 7.4 g Total Fat; 19 g Carbohydrate; 650 mg Sodium; 1 g Dietary Fibre

Pictured on pages 24/25.

Zucchini Treats

Parmesan cheese gives this its really good flavour. Cut larger squares if you like.

Large eggs, fork-beaten	4	4
Finely chopped onion	1/2 cup	125 mL
Cooking oil	1/2 cup	125 mL
Parsley flakes	1 tsp.	5 mL
Salt	1/2 tsp.	2 mL
Celery salt	1/2 tsp.	2 mL
Dried whole oregano	1/2 tsp	2 mL
Garlic powder	1/4 tsp.	1 mL
Grated Parmesan cheese	1/2 cup	125 mL
Biscuit mix	1 cup	250 mL
Thinly sliced zucchini, with peel	3 1/2 cups	875 mL
Grated Parmesan cheese	1/4 cup	60 mL

Combine first 9 ingredients in medium bowl. Beat well.

Stir in biscuit mix and zucchini. Turn into greased 9 x 13 inch (22 x 33 cm) pan.

Sprinkle with second amount of Parmesan cheese. Bake in 350°F (175°C) oven for about 30 minutes until browned. Cuts into 54 squares.

1 square: 44 Calories; 1 g Protein; 3.3 g Total Fat; 2 g Carbohydrate; 103 mg Sodium; trace Dietary Fibre

Pictured above.

Laurier Lake "Shrimp"

A great imitation since there weren't any shrimp in Laurier Lake, near where I grew up. Not only works as an appetizer but also for a meal. Even good cold. Serve with seafood sauce.

Pancake mix	2 cups	500 mL
Large egg, fork-beaten	1	1
Cooking oil	1 tbsp.	15 mL
Beer	3/4 cup	175 mL
Milk	1/4 cup	60 mL
Salt	1 tsp.	5 mL

Fish fillets, cut into 1 inch (2.5 cm) squares
Oil, for deep-frying

Stir pancake mix, egg, cooking oil, beer, milk and salt in medium bowl until smooth.

Dip a few fish pieces into batter. Drop carefully into 375°F (190°C) hot oil. Cook for about 2 minutes until browned. Remove with slotted spoon to paper towel-lined baking sheet. Keep warm in 200°F (95°C) oven while cooking remaining fish. Makes 4 cups (1 L), or about 30 appetizers.

1 appetizer: 78 Calories; 7 g Protein; 2 g Total Fat; 8 g Carbohydrate; 255 mg Sodium; trace Dietary Fibre

Garlic Dip

Make in the morning or up to two days ahead and keep refrigerated. Serve with an assortment of raw vegetables.

Light salad dressing (or mayonnaise)	3/4 cup	175 mL
Non-fat sour cream	1/4 cup	60 mL
Garlic cloves, minced (or 3/4 tsp., 4 mL, powder)	3	3
Parsley flakes	2 tsp.	10 mL
Lemon juice	1 tsp.	5 mL

Stir all 5 ingredients together in small bowl. Cover. Chill well. Makes 1 cup (250 mL) dip.

1 tbsp. (15 mL) dip: 34 Calories; trace Protein; 2.9 g Total Fat; 2 g Carbohydrate; 88 mg Sodium; trace Dietary Fibre

Pictured below.

Relish Cheese Ball, page 27   Cuke Spread 'R Dip, below

Garlic Dip

Cuke Spread 'R Dip

This needs to be made ahead and refrigerated for at least two hours. It is thick enough to serve as a spread with small, dark, cocktail-size bread slices, or as a dip with a selection of fresh vegetables.

Light cream cheese, softened	8 oz.	250 g
Finely chopped, peeled and seeded cucumber	2 cups	500 mL
Seasoned salt	1 tsp.	5 mL
Cayenne pepper	1/16 tsp.	0.5 mL

Mash cream cheese with fork. Add cucumber pieces, seasoned salt and cayenne pepper. Mix well. Chill for at least 2 hours to blend flavours. Makes 3 cups (750 mL) dip.

2 tbsp. (30 mL) dip: 22 Calories; 1 g Protein; 1.7 g Total Fat; 1 g Carbohydrate; 150 mg Sodium; trace Dietary Fibre

Pictured above.

Soy Fire Dip

Hot, spicy soy flavour.

Soy sauce	1/4 cup	60 mL
Apple cider vinegar	2 tbsp.	30 mL
Ketchup	2 tsp.	10 mL
Garlic clove (or 1/4 tsp., 1 mL, powder)	1	1
Dried crushed chilies	1 tsp.	5 mL

Combine all 5 ingredients in blender. Process until smooth. Let stand for about 1 hour at room temperature to blend flavours. Makes 1/2 cup (125 mL) dip.

1 tbsp. (15 mL) dip: 9 Calories; 1 g Protein; 0.1 g Total Fat; 2 g Carbohydrate; 546 mg Sodium; trace Dietary Fibre

Relish Cheese Ball

You can make two smaller balls and freeze one for later use. Make one or two days ahead to allow flavours to mingle. Serve with assorted crackers.

Light cream cheese, softened	2 x 8 oz.	2 x 250 g
Grated medium or sharp Cheddar cheese	2 cups	500 mL
Sweet pickle relish, drained	1/2 cup	125 mL
Onion powder	1/8 tsp.	0.5 mL
Finely chopped pecans (or walnuts)	1 cup	250 mL

Measure first 4 ingredients into medium bowl. Beat on low until well mixed. Shape into ball. If too soft to shape into ball, chill for at least 1 hour.

Roll ball in pecans to coat. Chill until needed. Makes 1 cheese ball, 3 1/2 cups (875 mL).

2 tbsp. (30 mL) cheese ball: 100 Calories; 4 g Protein; 8.5 g Total Fat; 2 g Carbohydrate; 232 mg Sodium; trace Dietary Fibre

Pictured on page 26.

Fluffy Salmon Spread

Makes a good spread for crackers or use as a filling for toast cups.

Light salad dressing (or mayonnaise)	1/2 cup	125 mL
Lemon juice	1 tbsp.	15 mL
Onion flakes	1 tbsp.	15 mL
Hot pepper sauce	1/2 tsp.	2 mL
Worcestershire sauce	1/2 tsp.	2 mL
Salt	1 tsp.	5 mL
Pepper, sprinkle		
Canned salmon, drained, skin and round bones removed, broken up (red is best for colour)	2 x 4 oz.	2 x 114 g
Creamed cottage cheese	1 cup	250 mL
Frozen whipped topping (in a tub), thawed	1 cup	250 mL

Measure first 7 ingredients into medium bowl. Stir.

Add salmon. Mix well.

Stir in cottage cheese. Fold in whipped topping. Turn into pretty glass bowl. Chill for 3 to 4 hours. Makes 4 cups (1 L) mousse.

2 tbsp. (30 mL) mousse: 33 Calories; 2 g Protein; 2 g Total Fat; 2 g Carbohydrate; 171 mg Sodium; trace Dietary Fibre

Pictured on this page.

Spinach Balls

Flavourful, moist and colourful. Pretty on a plate of mixed appetizers or piled on their own plate.

Frozen chopped spinach	10 oz.	300 g
Large eggs, fork-beaten	2	2
Grated Parmesan cheese	1/4 cup	60 mL
Parsley flakes	1 tsp.	5 mL
Poultry seasoning	3/4 tsp.	4 mL
Garlic salt	1/4 tsp.	1 mL
Salt	1/4 tsp.	1 mL
Pepper	1/4 tsp.	2 mL
Very finely chopped onion	1/2 cup	125 mL
Dry bread crumbs	1 1/2 cups	375 mL
Hard margarine (or butter), melted	1/4 cup	60 mL
Hard margarine (or butter), melted	2 tbsp.	30 mL

Cook spinach according to package directions. Drain. Squeeze dry.

Combine next 7 ingredients in medium bowl. Beat to mix.

Add onion and bread crumbs. Stir. Add first amount of melted margarine and spinach. Mix well. Shape into 1 inch (2.5 cm) balls. Arrange on greased baking sheet.

Brush with second amount of melted margarine. Bake in 325°F (160°C) oven for 10 to 12 minutes. Do not overcook. If desired these may be frozen on a tray before baking, then stored in containers. Makes 48 spinach balls.

3 spinach balls: 104 Calories; 4 g Protein; 5.8 g Total Fat; 10 g Carbohydrate; 247 mg Sodium; 1 g Dietary Fibre

Pictured below.

Fluffy Salmon Spread, this page   Spinach Balls, above

Parmesan Appies

Soft and creamy topping covers baguette slices. Serve hot.

Mayonnaise (not salad dressing)	1/2 cup	125 mL
Grated Parmesan cheese	1/2 cup	125 mL
Minced onion	1 tbsp.	15 mL
Garlic powder	1/8 tsp.	0.5 mL
Baguette, cut into 1/2 inch (12 mm) slices	1	1

Stir mayonnaise, Parmesan cheese, onion and garlic powder together in small bowl.

Arrange bread slices on ungreased baking sheet. Broil to toast 1 side. Turn slices over. Spread 2 tsp. (10 mL) on each slice. Broil until slightly browned. Makes 3/4 cup (175 mL) topping, enough for 18 slices.

1 slice: 134 Calories; 4 g Protein; 6.8 g Total Fat; 14 g Carbohydrate; 234 mg Sodium; trace Dietary Fibre

Pictured below.

Top right: Salami Rolls, this page
Centre left: Stuffed Mushrooms, this page
Bottom: Parmesan Appies, above

Salami Rolls

Great addition to an appetizer selection. And you made it yourself! Wrap well and freeze for up to six months.

Water	1 1/2 cups	375 mL
Quick curing salt (such as Morton's)	2 tbsp.	30 mL
Liquid smoke	1 tbsp.	15 mL
Mustard seed	2 tsp.	10 mL
Garlic salt	1 1/2 tsp.	7 mL
Pepper	1/2 tsp.	2 mL
Lean ground beef	3 lbs.	1.4 kg

Stir first 6 ingredients together in large bowl.

Add ground beef. Mix well. Shape into 3 rolls, 2 x 14 inches (5 x 35 cm) long. Wrap up tightly in foil on shiny side. Chill for 24 hours. Poke holes through foil with tip of sharp knife in bottom of rolls. Pour hot water into bottom of broiler pan. Set broiler rack on top. Arrange salami rolls on rack.

Bake in 300°F (150°C) oven for 2 hours. Cool. Makes 3 rolls, 2 1/4 lbs. (1 kg). Cuts into about 70 pieces each.

1 piece: 30 Calories; 4 g Protein; 1.6 g Total Fat; trace Carbohydrate; 236 mg Sodium; trace Dietary Fibre

Pictured on this page.

Stuffed Mushrooms

Always a welcome flavourful appetizer. Can be made ahead and popped in the oven when needed.

Medium fresh mushrooms	26	26
Hard margarine (or butter)	2 tbsp.	30 mL
Chopped onion	1 cup	250 mL
Finely diced pepperoni (or garlic sausage)	1/2 cup	125 mL
Water	1/4 cup	60 mL
Grated Parmesan cheese	1/4 cup	60 mL
Parsley flakes	1/2 tsp.	2 mL
Chopped chives	1 tsp.	5 mL
Chicken bouillon powder	1 tsp.	5 mL
Dried whole oregano, crushed	1/4 tsp.	1 mL
Garlic powder	1/4 tsp.	1 mL
Dry bread crumbs	3/4 cup	175 mL

Gently twist stems from mushrooms. Chop stems.

Melt margarine in non-stick frying pan. Add mushroom stems, onion and pepperoni. Sauté until onion is soft. Remove from heat.

Add remaining 8 ingredients. Mix well. Stuff mushroom caps. Arrange on greased baking sheet. Bake in 350°F (175°C) oven for 20 to 30 minutes. Makes about 26 stuffed mushrooms.

1 stuffed mushroom: 48 Calories; 2 g Protein; 2.7 g Total Fat; 4 g Carbohydrate; 139 mg Sodium; trace Dietary Fibre

Pictured on this page.

Apple Brie Pizza, below

Apple Brie Pizza

A thin, crispy appetizer. A delicious hint of sweetness from the apples. Cuts well. Easy to eat out of hand.

PIZZA CRUST

All-purpose flour	1 1/4 cups	300 mL
Instant yeast	1 tsp.	5 mL
Salt	1/4 tsp.	1 mL
Hot water	1/2 cup	125 mL
Cooking oil	4 tsp.	20 mL
Cornmeal	2 tsp.	10 mL

BRIE TOPPING

Brie cheese, with rind, softened	7 oz.	200 g
Sour cream	2 tbsp.	30 mL
Dill weed	1/4 tsp.	1 mL
Sherry (or alcohol-free sherry)	1 tsp.	5 mL
Medium red apple, with peel, cut into paper-thin wedges	1	1
Bacon slices, cooked crisp and crumbled (or 2 tbsp., 30 mL, real bacon bits)	3	3
Grated Parmesan cheese	2 tsp.	10 mL

Pizza Crust: Measure flour, yeast and salt into food processor.

With lid in place and machine running, pour hot water and cooking oil through food chute. Process for about 50 seconds until a ball is formed. Remove and wrap in plastic wrap. Let rest for 10 minutes.

Divide dough into 2 equal portions. Sprinkle 1 tsp. (5 mL) cornmeal on working surface. Roll 1 portion of dough over cornmeal to 10 inch (25 cm) diameter. Repeat with second portion of dough. Place on greased baking sheet. Poke holes all over dough with fork. Bake on bottom rack in 450°F (230°C) oven for about 10 minutes. You can bake these 1 at a time. Cool.

Brie Topping: Mash Brie cheese, sour cream, dill weed and sherry with fork on large plate. No need to mash until smooth but rather to coarsely mix. Divide between crusts.

Arrange apple slices in single layer over each. Sprinkle with bacon. Sprinkle with Parmesan cheese. Bake in centre of 450°F (230°C) oven for about 5 minutes until crust is crisp and surface is beginning to turn golden. Cut each pizza into 12 wedges, for a total of 24 wedges.

1 wedge: 71 Calories; 3 g Protein; 3.8 g Total Fat; 6 g Carbohydrate; 97 mg Sodium; trace Dietary Fibre

Pictured above.

Beef

Early in the twentieth century, there were few written recipes for meat. These early recipes mostly gave instructions for methods of cooking—broiling, braising, roasting and frying. In 1910, Campbell's published *Helps for the Hostess,* featuring recipes that combined their soups with beef. This led to the development of many more beef recipes, and today there are unlimited ways to prepare beef. The meat section in grocery stores is filled with trendy stir-fry strips, kabobs, and specialty barbecue and rouladen cuts, as well as the traditional roasts and steaks. Recipes in this section include casseroles, chilies, steaks, stews and stir-fries.

Short Rib Magic, page 31

Shipwreck

An old favourite many of us grew up with. Keep the salt and pepper handy to season each layer as you go.

Large onions, thinly sliced	2	2
Salt		
Pepper		
Medium potatoes, thinly sliced	2	2
Lean ground beef	1 lb.	454 g
Uncooked long grain white rice	1/2 cup	125 mL
Chopped celery	1 cup	250 mL
Condensed cream of tomato soup	10 oz.	284 mL
Soup can of boiling water	10 oz.	284 mL

Place onion in bottom of ungreased 2 quart (2 L) casserole. Sprinkle with salt and pepper. Lay potato over onion. Sprinkle with salt and pepper. Pat ground beef over potato. Sprinkle with salt and pepper. Scatter rice, then celery, over top. Sprinkle with salt and pepper.

Mix soup and boiling water in small bowl. Pour over top. Cover. Bake in 350°F (175°C) oven for 1 1/2 to 2 hours until vegetables are tender. Serves 4.

1 serving: 463 Calories; 27 g Protein; 18.7 g Total Fat; 48 g Carbohydrate; 1312 mg Sodium; 4 g Dietary Fibre

Pictured on this page.

Short Rib Magic

Very tender, dark and delicious. Beautifully glazed. Extra tasty.

Boneless beef short ribs	3 lbs.	1.4 kg
Envelope dry onion soup mix	1 x 1 1/2 oz.	1 x 42 g
Ketchup	3/4 cup	175 mL
Brown sugar, packed	1/2 cup	125 mL

Arrange short ribs in medium roaster. Stir onion soup mix and sprinkle over top. Pour ketchup over soup mix. Sprinkle with brown sugar. Cover. Bake in 325°F (160°C) oven for 2 1/2 to 3 hours until very tender. Serves 8.

1 serving: 399 Calories; 35 g Protein; 17.8 g Total Fat; 24 g Carbohydrate; 925 mg Sodium; 1 g Dietary Fibre

Pictured on page 30.

Swiss Steak Casserole

Baby carrots and baby potatoes make for a most appealing dish.

Beef sirloin (or round) steak, cut into 6 serving pieces	2 lbs.	900 g
All-purpose flour	1/4 cup	60 mL
Salt	1 tsp.	5 mL
Pepper	1/4 tsp.	1 mL
Cooking oil	1 tbsp.	15 mL
Chili sauce	1/2 cup	125 mL
Water	1/2 cup	125 mL
Beef bouillon powder	2 tsp.	10 mL
Tomato sauce	7 1/2 oz.	213 mL
Garlic powder	1/4 tsp.	1 mL
Baby red potatoes, with peel	12	12
Peeled baby carrots	24	24
Medium onions, cut into wedges	2	2

Pound steaks well with meat mallet.

Mix flour, salt and pepper in shallow dish. Dip both sides of steak in flour mixture to coat.

Heat 1/2 of cooking oil in non-stick frying pan. Add 3 steaks. Brown both sides well. Arrange in medium roaster. Repeat with remaining cooking oil and steaks.

Stir next 5 ingredients together in small bowl. Pour over steaks. Cover. Bake in 350°F (175°C) oven for 1 3/4 to 2 hours until tender.

Add potatoes, carrots and onion. Bake, covered, for about 1 1/2 hours until vegetables are tender. Add a touch more water if needed. Serves 6.

1 serving: 417 Calories; 37 g Protein; 8.6 g Total Fat; 47 g Carbohydrate; 1316 mg Sodium; 6 g Dietary Fibre

Pictured below.

Top right: Shipwreck, this page   Bottom: Swiss Steak Casserole, above

Noodle Casserole

Little chunks of cheese melt in this as it bakes.
A topping of onion rings sets it off.

Lean ground beef	1 1/2 lbs.	680 g
Chopped green pepper (optional)	1/2 cup	125 mL
Chopped onion	1 cup	250 mL
Medium noodles (8 oz., 225 g)	3 1/3 cups	825 mL
Boiling water	3 qts.	3 L
Cooking oil (optional)	1 tbsp.	15 mL
Salt	2 tsp.	10 mL
Condensed cream of tomato soup	10 oz.	284 mL
Condensed cream of mushroom soup	10 oz.	284 mL
Worcestershire sauce	1 tsp.	5 mL
Salt	3/4 tsp.	4 mL
Pepper	1/4 tsp.	1 mL
Canned sliced mushrooms, drained	10 oz.	284 mL
Small cubed medium Cheddar cheese	1 cup	250 mL
TOPPING		
Hard margarine (or butter)	1 tbsp.	15 mL
Water	1 tbsp.	15 mL
Dry bread crumbs	1/2 cup	125 mL
Canned french-fried onion rings	2 3/4 oz.	79 g

Scramble-fry ground beef, green pepper and onion in non-stick frying pan until onion is soft and beef is no longer pink. Drain.

Cook noodles in boiling water, cooking oil and first amount of salt in large uncovered pot or Dutch oven for 5 to 7 minutes until tender but firm. Drain. Return noodles to pot.

Empty both soups into medium bowl. Add Worcestershire sauce, second amount of salt and pepper. Stir vigorously. Add to noodles. Add beef mixture. Stir.

Add mushrooms and cheese. Stir. Turn into ungreased 3 quart (3 L) casserole.

Topping: Melt margarine in small saucepan. Stir in water and bread crumbs. Sprinkle over casserole. Bake, uncovered, in 350°F (175°C) oven for 25 to 30 minutes.

Top with onion rings. Bake for about 10 minutes until heated through. Serves 6.

1 serving: 593 Calories; 34 g Protein; 26.1 g Total Fat; 54 g Carbohydrate; 1537 mg Sodium; 3 g Dietary Fibre

Pictured on page 33.

Three Layer Pasta And Beef

Great mild flavour. Layers can
be seen when it is cut into to serve.

Fusilli pasta (8 oz., 225 g)	2 2/3 cups	650 mL
Boiling water	3 qts.	3 L
Cooking oil (optional)	1 tbsp.	15 mL
Salt	2 tsp.	10 mL
Lean ground beef	1 lb.	454 g
Chopped onion	1 cup	250 mL
All-purpose flour	1 tbsp.	15 mL
Ground allspice	1/4 tsp.	1 mL
Salt	1/2 tsp.	2 mL
Pepper	1/4 tsp.	1 mL
Tomato sauce	7 1/2 oz.	213 mL
Milk	2 cups	500 mL
All-purpose flour	1/4 cup	60 mL
Salt	1/2 tsp.	2 mL
Pepper	1/8 tsp.	0.5 mL
Grated Parmesan cheese	1/3 cup	75 mL

Cook pasta in boiling water, cooking oil and first amount of salt in large uncovered pot or Dutch oven for 7 to 8 minutes until tender but firm. Drain. Turn pasta into ungreased 2 quart (2 L) casserole.

Scramble-fry ground beef and onion in non-stick frying pan until onion is soft and beef is no longer pink. Drain.

Mix in next 4 ingredients. Stir in tomato sauce until boiling. Spoon over pasta.

Gradually whisk milk into second amount of flour in small saucepan until no lumps remain. Add third amount of salt and second amount of pepper. Heat and stir until boiling.

Stir in Parmesan cheese. Pour over beef. Poke here and there with knife to allow some sauce to reach bottom. Bake, uncovered, in 350°F (175°C) oven for about 40 minutes until browned. Makes 8 cups (2 L) casserole.

1 1/2 cups (375 mL) casserole: 411 Calories; 28 g Protein; 10.9 g Total Fat; 48 g Carbohydrate; 967 mg Sodium; 2 g Dietary Fibre

Pictured on page 33.

1. Noodle Casserole, this page
2. Dairy Beef Bake, page 34
3. Chili Modern, page 34
4. Three Layer Pasta And Beef, above

Chili Modern

Contains salsa instead of tomatoes.
Add crusty bread for a complete meal.

Lean ground beef	1 1/2 lbs.	680 g
Chopped onion	1 cup	250 mL
Canned kidney beans, with liquid	2 x 14 oz.	2 x 398 mL
Frozen kernel corn	1 1/2 cups	375 mL
Canned chopped green chilies, with liquid	4 oz.	114 mL
Chili powder	2 tsp.	10 mL
Garlic powder	1/4 tsp.	1 mL
Salt	1/2 tsp.	2 mL
Pepper	1/8 tsp.	0.5 mL
Medium salsa	1 1/2 cups	375 mL

Scramble-fry ground beef and onion in large pot or Dutch oven until onion is soft and beef is no longer pink. Drain.

Add remaining 8 ingredients. Heat, stirring occasionally, until boiling. Simmer for 10 to 15 minutes. Makes 8 1/2 cups (2.1 L) chili.

1 1/2 cups (375 mL) chili: 399 Calories; 33 g Protein; 11 g Total Fat; 45 g Carbohydrate; 1989 mg Sodium; 12 g Dietary Fibre

Pictured on page 33.

Broiled Steak

A great time awaits when steaks are broiled or barbecued. This has unusual flavourings.

Red wine vinegar	1/4 cup	60 mL
Beef T-bone (or porterhouse) steaks (about 3 lbs., 1.4 kg)	4	4
Cooking oil	1 tbsp.	15 mL
Salt	1 tsp.	5 mL
Pepper	1 tsp.	5 mL
Dried sweet basil, crushed	1 tsp.	5 mL

Brush vinegar on both sides of each steak. Brush with cooking oil. Arrange on broiler tray.

Mix salt, pepper and basil in small cup. Sprinkle 1/2 over steaks. Broil for 5 minutes. Turn steaks over. Sprinkle with remaining 1/2 of seasoning. Broil for 5 minutes until desired degree of doneness. Serves 4.

1 serving: 603 Calories; 56 g Protein; 39.8 g Total Fat; 2 g Carbohydrate; 795 mg Sodium; trace Dietary Fibre

Pictured on this page.

BARBECUED STEAK: Instead of broiling in oven, barbecue steaks over medium for 5 minutes per side until desired degree of doneness is reached.

Dairy Beef Bake

So creamy tasting. Excellent.

Lean ground beef	1 1/2 lbs.	680 g
Chopped onion	1/2 cup	125 mL
Chopped celery	1/4 cup	60 mL
Broad egg noodles (8 oz., 225 g)	4 cups	1 L
Boiling water	3 qts.	3 L
Cooking oil (optional)	1 tbsp.	15 mL
Salt	2 tsp.	10 mL
Canned stewed tomatoes, with juice	14 oz.	398 mL
Chili sauce	1/2 cup	125 mL
Garlic powder	1/2 tsp.	2 mL
Salt	1/2 tsp.	2 mL
Pepper	1/8 tsp.	0.5 mL
Non-fat sour cream	1 cup	250 mL
Light cream cheese	4 oz.	125 g

Scramble-fry ground beef, onion and celery in non-stick frying pan until slightly browned. Drain.

Cook noodles in boiling water, cooking oil and first amount of salt in large uncovered pot or Dutch oven for 5 to 7 minutes until tender but firm. Drain. Return noodles to pot. Add beef mixture. Stir.

Add next 5 ingredients. Stir.

Beat sour cream and cream cheese together well in small bowl. Add to pot. Stir gently, just to marble through. Turn into ungreased 3 quart (3 L) casserole. Cover. Bake in 350°F (175°C) oven for about 30 minutes until heated through. Makes 8 cups (2 L) casserole.

1 1/2 cups (375 mL) casserole: 510 Calories; 36 g Protein; 19.6 g Total Fat; 47 g Carbohydrate; 1306 mg Sodium; 4 g Dietary Fibre

Pictured on page 33.

Broiled Steak, this page

Shepherd's Pie

*An old favourite generally made on Monday to use
up Sunday's leftover roast beef and potatoes.*

Cooked roast beef, chopped	3 cups	750 mL
Small onion	1	1
Beef gravy	1/2 – 1 cup	125 – 250 mL
Salt	1 tsp.	5 mL
Pepper	1/4 tsp.	1 mL
Leftover mashed potatoes	3 cups	750 mL
Paprika, sprinkle (optional)		

Put beef and onion through food chopper or processor. If
you don't have either, chop with knife into very small pieces.
Add gravy. Mix well. Should be pasty enough to hold
together. Pack in ungreased 9 x 9 inch (22 x 22 cm) pan.
Sprinkle with salt and pepper.

Spread potatoes over top of beef. Sprinkle with paprika. Bake
in 350°F (175°C) oven for 30 minutes until hot and potatoes
are browned. Serves 4.

*1 serving: 387 Calories; 36 g Protein; 13.7 g Total Fat; 31 g Carbohydrate; 1414 mg Sodium;
4 g Dietary Fibre*

Pictured on page 36.

Crispy Minute Steak

Good flavour to this crispy-coated, tender steak.

Large egg	1	1
Water	2 tsp.	10 mL
Salt	1 tsp.	5 mL
Pepper	1/4 tsp.	1 mL
Fine dry bread crumbs	3/4 cup	175 mL
Hard margarine (or butter)	1 1/2 tbsp.	25 mL
Minute steak (tenderized beef steak)	1 1/2 lbs.	680 g

Beat egg, water, salt and pepper in shallow bowl.

Put bread crumbs into shallow dish.

Melt margarine in non-stick frying pan. Dip minute steak
into egg mixture, then into crumbs. Lay crumbed steak on
waxed paper. Press with your hand to ensure crumbs stay
on. Add to frying pan. Brown both sides, cooking to degree
of desired doneness. Serves 4.

*1 serving: 362 Calories; 41 g Protein; 13.7 g Total Fat; 16 g Carbohydrate; 1017 mg Sodium;
trace Dietary Fibre*

Pictured on this page.

Top: Crispy Minute Steak, this page
Bottom: Mellow Stew, below

Mellow Stew

*Rich-coloured sauce. Serve with mashed
potatoes for a complete meal.*

Beef stew meat, cut into 1 inch (2.5 cm) cubes	1 1/2 lbs.	680 g
Cooking oil	2 tsp.	10 mL
Water	2 cups	500 mL
Ketchup	1/2 cup	125 mL
White vinegar	3 tbsp.	50 mL
Brown sugar, packed	3 tbsp.	50 mL
Sliced carrot	2 cups	500 mL
Chopped onion	1 cup	250 mL
Salt	1 tsp.	5 mL
Pepper	1/4 tsp.	1 mL

Brown beef in cooking oil in large pot or Dutch oven.

Add water, ketchup, vinegar and brown sugar. Stir. Cover.
Boil slowly for 1 1/4 hours.

Add carrot, onion, salt and pepper. Stir. Cover. Boil gently for
30 to 40 minutes until beef and vegetables are tender. Makes
4 1/2 cups (1.1 L) stew.

*1 1/2 cups (375 mL) stew: 571 Calories; 51 g Protein; 23 g Total Fat; 40 g Carbohydrate;
1641 mg Sodium; 4 g Dietary Fibre*

Pictured above.

Left: Roast And Gravy, below   Right: Slow Stew, page 37   Bottom: Shepherd's Pie, page 35

Roast And Gravy

This has a different twist—gravy is made using the cooked vegetables.

Boneless beef roast (such as chuck or round)	3 lbs.	1.4 kg
Medium carrot, diced	1	1
Chopped onion	1/2 cup	125 mL
Water	2 cups	500 mL
Garlic powder	1/2 tsp.	2 mL
Ground sage	1/2 tsp.	2 mL
Salt	1/2 tsp.	2 mL
Pepper	1/8 tsp.	0.5 mL
All-purpose flour	2 tbsp.	30 mL

Place roast in centre of small roaster. Scatter carrot and onion around roast. Pour water over top.

Mix garlic powder, sage, salt and pepper in small cup. Sprinkle over vegetables. Cover. Bake in 350°F (175°C) oven for 2 to 2 1/2 hours until roast is very tender. Remove roast to platter.

Process drippings and vegetables in blender to make gravy. Add flour. Process until smooth. Pour into medium saucepan. Heat and stir until boiling and thickened. Makes 3 1/2 cups (875 mL) gravy. Serves 8.

1 serving: 402 Calories; 33 g Protein; 27.5 g Total Fat; 4 g Carbohydrate; 265 mg Sodium; trace Dietary Fibre

Pictured above.

Slow Stew

It is so easy to double this convenient recipe either to serve more people or to have leftovers for the next day.

Beef stew meat, cut into 3/4 inch (2 cm) cubes	1 lb.	454 g
Medium potatoes, cut bite-size	3	3
Medium carrots, cut bite-size	4	4
Cubed turnip (about 3/4 inch, 2 cm, size)	1 cup	250 mL
Medium onion, cut up	1	1
Sliced celery	1/2 cup	125 mL
Beef bouillon powder	2 tsp.	10 mL
Boiling water	1/2 cup	125 mL
Canned stewed tomatoes, with juice	14 oz.	398 mL
Minute tapioca	2 tbsp.	30 mL
Granulated sugar	1 tsp.	5 mL
Salt	3/4 tsp.	4 mL
Pepper	1/4 tsp.	1 mL

Combine first 6 ingredients in small roaster.

Stir bouillon powder into boiling water in medium bowl.

Add remaining 5 ingredients to bouillon mixture. Pour over beef and vegetables. Cover. Bake in 300°F (150°C) oven for 3 1/2 to 4 hours until beef is very tender. Serves 4.

1 serving: 369 Calories; 29 g Protein; 10.4 g Total Fat; 41 g Carbohydrate; 1216 mg Sodium; 6 g Dietary Fibre

Pictured on page 36.

Gravy Browner

There was no commercial gravy browner in the mid-1800s. This was used instead. Simply stir in a small amount at a time into gravy until darkened to your liking.

Granulated sugar	2 tbsp.	30 mL
Salt, just a pinch		
Water	2 tsp.	10 mL
Water	1 cup	250 mL

Combine sugar and salt in small saucepan. Heat and stir constantly until sugar is melted. It will darken until it looks slightly burnt.

When very dark brown, add first amount of water. It will spatter. Keep stirring.

Gradually stir in second amount of water. Be sure all hard sugar syrup is dissolved. Cool. Makes 1 cup (250 mL) gravy browner.

1 tsp. (5 mL) gravy browner: 2 Calories; 0 g Protein; 0 g Total Fat; 1 g Carbohydrate; trace Sodium; 0 g Dietary Fibre

Pictured on this page.

Boiled Roast

In days long past, when the oven was being used for baking bread, a roast was often boiled. Great nowadays for those tougher cuts and always-busy ovens. Best when you want sliced or shredded cooked beef. Use leftover beef stock for a soup base or as a dip for beef sandwiches.

Boneless beef roast (such as chuck or round)	3 lbs.	1.4 kg
Boiling water, to cover		
Garlic powder (optional)	1/2 tsp.	2 mL
Onion powder	1/2 tsp.	2 mL
Celery salt	1/2 tsp.	2 mL
Pepper	1/4 tsp.	1 mL
Chicken bouillon powder	1 tsp.	5 mL
Gravy Browner, this page	1 - 2 tsp.	5 - 10 mL

Set roast in centre of large pot or Dutch oven. Cover with boiling water 1/4 to 1/2 inch (6 to 12 mm) over top of roast.

Add remaining 6 ingredients to water. Stir. Cover. Boil gently for about 2 hours until tender. Serves 6 to 8.

1/6 recipe: 517 Calories; 43 g Protein; 36.7 g Total Fat; trace Carbohydrate; 344 mg Sodium; trace Dietary Fibre

Pictured below.

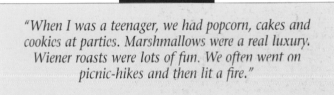

"When I was a teenager, we had popcorn, cakes and cookies at parties. Marshmallows were a real luxury. Wiener roasts were lots of fun. We often went on picnic-hikes and then lit a fire."

Jean Paré

Top: Gravy Browner in beef stock, this page
Bottom: Boiled Roast on a bun, above

Pacific Beef Stir-Fry,
below

Pacific Beef Stir-Fry

If you have everything prepared ahead, this cooks up in no time.

Medium onions, sliced	2	2
Red pepper slivers	1/3 cup	75 mL
Sliced fresh mushrooms	1 cup	250 mL
Cooking oil	2 tsp.	10 mL
Frozen whole green beans	2 1/2 cups	625 mL
Water	2 tbsp.	30 mL
Bean sprouts (large handful)	1 cup	250 mL
Cooking oil	1 tsp.	5 mL
Lean beef rump steak, cut into thin strips	1 lb.	454 g
Cooking oil	1 tsp.	5 mL
Soy sauce	3 tbsp.	50 mL
Granulated sugar	2 tsp.	10 mL
Ground ginger	1/8 tsp.	0.5 mL
Garlic powder	1/8 tsp.	0.5 mL
Cornstarch	1 1/2 tbsp.	25 mL

Stir-fry onion, red pepper and mushrooms in first amount of cooking oil in large non-stick wok or frying pan for 5 minutes. Vegetables will be tender crisp. Turn into medium bowl.

Combine green beans and water in wok. Cover. Cook for 4 minutes. Drain. Add bean sprouts and second amount of cooking oil to beans in wok. Stir-fry for about 4 minutes until hot. Add to vegetable mixture in bowl.

Stir-fry beef in wok in third amount of cooking oil for about 10 minutes until desired degree of doneness.

Combine remaining 5 ingredients in small cup. Stir well. Stir into beef until bubbling and thickened. Add vegetables and liquid in bowl to wok. Stir-fry until heated through. Makes 4 cups (1 L) stir-fry.

1 1/2 cups (375 mL) stir-fry: 439 Calories; 45 g Protein; 16.3 g Total Fat; 30 g Carbohydrate; 1310 mg Sodium; 6 g Dietary Fibre

Pictured above.

Layered Meatloaf

Using a large shallow pan rather than a loaf pan gives this a different shape. Just add a vegetable and you're set for supper.

Skim evaporated milk	13 1/2 oz.	385 mL
Finely chopped onion	3/4 cup	175 mL
Dry bread crumbs	1 cup	250 mL
Salt	1 tsp.	5 mL
Pepper	1/4 tsp.	1 mL
Lean ground beef	2 lbs.	900 g
Medium egg noodles (about 6 cups, 1.5 L)	10 oz.	285 g
Boiling water	2 qts.	2 L
Cooking oil (optional)	1 tbsp.	15 mL
Salt	2 tsp.	10 mL
Large eggs, fork-beaten	2	2
Grated Parmesan cheese	1/3 cup	75 mL
Canned chunky meatless spaghetti sauce	25 oz.	700 mL
Grated medium Cheddar cheese	1 cup	250 mL

Mix first 5 ingredients in medium bowl.

Add ground beef. Mix well. Pack in greased 9 x 13 inch (22 x 33 cm) pan. Bake in 350°F (175°C) oven for 30 to 35 minutes. Drain.

Cook noodles in boiling water, cooking oil and second amount of salt in large uncovered pot or Dutch oven for 5 to 7 minutes until tender but firm. Drain.

Combine eggs and Parmesan cheese in small bowl. Stir. Add to noodles. Mix well. Pour over beef. Spread to make even layer.

Drizzle spaghetti sauce over top. Sprinkle with Cheddar cheese. Return to oven for 15 minutes. Serves 8.

1 serving: 545 Calories; 39 g Protein; 19.8 g Total Fat; 52 g Carbohydrate; 1238 mg Sodium; 3 g Dietary Fibre

Pictured below.

Layered Meatloaf, above

Mexicali Special

A good one-dish meal.

Medium noodles	1 lb.	454 g
Boiling water	3 qts.	3 L
Salt	1 tbsp.	15 mL
Cooking oil (optional)	1 tbsp.	15 mL
Lean ground beef	2 lbs.	900 g
Chopped onion	1 cup	250 mL
Chopped celery	1/2 cup	125 mL
Sliced fresh mushrooms	1 cup	250 mL
Medium green pepper, chopped	1	1
Cooking oil	2 tbsp.	30 mL
Tomato juice	19 oz.	540 mL
Chili sauce	1/2 cup	125 mL
Canned chopped green chilies, with liquid	4 oz.	114 mL
Chili powder	1 tbsp.	15 mL
Dried whole oregano	1 tsp.	5 mL
Granulated sugar	1 tsp.	5 mL
Salt	2 tsp.	10 mL
Process cheese loaf (such as Velveeta), cut up	8 oz.	250 g

Cook noodles in boiling water and first amounts of salt and cooking oil in large uncovered pot or Dutch oven for 5 to 7 minutes until tender but firm. Drain. Set aside.

Scramble-fry ground beef, onion, celery, mushrooms and green pepper in 2 batches in second amount of cooking oil in same large pot or Dutch oven until browned. Drain. Return both batches to pot.

Add next 7 ingredients. Cover. Simmer gently, stirring occasionally, for about 30 minutes.

Add noodles and cheese. Heat and stir until cheese is melted. Serves 6.

1 serving: 756 Calories; 47 g Protein; 29 g Total Fat; 76 g Carbohydrate; 2526 mg Sodium; 5 g Dietary Fibre

Pictured below.

Top: Mexicali Special, above   Bottom: Lazy Ravioli, this page

Lazy Ravioli

This cooks and tastes better when baked in a shallow dish.

Lean ground beef	1 1/2 lbs.	680 g
Chopped onion	1 1/2 cups	375 mL
Coarsely chopped fresh mushrooms	1 1/2 cups	375 mL
Garlic clove, minced (or 1/4 tsp., 1 mL, powder)	1	1
Tomato paste	5 1/2 oz.	156 mL
Tomato sauce	7 1/2 oz.	213 mL
Hot water	1 cup	250 mL
Beef bouillon powder	1 tbsp.	15 mL
Parsley flakes	1 1/2 tsp.	7 mL
Dried sweet basil	1 1/2 tsp.	7 mL
Granulated sugar	3/4 tsp.	4 mL
Dried whole oregano	1/4 tsp.	1 mL
Dried thyme	1/4 tsp.	1 mL
Salt	1/2 tsp.	2 mL
Pepper	1/4 tsp.	1 mL
Frozen chopped spinach, cooked and drained	10 oz.	300 g
Large egg, fork-beaten	1	1
Dry bread crumbs	1/3 cup	75 mL
Parsley flakes	1 tbsp.	15 mL
Grated medium or sharp Cheddar cheese	1 cup	250 mL
Garlic salt	1/8 tsp.	0.5 mL
Ground nutmeg	1/8 tsp.	0.5 mL
Lasagna noodles, broken in half	8	8
Boiling water	4 qts.	4 L
Salt	1 tbsp.	15 mL
Cooking oil (optional)		
Grated part-skim mozzarella cheese	1 cup	250 mL

Scramble-fry ground beef, onion, mushrooms and garlic in large non-stick frying pan until beef is no longer pink. Drain. Return to frying pan.

Add next 11 ingredients. Stir. Bring to a boil. Cook, uncovered, until thickened.

Combine next 7 ingredients in small bowl. Mix.

Cook noodles in boiling water, second amount of salt and cooking oil for 14 to 16 minutes until tender but firm. Drain. Rinse with cold water. Drain well.

Arrange layers in ungreased 4 quart (4 L) casserole or small roaster as follows:

1. 1/2 of beef mixture
2. 1/2 of noodles
3. All of spinach mixture
4. 1/2 of noodles
5. 1/2 of beef mixture
6. All of mozzarella cheese

Cover. Bake in 350°F (175°C) oven for about 45 minutes. Serves 6 to 8.

1/6 recipe: 520 Calories; 40 g Protein; 21.6 g Total Fat; 42 g Carbohydrate; 1159 mg Sodium; 5 g Dietary Fibre

Pictured on this page.

Beverages

For centuries, water and milk were the most popular choices of non-alcoholic beverages. In the early 1900s, lemonade made from crystals mixed with water became a thirst-quenching drink. Today the varieties of fruit juice, soda pop and ice cream available offer us the chance to be creative in the liquid refreshments we serve. Whether it's a simple fruit drink or an ice cream shake, we can count on their diverse flavours to whet our appetite, complement a meal, or quench our thirst.

1. Cranberry Perc,
   page 43
2. Party Punch, this page
3. Pink Sunrise Punch,
   below
4. Orangeade, this page

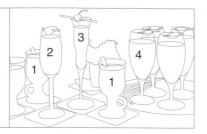

Pink Sunrise Punch

A refreshing drink without being sweet.

Pink grapefruit cocktail	2 cups	500 mL
Prepared orange juice	1 cup	250 mL
Grenadine syrup	1/4 cup	60 mL
Ginger ale	8 cups	2 L
Ice ring (or cubes)		
Maraschino cherries (optional)		

Combine grapefruit cocktail, orange juice and grenadine syrup in punch bowl.

Add ginger ale. Stir gently. Add ice ring. Serve in stemmed champagne glasses. Garnish each glass with a cherry. Makes 10 2/3 cups (2.75 L) punch.

1 cup (250 mL) punch: 123 Calories; trace Protein; 0.1 g Total Fat; 31 g Carbohydrate; 20 mg Sodium; trace Dietary Fibre

Pictured on page 40.

Party Punch

Pineapple and lemon-lime make a pretty party drink.

Pineapple juice	1 1/2 qts.	1.5 L
Water	1 qt.	1 L
Envelope unsweetened lemon-lime drink powder	1 x 1/4 oz.	1 x 6 g
Granulated sugar	1 cup	250 mL
Ginger ale	2 qts.	2 L
Ice ring (or cubes)		

Combine pineapple juice, water, drink powder and sugar in large container. Stir for several minutes until sugar is dissolved. Chill. Transfer to punch bowl.

Add ginger ale. Stir gently. Add ice ring. Makes 18 cups (4.5 L) punch.

1 cup (250 mL) punch: 133 Calories; trace Protein; 0.1 g Total Fat; 34 g Carbohydrate; 9 mg Sodium; trace Dietary Fibre

Pictured on page 40.

Orangeade

Vibrant orange colour. Very refreshing. Good to serve for any occasion—morning through evening.

Medium oranges, with peel, cut up	12	12
Water	12 cups	3 L
Citric acid (available at drug stores), generous 3 tbsp. (50 mL)	2 oz.	57 g
Granulated sugar	3 cups	750 mL
Ice cubes		

Put orange pieces through meat grinder or food processor being sure to catch all juice. Pour into large bowl or plastic pail.

Add water and citric acid. Stir well. Cover. Chill overnight.

Strain juice into large punch bowl. Add sugar. Stir until dissolved. Serve over ice in large glasses. Makes 14 cups (3.5 L) punch.

1 cup (250 mL) punch: 228 Calories; 2 g Protein; 0.4 g Total Fat; 66 g Carbohydrate; 3 mg Sodium; 1 g Dietary Fibre

Pictured on page 41.

Peach Shake

A tasty and healthy yogurt shake.

Canned sliced peaches, with juice	14 oz.	398 mL
Lemon juice	2 tsp.	10 mL
Brown sugar, packed	1 tbsp.	15 mL
Vanilla yogurt	1 cup	250 mL
Crushed ice (or 4 ice cubes)	1/2 cup	125 mL

Combine all 5 ingredients in blender. Process until smooth. Makes 3 1/2 cups (875 mL) shake.

1 cup (250 mL) shake: 115 Calories; 5 g Protein; 1.2 g Total Fat; 23 g Carbohydrate; 58 mg Sodium; 1 g Dietary Fibre

Pictured on page 43.

PEAR SHAKE: Use canned pears instead of peaches.

APRICOT SHAKE: Use canned apricots instead of peaches.

> *"When my eldest child was a baby, I kept his bottles chilled in the winter by putting them between the doors. In the summer, I had to go downstairs and use Grandad's refrigerator."*
>
> Jean Paré

Fruit Shake,
this page

Peach Shake,
page 42

Fruit Shake

Deliciously thick. Bananas and strawberries are a natural combination. Garnish with additional strawberries.

Medium bananas, cut up	2	2
Frozen whole strawberries	2 cups	500 mL
Milk	2 cups	500 mL
Granulated sugar	2 tbsp.	30 mL

Put all 4 ingredients into blender. Process until smooth. Pour into glasses. Makes 4 cups (1 L) shake.

1 cup (250 mL) shake: 156 Calories; 5 g Protein; 1.7 g Total Fat; 32 g Carbohydrate; 67 mg Sodium; 2 g Dietary Fibre

Pictured on this page.

Cranberry Perc

Spicy aroma fills the room. A warming but lively drink Serve with whole cinnamon sticks.

Cranberry cocktail	2 qts.	2 L
Apple juice	2 qts.	2 L
Frozen concentrated orange juice, thawed	12 oz.	341 mL
Granulated sugar	1/2 cup	125 mL
Cinnamon sticks (3 inches, 7.5 cm, each), smashed with hammer	2	2
Whole allspice	2 tsp.	10 mL
Whole cloves	1 tsp.	5 mL

Pour cranberry cocktail, apple juice and concentrated orange juice into percolator that has been washed with vinegar and baking soda. Put stem and basket into place.

Tie remaining 4 ingredients in double-layer of cheesecloth or filter bag. Set in basket. Cover. Perk as usual. Makes 17 1/2 cups (4.4 L) punch.

1 cup (250 mL) punch: 188 Calories; 1 g Protein; 0.2 g Total Fat; 47 g Carbohydrate; 9 mg Sodium; trace Dietary Fibre

Pictured on pages 40 and 41.

Slow Cooker Variation: Instead of using a percolator, pour first 3 ingredients into 5 to 6 quart (5 to 6 L) slow cooker. Tie remaining 4 ingredients in cheesecloth or filter bag. Add to slow cooker. Cook on Low for at least 2 hours until hot.

Hot Mocha Drink

This is decadent, especially with whipped topping.

Water	2 cups	500 mL
Unsweetened chocolate baking square, cut up	1 x 1 oz.	1 x 28 g
Instant coffee granules	1/4 cup	60 mL
Granulated sugar	2 tbsp.	30 mL
Milk	2 cups	500 mL
Vanilla	1/2 tsp.	2 mL
Frozen whipped topping (in a tub), thawed (or whipped cream or tiny marshmallows), optional	1/2 cup	125 mL
Chocolate curls, for garnish (optional)		

Stir first 6 ingredients in small saucepan. Heat slowly, stirring often, until chocolate is melted and mixture is steaming hot. Pour into mugs. Stir in a bit more sugar if desired.

Top with a dollop of whipped topping. Garnish with chocolate curls. Makes 4 cups (1 L) hot mocha.

1 cup (250 mL) hot mocha: 126 Calories; 6 g Protein; 5.1 g Total Fat; 16 g Carbohydrate; 66 mg Sodium; 1 g Dietary Fibre

Pictured below.

Rhubarb Punch, below

Hot Mocha Drink, above

Rhubarb Punch

This refreshing drink can be made any time of the year. Garnish punch with pineapple rings and maraschino cherries.

Fresh (or frozen) rhubarb, cut into 1/2 inch (12 mm) lengths (about 10 cups, 2.5 L)	2 lbs.	900 g
Water	3 cups	750 mL
Granulated sugar	1 cup	250 mL
Prepared orange juice	1 cup	250 mL
Lemon juice	3 tbsp.	50 mL
Ginger ale (equal to above mixture), approximately	5 1/4 cups	1.3 L
Ice cubes		

Cook rhubarb in water in large pot or Dutch oven until soft and tender. Place colander over large bowl. Pour rhubarb and juice into colander. Allow 30 minutes to drain. Discard rhubarb.

Add sugar to warm juice. If too cooled, warm slightly. Stir until sugar is dissolved.

Add orange juice and lemon juice. Stir. Pour into pitcher. Cover. Chill.

When ready to serve, pour into punch bowl. Add ginger ale. Pour over ice cubes in glasses. For single serving, fill glass with 1/2 juice mixture and 1/2 ginger ale. Makes 10 1/2 cups (2.6 L) punch.

1 cup (250 mL) punch: 140 Calories; 1 g Protein; 0.1 g Total Fat; 36 g Carbohydrate; 11 mg Sodium; 1 g Dietary Fibre

Pictured above.

Breads & Quick Breads

Prior to the 1850s, people relied on slow-growing yeast to leaven their breads. Soon after, single-acting baking powders became popular and in 1889, double-acting baking powder was introduced. In 1902, we began to see cookbooks using baking powder in recipes for biscuits, scones, muffins, waffles and batter bread. Today there are all kinds of exciting variations to these bread and quick-bread classics, made even easier with the introduction of instant yeast. For years muffins were either bran, blueberry, corn, date, apple or oatmeal. In the 1970s and 1980s, they became a trend, setting off a new generation of mega-muffins, three or four times their original size and featuring ingredients such as grated carrot or zucchini, chocolate chips, nuts and streusel toppings.

Bran Buns

Sweet with light bran flavour. Fluffy texture inside, crispy outside.

Granulated sugar	1 tsp.	5 mL
Warm water	1/2 cup	125 mL
Envelope active dry yeast	1 x 1/4 oz.	1 x 8 g
(1 scant tbsp., 15 mL)		
All-bran cereal (100% bran)	1/2 cup	125 mL
Granulated sugar	1/3 cup	75 mL
Hard margarine (or butter)	6 tbsp.	100 mL
Salt	1/2 tsp.	2 mL
Boiling water	1/2 cup	125 mL
Large egg, fork-beaten	1	1
All-purpose flour, approximately	3 cups	750 mL

Stir first amount of sugar and warm water in small bowl until sugar is dissolved. Sprinkle yeast over top. Let stand for 10 minutes. Stir until yeast is dissolved.

Combine next 5 ingredients in large bowl. Stir until margarine is melted. Cool to lukewarm. Add yeast mixture. Add egg. Mix well.

Work in flour. Turn out onto lightly floured surface. Knead for 8 to 10 minutes until smooth and elastic. Place in large greased bowl, turning once to grease top. Cover with tea towel. Let stand in oven with light on and door closed for about 50 minutes until doubled in size. Punch down dough. Shape into 18 buns. Place on greased 11 x 17 inch (28 x 43 cm) baking sheet. Cover with tea towel. Let stand in oven with light on and door closed for about 20 minutes until doubled in size. Bake in 375°F (190°C) oven for about 15 minutes until browned. Makes 18 buns.

1 bun: 141 Calories; 3 g Protein; 4.5 g Total Fat; 23 g Carbohydrate; 143 mg Sodium; 1 g Dietary Fibre

Pictured on page 46 and on front cover.

Brown Bread

A quick way to add hot bread to a meal.

All-purpose flour	2 1/3 cups	575 mL
Natural bran	1 cup	250 mL
Granulated sugar	2 tsp.	10 mL
Baking powder	4 tsp.	20 mL
Baking soda	1 tsp.	5 mL
Salt	1 tsp.	5 mL
Hard margarine (or butter), melted	1/4 cup	60 mL
Buttermilk (or reconstituted from powder)	1 cup	250 mL
Large egg, fork-beaten	1	1

Measure first 6 ingredients into medium bowl. Stir. Make a well in centre.

Combine margarine, buttermilk and egg in small bowl. Pour into well. Stir to make a soft ball. Turn out onto lightly floured surface. Knead 8 times. Shape into loaf. Place in greased 9 x 5 x 3 inch (22 x 12.5 x 7.5 cm) loaf pan. Bake in 350°F (175°C) oven for about 50 minutes until wooden pick inserted in centre comes out clean. Turn out onto rack to cool. Cuts into 16 slices.

1 slice: 119 Calories; 4 g Protein; 3.6 g Total Fat; 19 g Carbohydrate; 314 mg Sodium; 2 g Dietary Fibre

Pictured on page 46.

1. Brown Bread, page 45
2. Bran Buns, page 45
3. Chelsea Buns, page 47
4. White Bread, page 47

White Bread

Wonderfully flavoured bread. Slices well.

Milk	1 cup	250 mL
Water	1/2 cup	125 mL
Granulated sugar	2 tbsp.	30 mL
Hard margarine (or butter)	2 tbsp.	30 mL
Salt	2 tsp.	10 mL
Lukewarm water	1/2 cup	125 mL
Granulated sugar	1 tsp.	5 mL
Envelope active dry yeast (1 scant tbsp., 15 mL)	1 x 1/4 oz.	1 x 8 g
All-purpose flour	2 1/2 cups	625 mL
All-purpose flour, approximately	2 1/4 cups	550 mL
Hard margarine (or butter), softened	2 tsp.	10 mL

Heat milk, first amounts of water, sugar, margarine and salt in small saucepan until margarine is melted and sugar is dissolved. Pour into large bowl. Cool to lukewarm.

Stir second amounts of water and sugar in small bowl until sugar is dissolved. Sprinkle with yeast. Let stand for 10 minutes. Stir until yeast is dissolved. Add to lukewarm mixture. Stir.

Add first amount of flour. Beat well.

Work in second amount of flour until no longer sticky. Turn out onto lightly floured surface. Knead for 8 to 10 minutes until smooth and elastic. Place in large greased bowl, turning once to grease top. Cover with tea towel. Let stand in oven with light on and door closed for about 1 hour until doubled in size. Punch down dough. Divide in half. Shape into loaves. Place in 2 greased 8 x 4 x 3 inch (20 x 10 x 7.5 cm) loaf pans. Cover with tea towel. Let stand in oven with light on and door closed for 30 to 40 minutes until doubled in size. Remove to preheat oven. Bake in 375°F (190°C) oven for about 30 minutes. Turn out onto racks to cool.

Brush warm tops with second amount of margarine. Makes 2 loaves. Each loaf cuts into 16 slices, for a total of 32 slices.

1 slice: 88 Calories; 2 g Protein; 1.3 g Total Fat; 16 g Carbohydrate; 186 mg Sodium; 1 g Dietary Fibre

Pictured on page 46.

WHOLE WHEAT BREAD: Substitute whole wheat flour for 1/2 of all-purpose flour.

Chelsea Buns

A pretty bun. Fluffy soft, golden brown and glistening with a glaze. Sweet, buttery and fruity.

Granulated sugar	1 tsp.	5 mL
Warm water	1/2 cup	125 mL
Envelope active dry yeast (1 scant tbsp., 15 mL)	1 x 1/4 oz.	1 x 8 g
Hard margarine (or butter)	1/4 cup	60 mL
Granulated sugar	1/2 cup	125 mL
Large eggs	2	2
Salt	1/2 tsp.	2 mL
All-purpose flour	1 cup	250 mL
Milk, heated to lukewarm	1 cup	250 mL
All-purpose flour, approximately	4 cups	1 L
FILLING		
Hard margarine (or butter), melted	1/4 cup	60 mL
Raisins	3/4 cup	175 mL
Chopped mixed peel	1/2 cup	125 mL
Brown sugar, packed	3/4 cup	175 mL
GLAZE		
Liquid honey, warmed	3 tbsp.	50 mL

Stir first amount of sugar and warm water in small bowl until sugar is dissolved. Sprinkle yeast over top. Let stand for 10 minutes. Stir until yeast is dissolved.

Beat margarine and second amount of sugar in large bowl. Beat in eggs, 1 at a time. Add salt and first amount of flour. Beat on high until smooth. Add yeast mixture. Mix well.

Add milk. Stir. Work in second amount of flour until dough pulls away from sides of bowl. Turn out onto lightly floured surface. Knead for 5 to 10 minutes until smooth and elastic. Place in large greased bowl, turning once to grease top. Cover with tea towel. Let stand in oven with light on and door closed for about 1 hour until doubled in size. Punch down dough. Divide into 2 equal portions. Roll out each portion on lightly floured surface into 10 x 14 inch (25 x 35 cm) rectangle.

Filling: Brush each rectangle of dough with 1/2 of margarine. Sprinkle with 1/2 of raisins, 1/2 of mixed peel and 1/2 of brown sugar. Roll up from long side like jelly roll. Cut each roll into 12 slices. Place cut side down on greased 11 x 17 inch (28 x 43 cm) baking sheet. Cover with tea towel. Let stand in oven with light on and door closed for about 1 hour until doubled in size. Remove to preheat oven. Bake in 375°F (190°C) oven for 15 to 18 minutes.

Glaze: While still warm, dip wet brush into honey and brush tops of buns. Makes 24 buns.

1 bun: 227 Calories; 4 g Protein; 4.8 g Total Fat; 43 g Carbohydrate; 117 mg Sodium; 1 g Dietary Fibre

Pictured on page 46.

Apple Cheese Muffins

Like having a piece of cheese with apple pie.
Very moist because of the apple.

All-purpose flour	1 1/2 cups	375 mL
Baking soda	1 tsp.	5 mL
Salt	1/2 tsp.	2 mL
Hard margarine (or butter), softened	1/2 cup	125 mL
Granulated sugar	1/2 cup	125 mL
Large eggs	2	2
Milk	1/4 cup	60 mL
Grated cooking apple (such as McIntosh), approximately 1 large	3/4 cup	175 mL
Grated sharp Cheddar cheese	3/4 cup	175 mL
Ground cinnamon	1/2 tsp.	2 mL
Granulated sugar	1 tbsp.	15 mL

Stir flour, baking soda and salt in large bowl. Make a well in centre.

Cream margarine and first amount of sugar together in separate large bowl. Beat in eggs, 1 at a time. Add milk. Beat. Stir in apple and cheese. Pour into well. Stir just to moisten. Fill greased muffin cups almost full.

Mix cinnamon and second amount of sugar in small cup. Sprinkle over muffins. Bake in 400°F (205°C) oven for about 20 minutes until wooden pick inserted in centre comes out clean. Let stand for 5 minutes before removing to rack to cool. Makes 12 muffins.

1 muffin: 220 Calories; 5 g Protein; 11.7 g Total Fat; 24 g Carbohydrate; 383 mg Sodium; 1 g Dietary Fibre

Pictured below.

Banana Graham Muffins

The ultimate tender muffin. Excellent.

All-purpose flour	3/4 cup	175 mL
Graham cracker crumbs	1 cup	250 mL
Brown sugar, packed	1/2 cup	125 mL
Baking powder	1 tsp.	5 mL
Baking soda	1 tsp.	5 mL
Salt	1/4 tsp.	1 mL
Large egg, fork-beaten	1	1
Cooking oil	1/4 cup	60 mL
Mashed banana (about 3 medium)	1 cup	250 mL
Chopped walnuts (optional)	2/3 cup	150 mL

Measure first 6 ingredients into large bowl. Stir together. Make a well in centre.

Combine egg, cooking oil and banana in medium bowl. Beat to mix well. Stir in walnuts. Turn into well. Stir just to moisten. Fill greased muffin cups almost full. Bake in 400°F (205°C) oven for about 15 minutes until wooden pick inserted in centre comes out clean. Let stand for 5 minutes before removing to rack to cool. Makes 12 muffins.

1 muffin: 171 Calories; 2 g Protein; 6.3 g Total Fat; 28 g Carbohydrate; 245 mg Sodium; 1 g Dietary Fibre

Pictured below.

Top left: Apple Cheese Muffins, above
Top right: Banana Graham Muffins, above
Bottom: Lemon Muffins, page 49

Apricot Bran Muffins

A healthy muffin. Not sweet.

All-purpose flour	1 1/4 cups	300 mL
Natural bran	1 cup	250 mL
Granulated sugar	1/2 cup	125 mL
Baking powder	4 tsp.	20 mL
Salt	1/2 tsp.	2 mL
Large eggs	2	2
Apricot nectar (or apricot baby food)	1/2 cup	125 mL
Cooking oil	1/2 cup	125 mL
Dried apricots, cut up	1/2 cup	125 mL
Ground nutmeg	1/4 tsp.	1 mL

Combine first 5 ingredients in large bowl. Stir. Make a well in centre.

Put remaining 5 ingredients into blender. Process until dried apricots are finely chopped. Pour into well. Stir just to moisten. Fill greased muffin cups almost full. Bake in 400°F (205°C) oven for about 15 minutes until wooden pick inserted in centre comes out clean. Let stand for 5 minutes before removing to rack to cool. Makes 12 muffins.

1 muffin: 215 Calories; 4 g Protein; 10.9 g Total Fat; 28 g Carbohydrate; 131 mg Sodium; 3 g Dietary Fibre

Pictured on this page.

Lemon Muffins

Lemon flavour is mild. Can be enhanced by adding more peel.

Hard margarine (or butter), softened	1/3 cup	75 mL
Granulated sugar	1/2 cup	125 mL
Large egg	1	1
Lemon juice	2 tbsp.	30 mL
Grated lemon peel	1 tbsp.	15 mL
Milk	3/4 cup	175 mL
Lemon flavouring (optional)	1/2 tsp.	2 mL
All-purpose flour	2 cups	500 mL
Baking powder	2 1/2 tsp.	12 mL
Salt	1/2 tsp.	2 mL

Beat margarine, sugar and egg together well in medium bowl. Beat in lemon juice, lemon peel, milk and lemon flavouring.

Measure flour, baking powder and salt into large bowl. Stir. Make a well in centre. Pour lemon batter into well. Stir just to moisten. Fill greased muffin cups almost full. Bake in 400°F (205°C) oven for about 20 minutes until wooden pick inserted in centre comes out clean. Let stand for 5 minutes before removing to rack to cool. Makes 12 muffins.

1 muffin: 177 Calories; 3 g Protein; 6.2 g Total Fat; 27 g Carbohydrate; 194 mg Sodium; 1 g Dietary Fibre

Pictured on page 48.

Pineapple Muffins, below   Apricot Bran Muffins, this page

Pineapple Muffins

The pineapple makes this a particularly moist muffin.

All-purpose flour	2 cups	500 mL
Brown sugar, packed	3/4 cup	175 mL
Baking powder	1 1/2 tsp.	7 mL
Baking soda	1/2 tsp.	2 mL
Salt	1/2 tsp.	2 mL
Large egg, fork-beaten	1	1
Cooking oil	1/4 cup	60 mL
Sour cream	1 cup	250 mL
Canned crushed pineapple, with juice	8 oz.	227 mL
Chopped walnuts (or pecans)	1/2 cup	125 mL

Combine first 5 ingredients in large bowl. Make a well in centre.

Combine egg, cooking oil and sour cream in medium bowl. Beat. Stir in pineapple with juice and walnuts. Turn into well. Stir just to moisten. Fill greased muffin cups almost full. Bake in 400°F (205°C) oven for 15 to 20 minutes until wooden pick inserted in centre comes out clean. Let stand for 5 minutes before removing to rack to cool. Makes 14 muffins.

1 muffin: 225 Calories; 4 g Protein; 10.1 g Total Fat; 31 g Carbohydrate; 164 mg Sodium; 1 g Dietary Fibre

Pictured above.

Variation: Add 1/2 cup (125 mL) toasted long thread or fancy flake coconut.

Month Of Muffins

Keep batter in the refrigerator and enjoy fresh muffins all month.

Crushed shredded wheat cereal (4 – 5 biscuits)	2 cups	500 mL
Quick-cooking rolled oats (not instant)	2 cups	500 mL
All-bran cereal (100% bran)	2 cups	500 mL
Hard margarine (or butter), cut up	1 cup	250 mL
Boiling water	2 cups	500 mL
Large eggs, fork-beaten	4	4
Buttermilk (or reconstituted from powder)	4 cups	1 L
All-purpose flour	5 cups	1.25 L
Granulated sugar	2 cups	500 mL
Baking powder	1 tbsp.	15 mL
Baking soda	1 tbsp.	15 mL
Salt	1 tbsp.	15 mL
Raisins (optional)	2 cups	500 mL

Measure shredded wheat cereal into large bowl. Add next 4 ingredients. Stir well until margarine is melted.

Mix eggs well in batter. Stir in buttermilk.

Combine remaining 6 ingredients in separate large bowl. Add to batter. Stir just to moisten. Cover. Refrigerate for up to 1 month. To bake, fill greased muffin cups almost full. Bake in 400°F (205°C) oven for about 20 minutes until wooden pick inserted in centre comes out clean. Let stand for 5 minutes before removing to rack to cool. Makes 4 1/2 dozen muffins.

1 muffin: 151 Calories; 4 g Protein; 4.6 g Total Fat; 25 g Carbohydrate; 288 mg Sodium; 2 g Dietary Fibre

Pictured below.

Coconut Muffins

Wonderful with fresh fruit.

All-purpose flour	1 3/4 cups	425 mL
Granulated sugar	1/2 cup	125 mL
Medium coconut (see Note)	1 cup	250 mL
Baking powder	1 tbsp.	15 mL
Salt	1/2 tsp.	2 mL
Large egg, fork-beaten	1	1
Milk	1 cup	250 mL
Cooking oil	1/4 cup	60 mL
Coconut flavouring	1 tsp.	5 mL

Measure flour, sugar, coconut, baking powder and salt into large bowl. Stir. Make a well in centre.

Combine remaining 4 ingredients in small bowl. Beat slowly to mix. Pour into well. Stir just to moisten. Fill greased muffin cups almost full. Bake in 400°F (205°C) oven for 15 to 20 minutes until golden and wooden pick inserted in centre comes out clean. Let stand for 5 minutes before removing to rack to cool. Makes 12 muffins.

1 muffin: 216 Calories; 4 g Protein; 10.8 g Total Fat; 27 g Carbohydrate; 137 mg Sodium; 1 g Dietary Fibre

Pictured below.

Note: Toast coconut first on ungreased baking sheet in 350°F (175°C) oven for about 5 minutes until browned for a nice flavour change.

Centre left: Coconut Muffins, this page
Centre right: French Puffins, page 51
Bottom left: Month Of Muffins, this page
Bottom right: Apricot Date Loaf, page 51

French Puffins

Taste like cake doughnuts. Very tender.

All-purpose flour	2 cups	500 mL
Baking powder	2 1/2 tsp.	12 mL
Ground nutmeg	1/2 tsp.	2 mL
Salt	1/2 tsp.	2 mL
Hard margarine (or butter), softened	1/4 cup	60 mL
Granulated sugar	1/2 cup	125 mL
Large egg	1	1
Milk	2/3 cup	150 mL
Granulated sugar	1/4 cup	60 mL
Ground cinnamon	1/2 tsp.	2 mL
Hard margarine (or butter), melted	3 tbsp.	50 mL

Stir first 4 ingredients in large bowl. Make a well in centre.

Cream first amounts of margarine and sugar in medium bowl until smooth. Beat in egg. Add milk. Beat. Pour into well in flour mixture. Stir just to mix. Fill greased muffin cups almost full. Bake in 375°F (190°C) oven for 20 to 25 minutes until wooden pick inserted in centre comes out clean. Let stand for 5 minutes before removing to rack.

Mix second amount of sugar and cinnamon in small bowl. Brush hot muffin tops generously with melted margarine. Dip buttered tops into sugar mixture. Makes 12 muffins.

1 muffin: 206 Calories; 3 g Protein; 7.6 g Total Fat; 31 g Carbohydrate; 209 mg Sodium; 1 g Dietary Fibre

Pictured on page 50.

Apricot Date Loaf

Perfect choice for tea. Serve lightly buttered.

Hard margarine (or butter), softened	1/4 cup	60 mL
Chopped dates	1/2 cup	125 mL
Chopped dried apricot	1/2 cup	125 mL
Baking soda	1 tsp.	5 mL
Boiling water	3/4 cup	175 mL
Large egg, fork-beaten	1	1
Brown sugar, packed	1/2 cup	125 mL
Salt	1/2 tsp.	2 mL
Vanilla	1 tsp.	5 mL
All-purpose flour	1 cup	250 mL
Whole wheat (or all-purpose) flour	1 cup	250 mL
Baking powder	1 1/2 tsp.	7 mL

Combine first 5 ingredients in small bowl. Let stand until cool.

Combine egg, brown sugar, salt and vanilla in large bowl. Beat. Stir in date mixture.

Add both flours and baking powder. Stir just to moisten. Turn into greased 9 x 5 x 3 inch (22 x 12.5 x 7.5 cm) loaf pan. Bake in 350°F (175°C) oven for about 1 hour. Cool in pan for 5 minutes. Remove to rack to cool completely. Cuts into 18 slices.

1 slice: 120 Calories; 2 g Protein; 3.3 g Total Fat; 23 g Carbohydrate; 191 mg Sodium; 2 g Dietary Fibre

Pictured on page 50.

Barm Brack, below

Barm Brack

To make this Irish loaf, it must be planned the previous evening. You will find this a moist, different loaf. Serve warm with butter.

Cold tea	1 cup	250 mL
Raisins	1 cup	250 mL
Cut mixed peel	1/2 cup	125 mL
Currants	1/2 cup	125 mL
Granulated sugar	1 cup	250 mL
Large egg, fork-beaten	1	1
Hard margarine (or butter), melted	1/4 cup	60 mL
All-purpose flour	2 cups	500 mL
Baking powder	1 tsp.	5 ml
Baking soda	1/4 tsp.	1 mL
Salt	1/4 tsp.	1 mL

Combine first 5 ingredients in large bowl. Cover. Let stand overnight.

Stir egg and margarine into fruit mixture.

Combine remaining 4 ingredients in small bowl. Stir. Add to fruit batter. Stir until well blended. Spoon into greased 9 x 5 x 3 inch (22 x 12.5 x 7.5 cm) loaf pan. Bake in 350°F (175°C) oven for 60 to 70 minutes. Let stand for 10 minutes before removing to rack. Cuts into 18 slices.

1 slice: 180 Calories; 2 g Protein; 3 g Total Fat; 37 g Carbohydrate; 93 mg Sodium; 1 g Dietary Fibre

Pictured above.

Brunches & Lunches

At the turn of the century, mid-morning or afternoon teas and picnics consisted mainly of soups and sandwiches. Sandwich fillings were very different: lettuce, sardine, anchovy, oyster, sliced candied ginger and sliced fruit. When we think of brunches or lunches today, we have a vast selection of dishes from which to choose. These can include stratas, stir-fries and pasta salads. However, if you prefer the more traditional, serve Macaroni and Cheese (page 54), Tuna Biscuits (page 55) or Baked Pancake with Maple-flavoured Syrup (page 60).

1. **Granola Bars, page 60**
2. **Swedish Tea Ring, page 58**
3. **Beacon Shrimp Omelet, page 55**
4. **Sweet Swirl Rolls, page 58**
5. **Stir-Fry Salad, page 57**

Turkey Strata

It will remind you of a hot chicken salad sandwich.

White (or brown) bread slices, with crusts, trimmed to fit	6	6
Grated medium Cheddar cheese	1 cup	250 mL
Light salad dressing (or mayonnaise)	1/2 cup	125 mL
Sweet pickle relish	1/4 cup	60 mL
Finely chopped cooked turkey	2 cups	500 mL
White (or brown) bread slices, with crusts, trimmed to fit	6	6
Large eggs	6	6
Salt	3/4 tsp.	4 mL
Pepper	1/8 tsp.	0.5 mL
Milk	2 3/4 cups	675 mL
Sliced almonds, toasted in 350°F (175°C) oven for 5 to 8 minutes	1/2 cup	125 mL

Cover bottom of greased 9 x 13 inch (22 x 33 cm) pan with first amount of bread slices.

Stir next 4 ingredients together in medium bowl. Spread over bread slices. Cover with second amount of bread slices.

Beat eggs, salt and pepper in medium bowl. Stir in milk. Pour over all. Cover. Refrigerate several hours or overnight. Cover. Bake in 350°F (175°C) oven for 45 to 50 minutes.

Sprinkle with almonds. Bake, uncovered, for about 15 minutes. Serves 6.

1 serving: 539 Calories; 37 g Protein; 24.6 g Total Fat; 42 g Carbohydrate; 1098 mg Sodium; 2 g Dietary Fibre

Pictured below.

CHICKEN STRATA: Substitute finely chopped cooked chicken for turkey.

Macaroni And Cheese

A mainstay of many families way back when—and still today!

Elbow macaroni	2 cups	500 mL
Chopped onion	1/2 cup	125 mL
Boiling water	3 qts.	3 L
Cooking oil (optional)	1 tbsp.	15 mL
Salt	2 tsp.	10 mL
Milk	1 1/4 cups	300 mL
All-purpose flour	3 tbsp.	50 mL
Grated medium or sharp Cheddar cheese	2 cups	500 mL
Dry mustard	1 tsp.	5 mL
Salt	1/2 tsp.	2 mL
Pepper	1/8 tsp.	0.5 mL
Paprika, sprinkle		

Cook macaroni and onion in boiling water, cooking oil and first amount of salt in large uncovered pot or Dutch oven for 7 to 8 minutes until macaroni is tender but firm. Drain well. Return to pot.

Gradually whisk milk into flour in medium saucepan. Stir until smooth. Heat over medium, stirring continually, until thickened. Stir in cheese, dry mustard, second amount of salt and pepper. Stir to melt cheese. Pour over macaroni mixture. Stir. Pour into ungreased shallow 2 quart (2 L) casserole.

Sprinkle with paprika. Cover. Bake in 350°F (175°C) oven for about 35 minutes until thickened and bubbling. Remove cover. Bake for 10 minutes. Serves 4.

1 serving: 514 Calories; 26 g Protein; 21.9 g Total Fat; 53 g Carbohydrate; 755 mg Sodium; 2 g Dietary Fibre

Pictured below.

Left: Turkey Strata, above

Right: Macaroni And Cheese, above, with Turkey Sandwiches, page 55

Beacon Shrimp Omelet

This is a real breakfast or brunch treat.

SEAFOOD SAUCE

Ketchup	3 tbsp.	50 mL
Lemon juice	1 1/2 tsp.	7 mL
Creamed horseradish	1 tsp.	5 mL
Worcestershire sauce	1/4 tsp.	1 mL

OMELET

Hard margarine (or butter)	1/2 tsp.	2 mL
Large eggs, fork-beaten	2	2
Light cream cheese, softened and cut up	3 tbsp.	50 mL
Chopped green onion	2 tbsp.	30 mL
Cooked fresh baby shrimp	1/3 cup	75 mL

Seafood Sauce: Combine all 4 ingredients in small bowl. Makes 3 tbsp. (50 mL) sauce.

Omelet: Melt margarine in 8 inch (20 cm) non-stick frying pan over medium. Pour in eggs. Cover. Cook for 1 minute. Push 1 side of egg away from edge, tipping pan so some uncooked egg flows underneath. Cover. Cook for 1 minute.

Scatter cream cheese over top. Drizzle with sauce. Sprinkle with green onion and shrimp. Cover. Cook over low for 1 to 2 minutes until cheese is melted and shrimp is hot. Slide onto plate, folding one half over the other. Serves 1.

1 serving: 363 Calories; 28 g Protein; 19.8 g Total Fat; 19 g Carbohydrate; 1309 mg Sodium; 1 g Dietary Fibre

Pictured on page 53.

Turkey Sandwiches

You would never know canned turkey was used.

TURKEY FILLING

Canned flaked turkey, with liquid	6 1/2 oz.	184 g
Grated medium Cheddar cheese	1/2 cup	125 mL
Sweet pickle relish	2 tbsp.	30 mL
Light salad dressing (or mayonnaise)	2 tbsp.	30 mL
Finely chopped celery	2 tbsp.	30 mL
Finely chopped onion (or 1/2 tsp., 2 mL, powder)	2 tbsp.	30 mL
Salt, sprinkle		
Pepper, sprinkle		
Bread slices (buttered, optional)	8	8

Turkey Filling: Mix first 8 ingredients well in small bowl.

Spread 1/4 of filling on each of 4 bread slices. Cover with remaining 4 bread slices. Cut diagonally into quarters. Makes 16 small sandwiches, enough to serve 4.

1 serving: 302 Calories; 18 g Protein; 11 g Total Fat; 31 g Carbohydrate; 648 mg Sodium; 1 g Dietary Fibre

Pictured on page 54.

Tuna Biscuits,
below

Tuna Biscuits

A novel way to serve a tuna sandwich.

TUNA FILLING

Canned tuna, drained and flaked	6 1/2 oz.	184 g
Finely diced celery	1/3 cup	75 mL
Grated carrot	1/3 cup	75 mL
Light salad dressing (or mayonnaise)	1/3 cup	75 mL
Sweet pickle relish	2 tbsp.	30 mL
Lemon juice	1/2 tsp.	2 mL
Salt	1/8 tsp.	0.5 mL
Pepper, sprinkle		

BISCUIT DOUGH

All-purpose flour	2 cups	500 mL
Baking powder	4 tsp.	20 mL
Granulated sugar	1 tsp.	5 mL
Salt	1 tsp.	5 mL
Milk	3/4 cup	175 mL
Cooking oil	1/3 cup	75 mL

Tuna Filling: Combine all 8 ingredients in small bowl.

Biscuit Dough: Stir flour, baking powder, sugar and salt in medium bowl.

Add milk and cooking oil. Mix to form soft ball. Knead on lightly floured surface 8 times. Roll 1/2 of dough 1/4 inch (6 mm) thick. Cut into 6 rounds, 4 inches (10 cm) in diameter.

Place 3 tbsp. (50 mL) filling in centre of each round. Roll out second 1/2 of dough. Cut into 6 more circles. Dampen edge of filled rounds with water. Cover with second round. Press edges to seal. Arrange on ungreased baking sheet. Bake in 375°F (190°C) oven for 15 to 20 minutes until golden. Scraps of dough may be made into biscuits and baked as well. Makes 6 filled biscuits.

1 filled biscuit: 376 Calories; 13 g Protein; 17.7 g Total Fat; 41 g Carbohydrate; 775 mg Sodium; 2 g Dietary Fibre

Pictured above.

Niçoise Pasta Salad

Decorative. Serve with crusty bread for a great lunch.

Tri-coloured fusilli (or other medium) pasta	8 oz.	225 g
Boiling water	2 qts.	2 L
Cooking oil (optional)	1 tbsp.	15 mL
Salt	2 tsp.	10 mL
Small head of iceberg lettuce, coarsely shredded	1	1
Small red onion, sliced paper thin and separated into rings	1	1
Canned solid tuna, drained and broken into chunks	2 x 6 1/2 oz.	2 x 184 g
Fresh (or frozen) cooked green beans, cooled, cut or french cut	1 1/2 cups	375 mL
Whole pitted ripe olives, halved	1/3 cup	75 mL
DRESSING		
Cooking oil	1/3 cup	75 mL
Red wine vinegar	1/3 cup	75 mL
Dried sweet basil	1/2 tsp.	2 mL
Salt	1/2 tsp.	2 mL
Pepper	1/4 tsp.	1 mL
Garlic powder	1/4 tsp.	1 mL
Medium tomatoes, cut into wedges	2	2
Large hard-boiled eggs, quartered (or sliced)	3	3

Cook pasta in boiling water, cooking oil and salt in large uncovered pot or Dutch oven for 8 to 10 minutes until tender but firm. Drain. Rinse with cold water. Drain well. Transfer to large bowl. Cool completely.

Add next 5 ingredients. Mix.

Dressing: Stir first 6 ingredients in small bowl. Pour over tuna mixture. Toss. Divide among 6 plates.

Garnish each plate with tomato and egg wedges. Serves 6.

1 serving: 397 Calories; 23 g Protein; 18.1 g Total Fat; 36 g Carbohydrate; 516 mg Sodium; 3 g Dietary Fibre

Pictured below.

> "My first experience in the kitchen, when I was about eight years old, was making porridge for the family in the early morning because everyone else was doing various chores."
>
> "A prairie dust storm meant you had to wash dishes before a meal! I was lucky though–our house was pretty airtight."
>
> Jean Paré

Niçoise Pasta Salad, above

Saucy Asparagus

Baked on a tender biscuit crust. A very different presentation.

Milk	1 1/2 cups	375 mL
All-purpose flour	3 tbsp.	50 mL
Grated medium Cheddar cheese	1 cup	250 mL
Salt	1/4 tsp.	1 mL
Pepper	1/4 tsp.	1 mL
Refrigerator country-style biscuits (10 per tube)	12 oz.	340 g
Canned asparagus tips, drained	12 oz.	341 mL
Sliced almonds, toasted in 350°F (175°C) oven for 5 to 8 minutes	1/4 cup	60 mL

Gradually whisk milk into flour in small saucepan until smooth. Heat and stir until boiling and thickened.

Stir in cheese, salt and pepper. Heat until cheese is melted.

Press biscuits to make crust in greased 9 inch (22 cm) pie plate.

Arrange asparagus over crust. Pour sauce over asparagus. Sprinkle with almonds. Bake in 450°F (230°C) oven for about 15 minutes. Cuts into 8 wedges.

1 wedge: 236 Calories; 10 g Protein; 10.1 g Total Fat; 26 g Carbohydrate; 736 mg Sodium; 1 g Dietary Fibre

Pictured on this page.

Apple Scallop

A wonderful addition to breakfast. Double or triple the recipe for a buffet breakfast. A dollop of whipped topping finishes it nicely.

Granulated sugar	1/4 cup	60 mL
All-purpose flour	1 1/2 tbsp.	25 mL
Ground cinnamon	1 tsp.	5 mL
Medium cooking apples, (such as McIntosh), peeled and sliced	4	4
Hard margarine (or butter)	1 tbsp.	15 mL

Measure sugar, flour and cinnamon into ungreased 1 1/2 quart (1.5 L) casserole. Stir.

Add apple. Stir well.

Dab pieces of margarine here and there. Cover. Bake in 350°F (175°C) oven for 45 to 55 minutes until tender. Serves 4.

1 serving: 164 Calories; 1 g Protein; 3.4 g Total Fat; 35 g Carbohydrate; 35 mg Sodium; 3 g Dietary Fibre

Pictured on this page.

Top left and bottom: Saucy Asparagus, this page
Top right: Apple Scallop, this page

Stir-Fry Salad

A most attractive presentation. Contains tender strips of beef.

DRESSING

Cooking oil	1/4 cup	60 mL
Brown sugar, packed	1 tbsp.	15 mL
Ground cumin	1 tsp.	5 mL
Ground coriander	1 tsp.	5 mL
Dried crushed chilies, finely crushed	1 tsp.	5 mL
Garlic powder	1/2 tsp.	2 mL
Lime juice	2 tbsp.	30 mL
Beef flank (or top round) steak, cut on angle across grain into very thin strips	1 lb.	454 g
Medium green pepper, slivered	1	1
Medium red pepper, slivered	1	1
Medium red onion, halved lengthwise and sliced crosswise, 1/4 inch (6 mm) thick	1	1
Green jalapeño pepper, seeds and ribs removed, finely chopped	1	1
Shredded romaine lettuce	4 cups	1 L

Dressing: Combine first 6 ingredients in small cup.

Put lime juice and beef strips into medium bowl. Add 1 tbsp. (15 mL) dressing. Stir to coat well. Let stand at room temperature for 30 minutes.

Heat 1 tbsp. (15 mL) dressing in large non-stick frying pan. Add green pepper, red pepper, red onion and jalapeño pepper. Sauté until tender crisp. Transfer vegetables and any remaining dressing into large bowl.

Add beef strips with liquid to same hot frying pan. Stir-fry for 3 to 4 minutes until desired doneness. Add to vegetables in bowl. Toss well with remaining dressing. Divide lettuce among 4 plates. Divide beef mixture over top. Serve immediately. Serves 4.

1 serving: 318 Calories; 26 g Protein; 25 g Total Fat; 11 g Carbohydrate; 85 mg Sodium; 2 g Dietary Fibre

Pictured on page 53.

Swedish Tea Ring

Sweet biscuit taste with a delicate cream cheese flavour.
Very attractive. Best served warm but good either way.

CHEESE FILLING		
Light cream cheese, softened	4 oz.	125 g
Granulated sugar	3 tbsp.	50 mL
Vanilla	1/2 tsp.	2 mL
BREAD		
All-purpose flour	1 3/4 cups	425 mL
Granulated sugar	1 tbsp.	15 mL
Baking powder	1 tbsp.	15 mL
Salt	1/2 tsp.	2 mL
Hard margarine (or butter)	1/4 cup	60 mL
Milk	3/4 cup	175 mL
Chopped glazed cherries	1/3 cup	75 mL
Raisins	1/4 cup	60 mL
GLAZE		
Icing (confectioner's) sugar	1/2 cup	125 mL
Water	1 1/2 tsp.	7 mL
Sliced almonds, toasted in 350°F (175°C) oven for 5 to 8 minutes (optional)	1/4 cup	60 mL

Cheese Filling: Beat cream cheese, sugar and vanilla in small bowl until smooth.

Bread: Measure flour, sugar, baking powder, salt and margarine into medium bowl. Cut in margarine with pastry cutter until crumbly.

Stir in milk until ball is formed. Turn out onto lightly floured surface. Knead 8 times. Roll into 8 x 16 inch (20 x 40 cm) rectangle. Spread with filling.

Sprinkle with cherries and raisins. Roll up from long side like jelly roll. Seal long edge. Place seam side down on greased baking sheet. Form into ring. Pinch ends together to seal. Using scissors, cut from outside edge toward middle, over halfway through roll at 1 inch (2.5 cm) intervals. Turn each cut section on its side. Bake in 425°F (220°C) oven for 18 to 20 minutes until golden. Cool slightly.

Glaze: Stir icing sugar and water in small bowl, adding more icing sugar or water if needed to make a barely pourable consistency. Drizzle over barely warm tea ring.

Sprinkle almonds over glaze. Cuts into 12 pieces.

1 piece: 200 Calories; 4 g Protein; 6.2 g Total Fat; 33 g Carbohydrate; 274 mg Sodium; 1 g Dietary Fibre

Pictured on page 53.

Sweet Swirl Rolls

Very decorative with a bit of red jam showing through a white glaze.

Large egg, fork-beaten	1	1
Granulated sugar	2 tbsp.	30 mL
Envelope instant yeast (1 scant tbsp., 15 mL)	1 x 1/4 oz.	1 x 8 g
Warm milk	3/4 cup	175 mL
Warm water	1/3 cup	75 mL
Salt	1 tsp.	5 mL
All-purpose flour	1 1/2 cups	375 mL
All-purpose flour, approximately	2 cups	500 mL
Red jam	1/2 cup	125 mL
GLAZE		
Icing (confectioner's) sugar	1 cup	250 mL
Milk (or water)	1 tbsp.	15 mL
Vanilla	1/4 tsp.	1 mL

Combine egg, sugar and yeast in large bowl. Beat to mix. Add warm milk, warm water and salt. Mix.

Add first amount of flour. Beat well.

Stir and knead in second amount of flour until no longer sticky. Divide dough into 20 pieces. Roll each piece into 14 inch (35 cm) rope. Coil each into circle like a pinwheel on 2 greased baking sheets, pinching ends underneath to seal. Cover with tea towel. Let stand in oven with light on and door closed for about 1 hour until doubled in size.

Make indentation in centre of each roll using thumb. Fill with 1 tsp. (5 mL) jam. Bake in 375°F (190°C) oven for about 15 minutes until browned. Cool.

Glaze: Stir icing sugar, milk and vanilla together in small bowl. Add more icing sugar or milk if needed to make barely pourable consistency. Drizzle over rolls. Makes 20 rolls.

1 roll: 145 Calories; 3 g Protein; 0.6 g Total Fat; 32 g Carbohydrate; 146 mg Sodium; 1 g Dietary Fibre

Pictured on page 53.

Cheese Brunch Cake

Makes two wonderful yeast coffee cakes.
Serve one warm and freeze the other.

Milk	1/2 cup	125 mL
Hard margarine (or butter)	6 tbsp.	100 mL
Granulated sugar	1/3 cup	75 mL
Salt	3/4 tsp.	4 mL
Envelope instant yeast (1 scant tbsp., 15 mL)	1 x 1/4 oz.	1 x 8 g
All-purpose flour	1/2 cup	125 mL
Large eggs, room temperature	3	3
Golden raisins	1/2 cup	125 mL
Grated lemon peel	2 tsp.	10 mL
All-purpose flour, approximately	3 1/4 cups	800 mL

CHEESE FILLING

Light cream cheese	8 oz.	250 g
Dry curd cottage cheese	1/2 cup	125 mL
Granulated sugar	1/4 cup	60 mL
Large egg	1	1
Grated lemon peel	1 tsp.	5 mL
Vanilla	1 tsp.	5 mL
Ground cinnamon	1/4 tsp.	1 mL

CRUMB TOPPING

All-purpose flour	1/4 cup	60 mL
Granulated sugar	1/4 cup	60 mL
Finely chopped nuts	1/3 cup	75 mL
Ground cinnamon	1/4 tsp.	1 mL
Hard margarine (or butter), softened	1/4 cup	60 mL

Combine first 4 ingredients in small saucepan. Heat until margarine is melted. Pour into large bowl. Cool slightly until still very warm but not hot.

Combine yeast and first amount of flour in small bowl. Whisk into milk mixture until smooth and yeast is dissolved.

Beat eggs in medium bowl until frothy. Stir into yeast mixture. Add raisins and lemon peel. Stir.

Knead in second amount of flour until dough is elastic and no longer sticky. Place in large greased bowl, turning once to grease top. Cover with tea towel. Let stand in oven with light on and door closed for 1 hour. Punch down dough. Divide into 4 portions. Press 1 portion in greased 8 or 9 inch (20 or 22 cm) round cake pan, covering bottom and 1 inch (2.5 cm) up side. Repeat with second portion in second cake pan. Set remaining 2 portions aside.

Cheese Filling: Beat all 7 ingredients together well in medium bowl until fairly smooth. Spread 1/2 over each crust in pans. Roll remaining 2 portions of dough into circles large enough to fit tops. Place over cheese filling. Pinch edges of crusts together to seal.

Crumb Topping: Mix all 5 ingredients in small bowl until crumbly. Sprinkle 1/2 over each coffee cake. Cover with tea towel. Let stand in oven with light on and door closed for 1 hour until doubled in size. Bake in 350°F (175°C) oven for about 30 minutes until golden. Remove from pans to racks to cool for 30 minutes before serving. Each cake cuts into 6 wedges, for a total of 12 wedges.

1 wedge: 430 Calories; 11 g Protein; 18 g Total Fat; 56 g Carbohydrate; 515 mg Sodium; 2 g Dietary Fibre

Pictured below.

Top left: Maple-Flavoured Syrup, page 60
Top right: Cheese Brunch Cake, this page
Centre left: Marshmallow Puffs, page 60
Bottom right: Baked Pancake, page 60

Granola Bars

*Soft and chewy. Perfect for breakfast
on the go or school lunches.*

Quick-cooking rolled oats (not instant)	3 cups	750 mL
Brown sugar, packed	1/4 cup	60 mL
Flake coconut	1/4 cup	60 mL
Salt	1/2 tsp.	2 mL
Wheat germ	1/4 cup	60 mL
Hard margarine (or butter)	1/2 cup	125 mL
Corn syrup	1/3 cup	75 mL
Liquid honey	1/3 cup	75 mL
Vanilla	1 tsp.	5 mL
Semi-sweet chocolate chips	1/2 cup	125 mL

Stir rolled oats, brown sugar, coconut, salt and wheat germ in large bowl. Cut in margarine until mixture is crumbly and no large pieces remain.

Add corn syrup, honey and vanilla. Stir well.

Add chocolate chips. Work in. Press firmly in greased 9 x 9 inch (22 x 22 cm) pan. Bake in 350°F (175°C) oven for 30 to 40 minutes until golden. Chill for several hours or overnight. Cuts into 24 bars.

1 bar: 159 Calories; 2 g Protein; 7.5 g Total Fat; 22 g Carbohydrate; 111 mg Sodium; 2 g Dietary Fibre

Pictured on page 52.

Baked Pancake

Feed a morning grouch this Yorkshire Pudding-like pancake and watch a transformation before your eyes. Serve with warm Maple-Flavoured Syrup, this page.

Large eggs	3	3
All-purpose flour	1/2 cup	125 mL
Milk	1/2 cup	125 mL
Salt	1/4 tsp.	1 mL
Hard margarine (or butter), melted	2 tbsp.	30 mL

Beat all 5 ingredients together in small bowl or process in blender. Pour into greased 8 x 8 inch (20 x 20 cm) pan. Bake in 400°F (205°C) oven for about 20 minutes until lightly browned. Cuts into 4 pieces.

1 piece: 177 Calories; 8 g Protein; 9.6 g Total Fat; 15 g Carbohydrate; 296 mg Sodium; 1 g Dietary Fibre

Pictured on page 59.

Marshmallow Puffs

It's magic! The marshmallow disappears leaving delicious hollow buns. Serve warm with a fruit salad for a special brunch.

Refrigerator crescent-style rolls (8 per tube)	2 x 8 1/2 oz.	2 x 235 g
Hard margarine (or butter), melted	1 tbsp.	15 mL
Finely chopped pecans (or walnuts)	3 tbsp.	50 mL
Large marshmallows	16	16
Granulated sugar	2 tbsp.	30 mL
Ground cinnamon	1/2 tsp.	2 mL

Separate crescent rolls into 16 triangles.

Put margarine and pecans into 2 small dishes. Dip 1 end of each marshmallow into margarine, then into pecans. Place each marshmallow on each triangle of dough.

Combine sugar and cinnamon in small cup. Sprinkle 1/4 tsp. (1 mL) over each marshmallow. Pinch dough around marshmallow to seal. Gently roll each into ball. Set in greased muffin cup. Bake in 375°F (190°C) oven for 10 to 15 minutes until golden. Makes 16 marshmallow puffs.

1 puff: 92 Calories; 1 g Protein; 4 g Total Fat; 13 g Carbohydrate; 157 mg Sodium; trace Dietary Fibre

Pictured on page 59.

Maple-Flavoured Syrup

This is always close by on the shelf to make at a moment's notice. Serve with Baked Pancake, this page, regular pancakes, waffles or French toast.

Brown sugar, packed	2 cups	500 mL
Water	1 cup	250 mL
Maple flavouring	1 tsp.	5 mL

Combine brown sugar and water in small saucepan. Bring to a boil. Boil for 2 to 3 minutes. Remove from heat.

Add maple flavouring. Makes 2 cups (500 mL) syrup.

2 tbsp. (30 mL) syrup: 104 Calories; 0 g Protein; 0 g Total Fat; 27 g Carbohydrate; 8 mg Sodium; trace Dietary Fibre

Pictured on page 59.

"Real maple syrup in the 1950s was not considered an extravagant ingredient and was not expensive. Today, it's quite expensive and a real treat."

Jean Paré

Cakes

Orange Cake with Chocolate Orange Icing, page 62

Cakes

Fruit cakes, pound cakes, sponge cakes and jelly rolls date way back. Angel food cake was quite popular in the 1880s and chocolate marble cakes became the rage after the American Civil War in 1865. The Great War created the necessity of making cakes with less butter, sugar and eggs; applesauce cake was the answer. Cake baking remained strong, even throughout the Great Depression, but then came the rationing of butter and sugar because of the Second World War. Fewer ingredients meant cakes were able to be made in one bowl, a preference which eventually led to the development of the commercial cake mix in 1947. The first cake mixes called only for the addition of water—a true cake mix! During the 1990s, when an appreciation of fitness and health became fashionable, non-fat and low-fat cake recipes that used applesauce or other puréed fruits as a substitute for fat, found their market. Likewise, using egg whites or egg substitute instead of the whole egg also helped to reduce cholesterol and fat. Cakes have evolved and changed over time, but their popularity remains steadfast. We offer a variety of delicious recipes—both old and new—in this section.

> *"Gram made cakes with cream instead of butter and then poured cream over the finished cake. Oh, the cholesterol—but they sure were delicious!"*
>
> Jean Paré

Orange Cake

Orange both in appearance and in flavour. For the final touch, ice with Chocolate Orange Icing, below.

All-purpose flour	2 1/4 cups	550 mL
Baking powder	4 tsp.	20 mL
Salt	1/2 tsp.	2 mL
Hard margarine (or butter), softened	1/2 cup	125 mL
Granulated sugar	1 1/2 cups	375 mL
Grated peel of 1 medium orange		
Large eggs	2	2
Frozen concentrated orange juice, thawed	1/3 cup	75 mL
Milk	1 cup	250 mL

Stir flour, baking powder and salt in medium bowl.

Cream margarine and sugar together in large bowl. Mix in orange peel. Beat in eggs, 1 at a time. Add concentrated orange juice. Mix.

Add flour mixture in 3 parts alternately with milk in 2 parts, beginning and ending with flour mixture. Turn into 2 greased 8 inch (20 cm) round cake pans. Bake in 350°F (175°C) oven for about 35 minutes until wooden pick inserted in centre comes out clean. Let stand for 10 minutes before removing to rack to cool. Cuts into 16 pieces.

1 piece (without icing): 227 Calories; 3 g Protein; 7.1 g Total Fat; 38 g Carbohydrate; 177 mg Sodium; 1 g Dietary Fibre

Pictured on page 61.

Chocolate Orange Icing

Chocolate and orange flavours are meant to be together. Use to ice Orange Cake, above.

Hard margarine (or butter), softened	6 tbsp.	100 mL
Icing (confectioner's) sugar	2 1/2 cups	625 mL
Cocoa	1/2 cup	125 mL
Frozen concentrated orange juice, thawed	2 tbsp.	30 mL

Combine all 4 ingredients in medium bowl. Beat on low to moisten. Beat on high to blend well. Add more icing sugar or liquid as needed to make proper spreading consistency. Makes about 2 cups (500 mL) icing.

2 tbsp. (30 mL) icing: 117 Calories; 1 g Protein; 4.5 g Total Fat; 21 g Carbohydrate; 50 mg Sodium; 1 g Dietary Fibre

Pictured on page 61.

Fruitcake

(old recipe)

This recipe is from my Grandma Elford's cookbook. I wonder how this would turn out at today's prices?

Fruitcake

1 ½ cups sugar
4 eggs, well beaten
½ cup coffee
½ cup chopped suet
1 teaspoon cinnamon
½ teaspoon allspice
1 cup butter
½ cup molasses
3 cups flour
1 teaspoon soda
½ teaspoon cloves
2 cups raisins
10 cents' worth of citron peel; 10 cents' worth of almond meats; 5 cents' worth of lemon and orange peel together; chop these very fine or put through a meat grinder.

Fruitcake, this page

Fruitcake

(new recipe)

In the past, it was common to serve fruitcake at weddings. Guests would take their piece home and place it under their pillow for sweet dreams.

Raisins	2 cups	500 mL
Chopped citron	1 cup	250 mL
Slivered almonds, toasted in 350°F (175°C) oven for 5 to 8 minutes	1 cup	250 mL
Holiday fruit mix, with peel	1 cup	250 mL
Glazed cherries, chopped	1/4 cup	60 mL
All-purpose flour	1/3 cup	75 mL
Hard margarine (or butter), softened	1 cup	250 mL
Granulated sugar	1 1/2 cups	375 mL
Large eggs	4	4
Fancy molasses	1/2 cup	125 mL
Prepared coffee	1/2 cup	125 mL
All-purpose flour	3 cups	750 mL
Ground cinnamon	1 tsp.	5 mL
Ground allspice	1/2 tsp.	2 mL
Ground cloves	1/2 tsp.	2 mL
Baking soda	1 tsp.	5 mL

Measure first 6 ingredients into medium bowl. Toss well to coat with flour.

Cream margarine and sugar together in large bowl. Beat in eggs, 1 at a time. Mix in molasses and prepared coffee.

Stir remaining 5 ingredients together in separate medium bowl. Add to coffee mixture. Stir just to moisten. Add fruit mixture. Mix. Line 2 greased 9 x 5 x 3 inch (22 x 12.5 x 7.5 cm) loaf pans with greased brown paper. Divide dough between pans. Place separate pan, with about 1 inch (2.5 cm) water, on bottom rack in oven. Bake cakes on centre rack in 275°F (140°C) oven for about 2 hours 50 minutes until wooden pick inserted in centre comes out clean. Let stand for 10 minutes before removing to rack to cool. Makes 2 cakes. Each cake cuts into 20 pieces, for a total of 40 pieces.

1 piece: 422 Calories; 6 g Protein; 14.6 g Total Fat; 70 g Carbohydrate; 233 mg Sodium; 2 g Dietary Fibre

Pictured on this page.

Boiled Raisin Cake

Moist with raisins and spices. Caramel icing tops it off.

Raisins	1 1/2 cups	375 mL
Water	2 cups	500 mL
All-purpose flour	1 3/4 cups	425 mL
Baking powder	1 1/2 tsp.	7 mL
Baking soda	1/2 tsp.	2 mL
Ground cinnamon	3/4 tsp.	4 mL
Ground nutmeg	1/2 tsp.	2 mL
Salt	1/2 tsp.	2 mL
Hard margarine (or butter), softened	1/2 cup	125 mL
Brown sugar, packed	1 cup	250 mL
Large egg, fork-beaten	1	1
Vanilla	1 tsp.	5 mL

Caramel Icing, page 158

Combine raisins and water in small saucepan. Boil gently for about 6 minutes. Drain, reserving 2/3 cup (150 mL) liquid.

Stir next 6 ingredients in medium bowl.

Cream margarine, brown sugar, egg and vanilla together well in large bowl.

Add flour mixture in 3 parts, and raisins and reserved liquid in 2 parts, beginning and ending with flour mixture, stirring just to blend. Turn into greased 9 x 9 inch (22 x 22 cm) pan. Bake in 350°F (175°C) oven for about 40 minutes until wooden pick inserted in centre comes out clean.

Ice with Caramel Icing. Cuts into 12 pieces.

1 piece with icing: 415 Calories; 3 g Protein; 13 g Total Fat; 74 g Carbohydrate; 335 mg Sodium; 1 g Dietary Fibre

Pictured below.

Boiled Raisin Cake, above

Piña Colada Cake

This PEEN-yah Koh-LAH-duh layer cake is nice and high, with a light and fluffy icing.

White cake mix (2 layer size)	1	1
Instant vanilla pudding powder (4 serving size)	1	1
Water	2/3 cup	150 mL
White (or light) rum	1/3 cup	75 mL
Cooking oil	1/2 cup	125 mL
Large eggs	4	4
Coconut flavouring (optional)	1 tsp.	5 mL
Long thread coconut, toasted in 350°F (175°C) oven, stirring often, for 5 to 8 minutes	1/2 cup	125 mL

PINEAPPLE ICING

Icing (confectioner's) sugar	1/2 cup	125 mL
Canned crushed pineapple, with juice	8 oz.	225 mL
Instant vanilla pudding powder (4 serving size)	1	1
White (or light) rum	1 tsp.	5 mL
Envelope dessert topping (not prepared)	1	1
Milk	1/3 cup	75 mL
Long thread coconut, toasted in 350°F (175°C) oven, stirring often, for 5 to 8 minutes, for garnish	2 tbsp.	30 mL

Combine first 7 ingredients in medium bowl. Beat on low until moistened. Beat on medium for about 2 minutes until smooth.

Stir in coconut. Turn into greased 9 x 13 inch (22 x 33 cm) pan. Bake in 350°F (175°C) oven for 35 to 45 minutes until wooden pick inserted in centre comes out clean. Cool.

Pineapple Icing: Mix first 4 ingredients in small bowl. Let stand for 5 minutes.

Beat dessert topping with milk until stiff. Fold into pineapple mixture. Ice cake.

Sprinkle with coconut. Cuts into 18 pieces.

1 piece (with icing): 305 Calories; 3 g Protein; 13.6 g Total Fat; 41 g Carbohydrate; 160 mg Sodium; 1 g Dietary Fibre

Note: For a layer cake, turn into 2 greased 8 inch (20 cm) round cake pans. Bake for 30 to 35 minutes.

Pictured on page 70.

Pineapple Nut Coffee Cake

Rather a solid texture. Makes a nice coffee cake.

All-purpose flour	2 1/2 cups	625 mL
Baking powder	1 1/2 tsp.	7 mL
Salt	1/2 tsp.	2 mL
Finely chopped walnuts (or pecans)	1 cup	250 mL
Finely chopped candied pineapple	3/4 cup	175 mL
Hard margarine (or butter), softened	1 cup	250 mL
Granulated sugar	1 cup	250 mL
Large eggs	5	5
Crushed pineapple, with juice	3/4 cup	175 mL
Brandy flavouring	2 tsp.	10 mL

Stir first 5 ingredients in large bowl. Make a well in centre.

Cream margarine and sugar together in medium bowl. Beat in eggs, 1 at a time. Stir in pineapple with juice and brandy flavouring. Add to well. Stir just to moisten. Turn into greased 10 inch (25 cm) angel food tube pan. Bake in 275°F (140°C) oven for 2 hours until wooden pick inserted in centre comes out clean. Let stand for 10 minutes before removing to rack to cool. Cuts into 24 pieces.

1 piece: 232 Calories; 4 g Protein; 12.8 g Total Fat; 27 g Carbohydrate; 168 mg Sodium; 1 g Dietary Fibre

Pictured on this page.

Lemon Rum Cake

A touch of the Caribbean.

Lemon cake mix (2 layer size)	1	1
Large eggs	4	4
Cooking oil	1/2 cup	125 mL
Milk	1/2 cup	125 mL
Grated peel of 1 medium lemon		
Dark rum	1/2 cup	125 mL
LEMON GLAZE		
Icing (confectioner's) sugar	1 cup	250 mL
Lemon juice	1 tbsp.	15 mL
Dark rum	1 1/2 tsp.	7 mL

Combine first 6 ingredients in medium bowl. Beat on low to moisten. Beat on medium for about 2 minutes until smooth. Turn into greased 12 cup (2.7 L) bundt pan. Bake in 350°F (175°C) oven for about 1 hour until wooden pick inserted in centre comes out clean. Let stand for 20 minutes. Invert onto plate or rack to cool.

Lemon Glaze: Mix icing sugar, lemon juice and rum in small bowl. Add a bit more icing sugar or lemon juice if needed to make a barely pourable consistency. Drizzle over cake. Cuts into 16 pieces.

1 piece: 273 Calories; 3 g Protein; 12.7 g Total Fat; 33 g Carbohydrate; 150 mg Sodium; trace Dietary Fibre

Pictured on this page.

Top: Lemon Rum Cake, this page
Centre: Pineapple Nut Coffee Cake, this page
Bottom: Sour Cream Cake, below

Sour Cream Cake

This was a regular on farms many years ago when cream was plentiful. Garnish this light cake with strawberries.

Cake flour (sift before measuring)	1 1/2 cups	375 mL
Baking powder	1 1/2 tsp.	7 mL
Baking soda	1/4 tsp.	1 mL
Salt	1/4 tsp.	1 mL
Large eggs (room temperature)	2	2
Granulated sugar	3/4 cup	175 mL
Vanilla	1 tsp.	5 mL
Sour cream (not light or low-fat)	2/3 cup	150 mL

Sift cake flour, baking powder, baking soda and salt 2 times on large plate or waxed paper.

Beat eggs in medium bowl until light in colour, very thick and increased in volume. This will take about 5 minutes. Gradually add sugar, 2 tbsp. (30 mL) at a time, beating well after each addition. Add vanilla. Stir.

Add flour mixture alternately in 3 parts with sour cream in 2 parts, beginning and ending with flour mixture. Turn into greased and floured 8 x 8 inch (20 x 20 cm) pan. Bake in 350°F (175°C) oven for 30 to 35 minutes until golden and wooden pick inserted in centre comes out clean. Cuts into 12 pieces.

1 piece: 137 Calories; 3 g Protein; 2.8 g Total Fat; 25 g Carbohydrate; 104 mg Sodium; trace Dietary Fibre

Pictured above.

Chocolate Date Cake

A cook's choice—a cake you don't need to ice.

Boiling water	1 1/4 cups	300 mL
Chopped dates	2 cups	500 mL
Hard margarine (or butter), softened	3/4 cup	175 mL
Granulated sugar	1 cup	250 mL
Large eggs	2	2
Vanilla	1 tsp.	5 mL
All-purpose flour	2 cups	500 mL
Cocoa	1 tbsp.	15 mL
Baking soda	1 tsp.	5 mL
Salt	1/2 tsp.	2 mL
Semi-sweet chocolate chips	1/2 cup	125 mL
Chopped walnuts (or pecans)	1/2 cup	125 mL

Pour boiling water over dates in small bowl. Let stand until cool.

Cream margarine and sugar together in large bowl. Beat in eggs, 1 at a time. Add vanilla. Add date mixture. Stir.

Add flour, cocoa, baking soda and salt. Mix. Turn into greased 9 x 13 inch (22 x 33 cm) pan.

Sprinkle with chocolate chips and walnuts. Bake in 350°F (175°C) oven for about 40 minutes. Cuts into 24 pieces.

1 piece: 208 Calories; 3 g Protein; 9.8 g Total Fat; 30 g Carbohydrate; 192 mg Sodium; 2 g Dietary Fibre

Pictured below.

Chocolate Date Cake, above

Dark Chocolate Cake

A very light texture to this delicious cake.
Ice with Chocolate Mocha Icing, below.

Cooking oil	1/2 cup	125 mL
Granulated sugar	3/4 cup	175 mL
Brown sugar, packed	1 cup	250 mL
Large eggs	2	2
Vanilla	1 tsp.	5 mL
Buttermilk (or reconstituted from powder)	1 cup	250 mL
Strong prepared coffee	1 cup	250 mL
All-purpose flour	2 cups	500 mL
Cocoa (sifted if lumpy)	3/4 cup	175 mL
Baking soda	2 tsp.	10 mL
Baking powder	1 tsp.	5 mL
Salt	1 tsp.	5 mL

Beat cooking oil and both sugars in large bowl. Beat in eggs, 1 at a time. Add vanilla. Mix.

Beat in buttermilk and prepared coffee.

Add remaining 5 ingredients. Beat until smooth. Batter will be thin. Pour into greased 9 x 13 inch (22 x 33 cm) pan. Bake in 350°F (175°C) oven for about 45 minutes until wooden pick inserted in centre comes out clean. Cool. Cuts into 18 pieces.

1 piece (without icing): 214 Calories; 3 g Protein; 7.5 g Total Fat; 35 g Carbohydrate; 331 mg Sodium; 2 g Dietary Fibre

Pictured on page 70.

Variation: For a layer cake, turn into 2 greased 8 inch (20 cm) round cake pans. Bake for 30 to 35 minutes.

Chocolate Mocha Icing

A wonderful blend of coffee and chocolate.
Use to ice Dark Chocolate Cake, above.

Icing (confectioner's) sugar	3 cups	750 mL
Hard margarine (or butter), softened	1/2 cup	125 mL
Cocoa	1/4 cup	60 mL
Vanilla	2 tsp.	10 mL
Strong prepared coffee	1/4 cup	60 mL

Measure all 5 ingredients into medium bowl. Beat on low to moisten. Beat on medium until smooth and creamy. Add more icing sugar or prepared coffee if needed to make proper spreading consistency. Makes 1 1/2 cups (375 mL) icing.

2 tbsp. (30 mL) icing: 189 Calories; 1 g Protein; 8 g Total Fat; 31 g Carbohydrate; 92 mg Sodium; 1 g Dietary Fibre

Pictured on page 70.

Mock Angel Cake

(old recipe)

*This is a recipe from my great-great-Aunt Frank (Frances).
No temperature, no time given—but I bet it always
turned out delicious!*

> From: Aunt Frank
>
> Mock Angel Cake
>
> 1 cup   Flour   1 cup Sugar
> 2 tsps   Baking Powder Pinch of Salt
>
> Put all into sifter, sift together 4 times;
> add 1 cup boiling milk; stir until smooth;
> lastly fold well beaten whites of 2 eggs;
> fold carefully until whites are evenly folded
> in batter; do not grease tin or flavor cake; ice to
> please

Mock Angel Cake

(new recipe)

*This recipe has an extra half recipe added to take
advantage of the larger modern angel food tube pan.
If you have the smaller eight-inch (20 cm) angel food
tube pan, you can use the original recipe, this page.*

All-purpose flour	1 1/2 cups	375 mL
Granulated sugar	1 1/2 cups	375 mL
Baking powder	1 tbsp.	15 mL
Salt	1/4 tsp.	1 mL
Milk	1 1/2 cups	375 mL
Egg whites (large), room temperature	3	3

Measure first 4 ingredients into flour sifter. Sift onto
large plate or waxed paper. Sift 3 more times, sifting
into large bowl for 4th sifting.

Heat milk in small saucepan until just boiling. Remove
from heat immediately. Stir into flour mixture until
smooth.

Beat egg whites in medium bowl until stiff. Fold into batter
until no streaks remain. Turn into ungreased 10 inch (25 cm)
angel food tube pan. Bake in 350°F (175°C) oven for about
45 minutes until golden. Invert pan onto rack to cool.
Remove cake from pan when completely cooled. Cuts into
16 pieces.

*1 piece: 135 Calories; 3 g Protein; 0.4 g Total Fat; 31 g Carbohydrate; 68 mg Sodium;
trace Dietary Fibre*

Pictured below.

Mock Angel Cake, above

Top: Coffee-Group Cake, this page
Bottom: Tomato Soup Cake, below

HEIRLOOM RECIPE

Tomato Soup Cake

An old family favourite without nuts or raisins. Cake is quite moist. Ice with your favourite chocolate icing or garnish with whipped topping and chopped walnuts.

Hard margarine (or butter)	1/2 cup	125 mL
Granulated sugar	1 cup	250 mL
Large egg	1	1
All-purpose flour	1 1/2 cups	375 mL
Ground cinnamon	1/2 tsp.	2 mL
Ground nutmeg	1/2 tsp.	2 mL
Ground cloves	1/2 tsp.	2 mL
Salt	1/2 tsp.	2 mL
Raisins (optional)	1 cup	250 mL
Chopped walnuts (optional)	3/4 cup	175 mL
Baking soda	1 tsp.	5 mL
Hot water	2 tsp.	10 mL
Condensed cream of tomato soup	10 oz.	284 mL

Cream margarine and sugar together in large bowl. Add egg. Beat well.

Measure next 7 ingredients into small bowl. Mix thoroughly.

Combine baking soda and hot water in small cup. Mix well. Stir into tomato soup in small bowl. Add tomato soup mixture to sugar mixture in 2 parts alternately with flour mixture in 3 parts, beginning and ending with flour mixture. Turn into greased 9 × 13 inch (22 × 33 cm) pan. Bake in 325°F (160°C) oven for 35 to 45 minutes until wooden pick inserted in centre comes out clean. Cool. Cuts into 18 pieces.

1 piece: 150 Calories; 2 g Protein; 6.1 g Total Fat; 22 g Carbohydrate; 336 mg Sodium; 1 g Dietary Fibre

Pictured above.

Coffee-Group Cake

Serve this warm for rave reviews.
Orange-flavoured with a crunchy topping. Scrumptious!

Boiling water	1 1/4 cups	300 mL
Quick-cooking rolled oats (not instant)	1 cup	250 mL
All-purpose flour	1 3/4 cups	425 mL
Baking powder	1 tsp.	5 mL
Baking soda	1 tsp.	5 mL
Salt	1/2 tsp.	2 mL
Ground cinnamon	1/2 tsp.	2 mL
Hard margarine (or butter), softened	1/2 cup	125 mL
Granulated sugar	1 cup	250 mL
Brown sugar, packed	1/2 cup	125 mL
Large eggs	2	2
Vanilla	1 tsp.	5 mL
Frozen concentrated orange juice, thawed	1/4 cup	60 mL
COCONUT TOPPING		
Hard margarine (or butter)	1/4 cup	60 mL
Brown sugar, packed	1/2 cup	125 mL
Frozen concentrated orange juice	2 tbsp.	30 mL
Flake coconut	1 cup	250 mL
Chopped walnuts	1/2 cup	125 mL

Pour boiling water over rolled oats in small bowl. Set aside.

Stir next 5 ingredients in separate small bowl.

Cream margarine and both sugars together in large bowl. Beat in eggs, 1 at a time. Add vanilla and concentrated orange juice. Mix.

Add flour mixture in 3 parts, alternately with rolled oat mixture in 2 parts, beginning and ending with flour mixture, stirring just to blend. Turn into greased 9 × 13 inch (22 × 33 cm) pan. Bake in 350°F (175°C) oven for about 40 minutes until wooden pick inserted in centre comes out clean.

Coconut Topping: Measure margarine, brown sugar and concentrated orange juice into small saucepan. Heat and stir until boiling. Boil for 1 minute.

Add coconut and walnuts. Stir. Spoon over hot cake. Return to oven. Broil until topping is golden. Cuts into 16 pieces.

1 piece: 348 Calories; 4 g Protein; 16.7 g Total Fat; 47 g Carbohydrate; 295 mg Sodium; 2 g Dietary Fibre

Pictured on this page.

Queen Cakes
(old recipe)

A turn-of-the-century recipe from a good friend's aunt who emigrated from England to Canada. Note that everything is weighed—the British method of measurements.

Queen Cakes

½ lb. fine flour, ¼ lb. butter, ¼ lb. castor sugar, ¼ lb. currants, grated rind of ½ lemon, 3 eggs

—Beat butter and sugar to a cream, sift in the flour and strain in the eggs by degrees, beating the mixture well. Add currants and flavoring. Beat for 10 minutes. Bake in small greased tins. ¼ hour.

Dainty Queen Cakes, this page

Dainty Queen Cakes
(new recipe)

Margarine was unknown at the time of the original recipe. We've made the switch to the less expensive margarine. Cherries have been added for colour.

Hard margarine (or butter), softened	1/2 cup	125 mL
Granulated sugar	1/2 cup	125 mL
Large eggs	3	3
Milk	1/4 cup	60 mL
Grated lemon peel	1 tsp.	5 mL
Vanilla	1 tsp.	5 mL
All-purpose flour	1 3/4 cups	425 mL
Baking powder	1 tsp.	5 mL
Salt	1/2 tsp.	2 ml
Currants	1/3 cup	75 mL
Chopped glazed cherries	1/2 cup	125 mL

Cream margarine and sugar together in large bowl. Beat in eggs, 1 at a time. Add milk, lemon peel and vanilla. Mix.

Stir in remaining 5 ingredients. Divide batter among 24 greased mini-muffin cups. Bake in 375°F (190°C) oven for 12 to 15 minutes until wooden pick inserted in centre comes out clean. Let stand for 5 minutes before turning out onto rack to cool. Makes 24 small cakes.

1 cake: 119 Calories; 2 g Protein; 4.8 g Total Fat; 17 g Carbohydrate; 115 mg Sodium; trace Dietary Fibre

Pictured on this page.

Red Velvet Cake

This red cake was all the rage at one time.
Tastes like a white cake. Three layers look impressive.

All-purpose flour	2 1/2 cups	625 mL
Cocoa	1 tsp.	5 mL
Salt	1 tsp.	5 mL
Hard margarine (or butter), softened	1/2 cup	125 mL
Granulated sugar	1 1/2 cups	375 mL
Large eggs	2	2
Red food colouring	2 oz.	56 mL
Vanilla	1 tsp.	5 mL
Buttermilk (or reconstituted from powder)	1 cup	250 mL
Baking soda	1 tsp.	5 mL
White vinegar	1 tsp.	5 mL
VANILLA ICING		
Milk	2 cups	500 mL
All-purpose flour	1/4 cup	60 mL
Hard margarine (or butter), softened	2 cups	500 mL
Granulated sugar	2 cups	500 mL
Vanilla	2 tsp.	10 mL

Stir flour, cocoa and salt in medium bowl.

Cream margarine and sugar together in large bowl. Beat in eggs, 1 at a time. Add food colouring and vanilla. Add flour mixture alternately with buttermilk, beginning and ending with flour mixture.

Mix baking soda into vinegar in small cup. Add to batter. Stir to mix. Divide among 3 greased 9 inch (22 cm) round cake pans. Bake in 350°F (175°C) oven for 25 to 30 minutes until wooden pick inserted in centre comes out clean. Let stand for 10 minutes before turning out onto racks to cool.

Vanilla Icing: Gradually whisk milk into flour in small saucepan until smooth. Heat and stir until boiling and thickened. Cook completely.

Beat margarine on high. Gradually add sugar until completely dissolved. Add vanilla and milk mixture. Beat on high until light and fluffy. Fill and ice cake. Cuts into 16 pieces.

1 piece (with icing): 565 Calories; 5 g Protein; 32 g Total Fat; 66 g Carbohydrate; 655 mg Sodium; 1 g Dietary Fibre

Pictured on page 71.

Note: 2 x 1 oz. (2 x 28 g) bottles of red food colouring equals 1/4 cup (60 mL). If you prefer to use only 1 bottle, it equals 2 tbsp. (30 mL).

1. Piña Colada Cake, page 64
2. Syrup Cake, page 74
3. Red Velvet Cake, above
4. Dark Chocolate Cake with Chocolate Mocha Icing, page 66

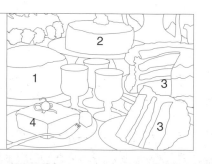

Top: Friendship Cake, this page   Bottom: Brown Sugar Pound Cake, below

HEIRLOOM RECIPE

Brown Sugar Pound Cake

This is it—that special cake from the past—before we started counting calories and fat grams! I found this in Great Grandma's cookbook. Absolutely incredible taste. A large, nutty, moist cake. Garnish with whipped topping.

All-purpose flour	3 cups	750 mL
Baking powder	1/2 tsp.	2 mL
Salt	1/2 tsp.	2 mL
Butter (or hard margarine), softened (butter is best)	1 1/2 cups	375 mL
Brown sugar, packed	4 cups	1 L
Large eggs	5	5
Vanilla	1 tsp.	5 mL
Maple flavouring	1/2 tsp.	2 mL
Milk	1 cup	250 mL
Finely chopped pecans (or walnuts)	1 cup	250 mL

Measure flour, baking powder and salt into medium bowl. Stir.

Cream butter in large bowl until fluffy. Gradually beat in brown sugar. Add eggs, 1 at a time, beating well after each addition. Mix in vanilla and maple flavouring.

Add flour mixture in 3 parts alternately with milk in 2 parts, beginning and ending with flour mixture. Fold in pecans. Turn into greased and floured 10 inch (25 cm) angel food tube pan. Bake in 325°F (160°C) oven for 1 1/4 to 1 1/2 hours until wooden pick inserted in centre comes out clean. Let stand for 10 minutes before turning out onto rack to cool. Cuts into 20 pieces.

1 piece: 443 Calories; 5 g Protein; 20.5 g Total Fat; 62 g Carbohydrate; 277 mg Sodium; 1 g Dietary Fibre

Pictured above.

Friendship Cake

Remember the one that took three weeks for the starter and 30 days to brandy the fruit? This is a much quicker and cheaper version.

INSTANT STARTER

Prepared orange (or pineapple or grapefruit) juice	3/4 cup	175 mL
Granulated sugar	2 cups	500 mL
Canned sliced peaches, with juice, cut up	3 x 14 oz.	3 x 398 mL
Canned pineapple chunks, with juice, cut up	19 oz.	540 mL
Maraschino cherries, drained and halved (or quartered)	2 cups	500 mL

Instant Starter: Combine all 5 ingredients in large plastic ice cream pail or glass container. Stir. Let stand at room temperature overnight. Next day, drain fruit. Reserve juice to give to friends to use instead of orange juice in the starter. Use juice within a few days.

CAKE

Fruit from above, well drained		
Yellow (or white) cake mixes (2 layer size, each)	2	2
Large eggs, fork-beaten	16	16
Cooking oil	1 1/2 cups	375 mL
Yellow (or white) cake mixes (2 layer size, each)	2	2
All-purpose flour	1 cup	250 mL
Chopped nuts	4 cups	1 L

Cake: Put drained fruit and first 2 cake mixes into large bowl. Toss to coat fruit. Set aside.

Combine eggs, cooking oil, remaining 2 cake mixes and flour in separate large bowl. Beat on high for about 2 minutes until smooth.

Add nuts and fruit mixture. Stir. Divide batter among 6 greased 9 x 5 x 3 inch (22 x 12.5 x 7.5 cm) loaf pans. Bake in 350°F (175°C) oven for 1 to 1 1/4 hours until wooden pick inserted in centre comes out clean. Let stand for 10 minutes before turning out onto racks to cool completely. Makes 6 cakes. Each cake cuts into 16 pieces, for total of 96 pieces.

1 piece: 207 Calories; 3 g Protein; 10.6 g Total Fat; 26 g Carbohydrate; 98 mg Sodium; 1 g Dietary Fibre

Pictured on this page.

Sweet Cream Sponge Cake

(old recipe)

This recipe is from an old church cookbook. The amount of cream would probably vary according to the size of teacup used. That would mean the amount of flour would vary. No time or temperature given.

Sweet Cream Sponge Cake

2 eggs broken into tea cup; fill the cup with sweet cream and beat until light: 1 cup sugar, 1-1/2 cups flour, 2 teaspoons baking powder, any desired flavouring and a pinch of salt; beat the sugar with the eggs and cream, and have the batter so that it will run easily from the spoon. The better way is not to put in all the flour at once, as a stiff batter will never make a light sponge cake.

HEIRLOOM RECIPE

Old Hermit Cake

This is a huge cake and so good, you will think it's full of hermit cookies. Recipe is over 100 years old so it uses butter instead of margarine.

Butter, softened	2 cups	500 mL
Brown sugar, packed	3 cups	750 mL
Large eggs	6	6
Juice of 1 lemon		
Vanilla	4 tsp.	20 mL
All-purpose flour	4 1/2 cups	1.1 L
Baking powder	4 tsp.	20 mL
Ground cinnamon	2 tsp.	10 mL
Salt	1/4 tsp.	1 mL
Chopped dates	3 cups	750 mL
Chopped walnuts	3 cups	750 mL

Cream butter and brown sugar together well in large bowl. Beat in eggs, 1 at a time. Mix in lemon juice and vanilla.

Add remaining 6 ingredients. Stir well. Turn into greased and floured 10 inch (25 cm) angel food tube pan. Bake in 275°F (140°C) oven for 2 1/2 to 3 hours until wooden pick inserted in centre comes out clean. Let stand for 10 minutes before turning out onto rack to cool. Cuts into 24 pieces.

1 piece: 525 Calories; 7 g Protein; 28 g Total Fat; 65 g Carbohydrate; 224 mg Sodium; 3 g Dietary Fibre

Pictured on this page.

Sweet Cream Sponge Cake

(new recipe)

In years gone by, whipping cream was practically a staple. Buy extra for garnish when making this recipe today.

Large eggs	2	2
Whipping cream	1 cup	250 mL
Granulated sugar	1 cup	250 mL
Vanilla	1 tsp.	5 mL
All-purpose flour	1 1/2 cups	375 mL
Baking powder	2 tsp.	10 mL
Salt	1/2 tsp.	2 mL

Beat eggs in large bowl until light in colour and thickened. Add whipping cream, sugar and vanilla. Beat well.

Add 1/2 of flour. Beat until smooth. Add second 1/2 of flour, baking powder and salt. Beat until smooth. Pour into greased 9 x 9 inch (22 x 22 cm) pan. Bake in 350°F (175°C) oven for about 30 minutes until wooden pick inserted in centre comes out clean. Cuts into 24 pieces.

1 piece: 103 Calories; 2 g Protein; 3.9 g Total Fat; 16 g Carbohydrate; 67 mg Sodium; trace Dietary Fibre

Pictured below.

Top: Old Hermit Cake, this page
Bottom: Sweet Cream Sponge Cake, above

Lazy Daisy Cake

Good warm or cold. Without the topping, it makes a good shortcake that doesn't crumble. A recipe this old and this good lasts through the years and stands the test of time.

Large eggs	2	2
Granulated sugar	1 cup	250 mL
Vanilla	1 tsp.	5 mL
All-purpose flour	1 cup	250 mL
Baking powder	1 tsp.	5 mL
Salt	1/2 tsp.	2 mL
Milk	1/2 cup	125 mL
Hard margarine (or butter)	1 tbsp.	15 mL
COCONUT TOPPING		
Hard margarine (or butter)	3 tbsp.	50 mL
Brown sugar, packed	1/2 cup	125 mL
Cream (or milk)	2 tbsp.	30 mL
Flake coconut	1/2 cup	125 mL

Beat eggs in medium bowl until frothy. Gradually add sugar while beating until thickened. Add vanilla. Mix.

Combine flour, baking powder and salt in small bowl. Stir into egg mixture.

Combine milk and margarine in small saucepan. Heat until hot and margarine is melted. Stir into batter. Turn into greased 9 × 9 inch (22 × 22 cm) pan. Bake in 350°F (175°C) oven for 25 to 30 minutes until wooden pick inserted in centre comes out clean.

Coconut Topping: Combine all 4 ingredients in small saucepan. Heat until margarine is melted and brown sugar is dissolved. Do not boil. Spread over cake. Return to oven for about 3 minutes until top is bubbling. Cuts into 12 pieces.

1 piece: 227 Calories; 3 g Protein; 7.9 g Total Fat; 37 g Carbohydrate; 182 mg Sodium; 1 g Dietary Fibre

Pictured below.

Lazy Daisy Cake, above

Syrup Cake

This has a taffy topping. For an extra special touch, sprinkle with finely chopped pecans or walnuts.

Cake flour (sift before measuring)	1 3/4 cups	425 mL
Baking powder	2 tsp.	10 mL
Salt	1/2 tsp.	2 mL
Hard margarine (or butter), softened	1/2 cup	125 mL
Granulated sugar	1/4 cup	60 mL
Vanilla	1 tsp.	5 mL
Large eggs	2	2
White corn syrup	3/4 cup	175 mL
Milk	1/2 cup	125 mL
TAFFY TOPPING		
Egg whites (large), room temperature	2	2
Golden corn syrup	3/4 cup	175 mL
Granulated sugar	1/4 cup	60 mL
Vanilla	1 tsp.	5 mL
Salt	1/8 tsp.	0.5 mL

Measure cake flour into medium bowl. Add baking powder and salt. Stir.

Cream margarine, sugar and vanilla together in large bowl. Beat in eggs, 1 at a time. Add corn syrup. Mix.

Add flour mixture in 3 parts alternately with milk in 2 parts, beginning and ending with flour mixture, stirring until just mixed. Turn into 2 greased and waxed paper-lined 8 inch (20 cm) round cake pans. Bake in 350°F (175°C) oven for about 30 minutes until wooden pick inserted in centre comes out clean. Cool.

Taffy Topping: Measure all 5 ingredients into top of double boiler. Place over boiling water. Beat continuously with electric beater until peaks stand up when beater is lifted. This will take about 7 minutes. Fill and frost cake. Cuts into 16 pieces.

1 piece: 238 Calories; 3 g Protein; 6.9 g Total Fat; 42 g Carbohydrate; 222 mg Sodium; trace Dietary Fibre

Pictured on page 71.

Candy & Snacks

Before the twentieth century, fudges, fondants, caramels and mints were commonplace. These were cumbersome to make as they required plenty of boiling, beating or pulling. The invention of candy thermometers has made judging the correct stage of sugar syrup much easier. Let Sponge Toffee (right) and Brown Sugar Fudge (page 79) bring back memories of childhood and the corner store as you enjoy these time-honoured recipes. But don't forget to try Polynesian Popcorn (page 80) for a burst of newer flavours.

Russian Toffee

Shiny deep brown. A delicious treat to be sure.

Hard margarine (or butter)	1 cup	250 mL
Corn syrup	1 cup	250 mL
Sweetened condensed milk	11 oz.	300 mL
Brown sugar, packed	2 cups	500 mL
Crushed pecans	1 cup	250 mL
Vanilla	1 tsp.	5 mL

Melt margarine, corn syrup and condensed milk in large saucepan. Add brown sugar. Bring mixture to a boil. Stir continually until mixture reaches firm ball stage on candy thermometer or until a small spoonful dropped into cold water forms a firm but pliable ball.

Stir in pecans and vanilla. Pour onto greased 11 × 17 inch (28 × 43 cm) baking sheet. Using a hot knife, cut into bite-size pieces while still warm. Cool. Wrap in waxed paper. Makes 3 lbs. (1.4 kg) toffee, about 70, 1 × 1 inch (2.5 × 2.5 cm) pieces.

1 piece: 94 Calories; 1 g Protein; 4.5 g Total Fat; 14 g Carbohydrate; 45 mg Sodium; trace Dietary Fibre

Pictured on this page.

Sponge Toffee

Looks just like a sea sponge. Melts in your mouth but be careful—it's chewy and sticky like toffee. Kids have been enjoying this for years and years.

Granulated sugar	1 cup	250 mL
Corn syrup	1 cup	250 mL
White vinegar	1 tbsp.	15 mL
Baking soda	1 tbsp.	15 mL

Grease 9 × 13 inch (22 × 33 cm) pan. Set aside. Put sugar, corn syrup and vinegar into heavy 3 quart (3 L) saucepan. Heat and stir over medium-low until sugar is dissolved and mixture is starting to boil. Boil, without stirring, until mixture reaches soft crack stage on candy thermometer or until a small spoonful dropped into cold water separates into hard strands that are still pliable. Remove from heat.

Put baking soda into small fine sieve. Quickly sieve over surface of sugar mixture. Stir immediately and just enough to mix in baking soda. Bubbles disappear quickly if touched too much. While mixture is foaming, pour into pan. Allow candy to spread by itself. Do not spread or it will collapse. Cool. Break into pieces. Store in airtight container. Makes about 1 lb. (454 g) candy.

1 oz. (28 g) candy: 112 Calories; 0 g Protein; 0 g Total Fat; 29 g Carbohydrate; 235 mg Sodium; 0 g Dietary Fibre

Pictured below.

Top: Sponge Toffee, above
Bottom: Russian Toffee, this page

Chocolate Crisps,
below

Chocolate Crisps

This will remind you of a famous chocolate bar from the 1950s.

Semi-sweet chocolate chips	2 cups	500 mL
Butterscotch chips	2 cups	500 mL
Peanuts, chopped	1/2 cup	125 mL
Box of ripple potato chips, crushed (about 1 1/3 cups, 325 mL, crushed)	1/2 × 6 1/2 oz.	1/2 × 180 g

Melt chocolate chips and butterscotch chips together in medium saucepan, stirring often, over low.

Add peanuts and crushed potato chips. Stir. Spoon 1 tbsp. (15 mL) into 1 1/4 inch (3 cm) double paper cups or foil candy cups. Makes about 32 chocolate crisps.

1 crisp: 134 Calories; 1 g Protein; 6 g Total Fat; 21 g Carbohydrate; 26 mg Sodium; 1 g Dietary Fibre

Pictured above.

PEANUT CRISPS: Omit potato chips. Add an extra 1/2 cup (125 mL) chopped peanuts. More like the real thing.

Honey Caramels

Mm-Mmm! Wonderful, buttery flavour. A soft caramel.

Granulated sugar	2 cups	500 mL
Creamed honey	1/4 cup	60 mL
Whipping cream	1 cup	250 mL
Butter (not margarine)	1/2 cup	125 mL
Vanilla	1 tsp.	5 mL

Measure all 5 ingredients into medium heavy saucepan. Boil over medium, stirring occasionally, until mixture reaches firm ball stage on candy thermometer or until a small spoonful dropped into cold water forms a firm but pliable ball. Remove from heat. Let stand for 10 minutes. Beat well, until signs of thickening appear. Quickly turn into greased 8 × 8 inch (20 × 20 cm) pan. Cool completely. Score into 64 squares. Makes 1 3/4 lbs. (790 g) candy, or 64 squares.

1 square: 55 Calories; trace Protein; 2.8 g Total Fat; 8 g Carbohydrate; 17 mg Sodium; 0 g Dietary Fibre

Pictured on page 77.

Date Loaf Candy

Tastes like a fudgy date-flavoured candy.

Granulated sugar	3 cups	750 mL
Milk	1 cup	250 mL
Hard margarine (or butter)	1 tbsp.	15 mL
Chopped dates (1 1/2 cups, 375 mL, lightly packed)	1/2 lb.	225 g
Chopped pecans (or walnuts)	1 cup	250 mL
Vanilla	1/2 tsp.	2 mL

Combine sugar, milk and margarine in 3 quart (3 L) heavy saucepan. Heat and stir over medium until boiling. Boil, without stirring, over medium-low until mixture reaches firm ball stage on candy thermometer or until a small spoonful dropped into cold water forms a firm but pliable ball. Remove from heat.

Add dates, pecans and vanilla. Mix well. Pour onto waxed paper. Cool enough to handle. Roll about 1/3 at a time into 5 inch (12 cm) roll. Wrap in plastic wrap. Chill. Cut each roll into about twenty 1/4 inch (6 mm) slices, making about 60 slices in total. Makes 1 3/4 lbs. (790 g) candy.

1 slice: 68 Calories; trace Protein; 1.7 g Total Fat; 14 g Carbohydrate; 5 mg Sodium; trace Dietary Fibre

Pictured on page 77.

HEIRLOOM RECIPE

Ryley's Toffee

I used to make this after school on the wood stove—and without a candy thermometer! A yummy toffee.

Sweetened condensed milk	11 oz.	300 mL
Brown sugar, packed	1 1/4 cups	300 mL
Hard margarine (or butter)	1/4 cup	60 mL
Corn syrup	1/4 cup	60 mL

Stir all 4 ingredients together in medium heavy saucepan. Bring to a boil, stirring constantly over medium-low, until mixture reaches firm ball stage on candy thermometer or until a small spoonful dropped into cold water forms a hard ball that is firm but pliable. Pour into well greased 8 × 8 inch (20 × 20 cm) pan. Cool slightly. Score toffee into 1 inch (2.5 cm) squares with knife before too hard. When cold, remove from pan. Break over edge of counter or sink. Makes 64 pieces.

1 piece: 47 Calories; trace Protein; 1.3 g Total Fat; 9 g Carbohydrate; 19 mg Sodium; trace Dietary Fibre

Pictured on page 77.

1. Ryley's Toffee, page 76
2. Honey Caramels, page 76
3. Double-Decker Fudge, page 78
4. Date Loaf Candy, page 76
5. Dipped Truffles, page 78

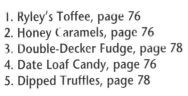 

Truffles

For an elegant evening of entertaining. Also makes a nice gift.

Sweetened condensed milk (see Note)	11 oz.	300 mL
Vanilla	1 tsp.	5 mL
Salt	1/2 tsp.	2 mL
Bittersweet chocolate baking squares, cut up	9 x 1 oz.	9 x 28 g
Chocolate sprinkles, for rolling	2 tbsp.	30 mL
Cocoa, for rolling	2 tbsp.	30 mL
Ground pecans (or hazelnuts), for rolling	1/4 cup	60 mL

Combine first 4 ingredients in medium heavy saucepan. Heat and stir over low until chocolate is melted and mixture is smooth. Cool.

With buttered fingers, shape into 1 inch (2.5 cm) balls. Roll 1/3 in chocolate sprinkles, 1/3 in cocoa and 1/3 in ground pecans. Keep chilled. Makes 4 dozen truffles.

1 coated truffle: 57 Calories; 1 g Protein; 3.2 g Total Fat; 7 g Carbohydrate; 39 mg Sodium; trace Dietary Fibre

Note: For 14 oz. (398 mL) can of sweetened condensed milk, use 12 x 1 oz. (12 x 28 g) chocolate baking squares.

Variation: Omit vanilla. Add 1 tbsp. (15 mL) of your favourite liqueur.

WHITE TRUFFLES: Use 9 x 1 oz. (9 x 28 g) squares of white chocolate instead of the bittersweet. Omit vanilla. Add 1 tbsp. (15 mL) of your favourite liqueur. Roll as for Truffles, above, or dip into chocolate as in Dipped Truffles, below.

DIPPED TRUFFLES: Melt 6 x 1 oz. (6 x 28 g) semi-sweet or white chocolate baking squares and 3 tbsp. (50 mL) paraffin wax in small saucepan over low, stirring often, until melted. Using fork, lower 1 truffle at a time into chocolate. Lift out, holding above saucepan to allow excess chocolate to drip, then transfer to waxed paper to set. Repeat with remaining truffles.

Pictured on page 77.

Vinegar Candy, this page

Double-Decker Fudge

Creamy smooth with both dark and light layers in every piece. Very attractive on a dessert platter.

Peanut butter chips	1 cup	250 mL
Semi-sweet chocolate chips	1 cup	250 mL
Granulated sugar	2 1/4 cups	550 mL
Marshmallow creme (7 oz., 200 g, jar)	1 1/2 cups	375 mL
Evaporated milk	3/4 cup	175 mL
Hard margarine (or butter)	1/4 cup	60 mL
Vanilla	1 tsp.	5 mL

Put peanut butter chips into medium bowl. Put chocolate chips into separate medium bowl.

Combine sugar, marshmallow creme, evaporated milk and margarine in 3 quart (3 L) heavy saucepan. Heat and stir until boiling. Boil slowly for 5 minutes, stirring constantly. Remove from heat.

Stir in vanilla. Measure 2 cups (500 mL) and pour over peanut butter chips. Stir vigorously until melted. Pour into greased 8 x 8 inch (20 x 20 cm) pan. Pour remaining marshmallow mixture over chocolate chips. Stir vigorously until melted. Pour over layer in pan. Cool. Makes 2 1/4 lbs. (1 kg) fudge. Cuts into 48 pieces.

1 piece: 107 Calories; 2 g Protein; 3.7 g Total Fat; 21 g Carbohydrate; 33 mg Sodium; trace Dietary Fibre

Pictured on page 77.

Vinegar Candy

A hard candy that lasts a long time and slowly disappears in the mouth. Shiny and looks like butterscotch.

Granulated sugar	2 cups	500 mL
White vinegar	1/2 cup	125 mL
Water	1/4 cup	60 mL
Hard margarine (or butter)	2 tbsp.	30 mL
Salt, just a pinch		

Measure all 5 ingredients into large saucepan. Heat and stir until sugar is dissolved. Boil until mixture reaches hard ball stage on candy thermometer or until a small spoonful dropped into cold water forms a hard ball that is firm and barely pliable. Pour into greased 8 x 8 inch (20 x 20 cm) pan. Cool. Makes 1 lb. (454 g) candy. Break into pieces.

1 oz. (28 g) candy: 128 Calories; trace Protein; 3 g Total Fat; 26 g Carbohydrate; 36 mg Sodium; 0 g Dietary Fibre

Pictured on this page.

On plate: Brown Sugar Fudge, below

Centre plate and top right: Sugar Nuts, below

Brown Sugar Fudge

This sets up firmly and melts in your mouth.

Brown sugar, packed	2 cups	500 mL
Granulated sugar	1 cup	250 mL
Corn syrup	2 tbsp.	30 mL
Hard margarine (or butter)	2 tbsp.	30 mL
Salt	1/8 tsp.	0.5 mL
Milk	2/3 cup	150 mL
Fine coconut (or finely ground nuts)	1/2 cup	125 mL

Measure first 6 ingredients into medium heavy saucepan. Heat over medium, stirring often, until boiling. Boil, without stirring, until mixture reaches soft ball stage on candy thermometer or until a small spoonful dropped into cold water forms a soft, very pliable ball. Remove from heat.

Cool until you can almost hold your hand against the bottom of saucepan. Beat until it has lost its gloss and begins to thicken. Stir in coconut. Pour into greased 8 x 8 inch (20 x 20 cm) pan. Cool. Cuts into 64 squares.

1 square: 51 Calories; trace Protein; 0.9 g Total Fat; 11 g Carbohydrate; 15 mg Sodium; trace Dietary Fibre

Pictured above.

Note: If you miss the crucial point of pouring fudge just before it sets, it can be shaped into rolls and coated with crushed or finely chopped nuts. Slice to serve.

Sugar Nuts

Addictive! Use whatever combination of nuts you prefer, for a total of 4 1/2 cups (1.1 L).

Egg whites (large), room temperature	2	2
Granulated sugar	1 cup	250 mL
Salt, just a pinch		
Pecans	1 1/2 cups	375 mL
Walnuts	1 1/2 cups	375 mL
Almonds	1 1/2 cups	375 mL
Hard margarine (or butter), melted	1/2 cup	125 mL

Beat egg whites in medium bowl until stiff. Beat in sugar and salt.

Fold in pecans, walnuts and almonds.

Pour margarine into 9 x 13 inch (22 x 33 cm) pan. Spread nut mixture over margarine. Bake in 325°F (160°C) oven for about 30 minutes, stirring every 10 minutes, until no margarine remains. Pour out onto waxed paper. Separate to cool. Makes 7 cups (1.75 L) nuts.

1/4 cup (60 mL) nuts: 180 Calories; 3 g Protein; 14.7 g Total Fat; 12 g Carbohydrate; 43 mg Sodium; 2 g Dietary Fibre

Pictured above.

Spicy Cheddar Popcorn,
this page

Polynesian
Popcorn,
this page

Chili Popcorn,
this page

Spicy Cheddar Popcorn

Add more cayenne pepper if you like it real spicy!

Hard margarine (or butter), melted	1/4 cup	60 mL
Popped corn (pop about 1/4 cup, 60 mL)	8 cups	2 L
Dry grated Cheddar cheese powder	1/3 cup	75 mL
Seasoned salt	1 tsp.	5 mL
Onion powder	1/8 tsp.	0.5 mL
Garlic powder	1/8 tsp.	0.5 mL
Chili powder	1/4 tsp.	1 mL
Cayenne pepper (optional)	1/8 tsp.	0.5 mL

Drizzle margarine over popped corn in large bowl. Toss well to coat.

Combine remaining 6 ingredients in small bowl. Sprinkle over popcorn. Toss well to coat each piece evenly. Makes 8 cups (2 L) flavoured popcorn.

1 cup (250 mL) popcorn: 114 Calories; 3 g Protein; 7.8 g Total Fat; 9 g Carbohydrate; 268 mg Sodium; 1 g Dietary Fibre

Pictured on this page.

Polynesian Popcorn

A very unusual flavour. A good conversation appetizer.

Hard margarine (or butter), melted	1/4 cup	60 mL
Soy sauce	2 tsp.	10 mL
Ground ginger	3/4 tsp.	4 mL
Onion salt	1/2 tsp.	2 mL
Popped corn (pop about 1/4 cup, 60 mL)	8 cups	2 L

Stir first 4 ingredients together in large bowl.

Add popped corn. Toss well to coat each piece evenly. Makes 8 cups (2 L) flavoured popcorn.

1 cup (250 mL) popcorn: 95 Calories; 2 g Protein; 6.2 g Total Fat; 9 g Carbohydrate; 238 mg Sodium; 1 g Dietary Fibre

Pictured on this page.

Chili Popcorn

Easy to add more or less flavour to this. Reddish tinge.

Popped corn (pop about 1/4 cup, 60 mL)	8 cups	2 L
Hard margarine, melted	1/4 cup	60 mL
Salt	1 tsp.	5 mL
Chili powder	1/2 tsp.	2 mL
Paprika	1/8 tsp.	0.5 mL

Toss hot popped corn with margarine in large bowl.

Stir salt, chili powder and paprika together in small cup. Sprinkle over popcorn. Toss well to coat each piece evenly. Makes 8 cups (2 L) flavoured popcorn.

1 cup (250 mL) popcorn: 96 Calories; 1 g Protein; 6.5 g Total Fat; 9 g Carbohydrate; 410 mg Sodium; 1 g Dietary Fibre

Pictured on this page.

Chicken

Many of us have special memories of Sunday roast chicken dinners. On homesteads during the Depression years, unplanned guests were made welcome with a chicken dinner, as fresh chicken was readily accessible right outside the back door! Chicken cooked up fast, either roasted or fried in a lot of grease, and was always delicious. Almost everyone today relies on the grocery store to supply us with our poultry. We have the luxury of choosing only selected parts, boned and skinned if we wish, to use in a wide variety of lighter, healthier recipes. Try Chicken Divan (below) for a full-meal selection, or Chicken and Chutney (page 85) for a newer flavour over rice or noodles.

Chicken Divan, this page

Chicken Divan

Delicate curry flavour. A divine dinner for six.

Boneless, skinless chicken breast halves (about 1 1/2 lbs., 680 g)	6	6
Water	2 cups	500 mL
Vegetable bouillon powder	2 tsp.	10 mL
Long grain white rice	1 1/4 cups	300 mL
Water	2 1/2 cups	625 mL
Condensed cream of chicken soup	10 oz.	284 mL
Light sour cream	1/2 cup	125 mL
Grated medium Cheddar cheese	1/2 cup	125 mL
Light salad dressing (or mayonnaise)	1/3 cup	75 mL
Curry powder	1 tsp.	5 mL
Water	1/2 cup	125 mL
Frozen cut broccoli, thawed and coarsely chopped	1 lb.	454 g

Cook chicken in first amount of water and bouillon powder in large uncovered saucepan for about 35 minutes until tender. Drain. Cool a bit. Cut chicken into cubes.

Cook rice in second amount of water in medium covered saucepan for about 20 minutes until water is absorbed and rice is tender.

Mix next 6 ingredients in medium bowl.

Spoon rice into ungreased 3 quart (3 L) casserole. Cover with broccoli. Scatter chicken over broccoli. Pour soup mixture over all. Poke with fork here and there to allow some liquid to drizzle down to bottom. Bake, uncovered, in 350°F (175°C) oven for about 1 hour. Serves 6.

1 serving: 445 Calories; 37 g Protein; 13.2 g Total Fat; 43 g Carbohydrate; 767 mg Sodium; 3 g Dietary Fibre

Pictured above.

Chicken Casserole

A stew-like meal with the delicious flavour of roast chicken.

Chicken parts, with skin (see Note)	3 lbs.	1.4 kg
Elbow macaroni (about 8 oz., 225 g)	2 cups	500 mL
Boiling water	3 qts.	3 L
Cooking oil (optional)	1 tbsp.	15 mL
Salt	2 tsp.	10 mL
Large onion, sliced	1	1
Medium carrots, cut into thin strips, 3 inches (7.5 cm) long	4	4
Thinly sliced celery	1 cup	250 mL
Frozen green beans (or peas)	2 cups	500 mL
Condensed cream of mushroom soup	2 x 10 oz.	2 x 284 mL
Canned sliced mushrooms, with liquid	10 oz.	284 mL
Salt	1/2 tsp.	2 mL
Pepper	1/4 tsp.	1 mL
Hard margarine (or butter)	2 tbsp.	30 mL
Dry bread crumbs	1/2 cup	125 mL
Grated medium Cheddar cheese	1/2 cup	125 mL

Arrange chicken in small roaster. Cover. Bake in 350°F (175°C) oven for 1 hour until tender. Remove chicken to large plate. Tilt roaster. Spoon off fat. Leave juices in roaster. Remove skin and bone from chicken. Chop chicken into bite-size pieces.

Cook macaroni in boiling water, cooking oil and first amount of salt in large uncovered pot or Dutch oven for 5 to 7 minutes until tender but firm. Drain. Turn into roaster. Add chicken.

Add onion, carrot, celery and green beans.

Mix soup, mushrooms with liquid, second amount of salt and pepper in medium bowl. Pour over all.

Melt margarine in small saucepan. Stir in bread crumbs and cheese. Sprinkle over top. Cover. Bake in 350°F (175°C) oven for 1 1/4 hours until carrot is tender. Remove cover. Bake for 10 minutes until topping dries a bit. Serves 8.

1 serving: 404 Calories; 27 g Protein; 14.5 g Total Fat; 41 g Carbohydrate; 1087 mg Sodium; 4 g Dietary Fibre

Pictured on this page.

Note: Substitute 4 cups (1 L) leftover chopped cooked chicken and 1/2 cup (125 mL) chicken broth for the chicken parts.

Chicken Fried Rice

Serve as a side dish or main dish.

Cooking oil	1 tbsp.	15 mL
Garlic clove, minced (or 1/4 tsp., 1 mL, powder)	1	1
Boneless, skinless chicken breast halves (about 1/2 lb., 225 g), cut into 3/4 inch (2 cm) cubes	2	2
Cooking oil	1 tsp.	5 mL
Large eggs	3	3
Salt, sprinkle		
Pepper, sprinkle		
Cooking oil	2 tsp.	10 mL
Chopped onion	1/2 cup	125 mL
Thinly sliced celery	3/4 cup	175 mL
Diced red or green pepper	3/4 cup	175 mL
Chopped fresh mushrooms	1 cup	250 mL
Cold cooked rice, crumbled	4 cups	1 L
Soy sauce	2 tbsp.	30 mL
Frozen baby peas, thawed	1 cup	250 mL
Green onions, sliced	2	2

Heat first amount of cooking oil in large non-stick wok or frying pan. Add garlic and chicken. Sauté for about 4 minutes until chicken is no longer pink. Transfer to medium bowl.

Heat second amount of cooking oil in same wok. Break eggs into pan. Pierce each yolk. Sprinkle with salt and pepper. Cook for about 1 minute. Turn eggs over. When cooked, transfer to cutting board. Cut into shreds. Add to chicken.

Heat third amount of cooking oil. Add onion, celery, red pepper and mushrooms. Sauté until onion is soft and clear.

Add rice. Drizzle mixture with soy sauce. Stir. Add peas, green onion and chicken mixture. Stir until heated through. Makes 8 cups (2 L) fried rice.

1 cup (250 mL) fried rice: 262 Calories; 14 g Protein; 6.2 g Total Fat; 36 g Carbohydrate; 339 mg Sodium; 2 g Dietary Fibre

Pictured on page 83.

Chicken Casserole, this page

Left: Broccoli Rice Chicken, below

Centre: Chicken Fried Rice, page 82

Right: Chicken Express, below

Broccoli Rice Chicken

A mild comfort food. A one-dish meal made in the frying pan.

Chicken thighs, skin removed (about 2 lbs., 900 g)	8	8
Garlic salt	1/2 tsp.	2 mL
Paprika	1/2 tsp.	2 mL
Pepper, sprinkle		
Cooking oil	1 tbsp.	15 mL
Large onion, sliced	1	1
Fresh broccoli, florets reserved and stems chopped	1 lb.	454 g
Condensed cream of mushroom (or celery) soup	10 oz.	284 mL
Water	1 2/3 cups	400 mL
White (or alcohol-free white) wine	1/3 cup	75 mL
Uncooked converted rice	1 1/2 cups	375 mL
Paprika, sprinkle		
Reserved broccoli florets		

Sprinkle chicken thighs with garlic salt, paprika and pepper. Brown both sides in cooking oil in non-stick frying pan. Transfer to medium bowl.

Sauté onion in same frying pan until soft.

Add broccoli stems, soup, water, wine and rice. Stir. Bring to a boil. Arrange chicken over top. Sprinkle generously with paprika. Cover. Cook over low for 30 minutes, stirring rice around chicken twice during cooking. Rice should be almost tender.

Stir in reserved broccoli florets. Cover. Cook for about 10 minutes until broccoli and rice are tender. Serves 4.

1 serving: 606 Calories; 37 g Protein; 15.5 g Total Fat; 75 g Carbohydrate; 935 mg Sodium; 5 g Dietary Fibre

Pictured above.

Chicken Express

This is served over a bed of rice. Sweet and sour flavour with lots of chicken and vegetables.

Boneless, skinless chicken breast halves (about 1 1/2 lbs., 680 g), cut bite-size	6	6
Cooking oil	2 tsp.	10 mL
Salt, sprinkle		
Pepper, sprinkle		
Sliced celery	2 cups	500 mL
Sliced fresh mushrooms	2 cups	500 mL
Chopped onion	1/2 cup	125 mL
Small green pepper, chopped	1	1
Canned crushed pineapple, with juice	14 oz.	398 mL
Water	2 tbsp.	30 mL
Cornstarch	2 tbsp.	30 mL
Soy sauce	1/4 cup	60 mL
Brown sugar, packed	2 tbsp.	30 mL
White vinegar	2 tbsp.	30 mL
Garlic powder	1/4 – 1/2 tsp.	1 – 2 mL
Ground ginger	1/4 – 1/2 tsp.	1 – 2 mL

Cook chicken in cooking oil in non-stick frying pan. Sprinkle with salt and pepper. Transfer to medium bowl.

Add celery, mushrooms, onion and green pepper to same frying pan. Sauté until soft.

Add pineapple with juice. Heat and stir until boiling.

Mix water and cornstarch in small bowl. Add remaining 5 ingredients. Mix. Stir into vegetable mixture until boiling. Add chicken. Return to a boil. Serve immediately. Serves 6.

1 serving: 243 Calories; 30 g Protein; 3.3 g Total Fat; 24 g Carbohydrate; 849 mg Sodium; 2 g Dietary Fibre

Pictured above.

Chicken Chow Mein

*A popular dish. To decrease the sodium, use
low-salt condensed soup and soy sauce.*

Cooking oil	1 tbsp.	15 mL
Boneless, skinless chicken breast halves (about 1 1/2 lbs., 680 g), cut into 1/4 inch (6 mm) wide strips	6	6
Condensed cream of mushroom soup	10 oz.	284 mL
Condensed cream of chicken soup	10 oz.	284 mL
Water	1 cup	250 mL
Soy sauce	1/4 cup	60 mL
Chicken bouillon powder	2 tsp.	10 mL
Chow mein noodles	2 cups	500 mL
Thinly sliced celery	2 cups	500 mL
Chopped onion	2 cups	500 mL
Chow mein noodles	2 cups	500 mL

Heat cooking oil in non-stick frying pan. Add chicken strips. Sauté quickly to brown.

Stir both soups, water, soy sauce and bouillon powder in large bowl. Add first amount of chow mein noodles. Add chicken. Stir. Add celery and onion. Mix in. Turn into ungreased 3 quart (3 L) casserole.

Sprinkle with second amount of chow mein noodles. Bake, uncovered, in 350°F (175°C) oven for 1 1/2 to 2 hours until bubbly hot. Serves 6.

1 serving: 455 Calories; 34 g Protein; 20.6 g Total Fat; 33 g Carbohydrate; 2004 mg Sodium; 3 g Dietary Fibre

Pictured below.

Easy Chicken

*Tender and tasty with a rich brown sauce. The addition
of thyme and rosemary enhances the flavour.*

Chicken parts, skin removed	3 lbs.	1.4 kg
Medium onion, thinly sliced	1	1
Water	1 cup	250 mL
All-purpose flour	3 tbsp.	50 mL
Worcestershire sauce	1 tsp.	5 mL
Lemon juice	2 tbsp.	30 mL
Granulated sugar	2 tbsp.	30 mL
Parsley flakes	1 tsp.	5 mL
Ground thyme	1 tsp.	5 mL
Chicken bouillon powder	2 tsp.	10 mL
Dried rosemary, crushed	1/2 tsp.	2 mL
Salt	1 tsp.	5 mL
Pepper	1/2 tsp.	2 mL
Liquid gravy browner	1 tsp.	5 mL

Arrange chicken in ungreased 3 quart (3 L) casserole or small roaster. Scatter onion slices over chicken.

Measure remaining 12 ingredients into small bowl. Mix well. Pour over chicken. Cover. Bake in 350°F (175°C) oven for about 1 1/2 hours until tender. Serves 4 to 6.

1/4 recipe: 268 Calories; 38 g Protein; 5.3 g Total Fat; 15 g Carbohydrate; 1197 mg Sodium; 1 g Dietary Fibre

Pictured below.

Left: Easy Chicken, above
Top centre: Chicken Chow Mein, this page
Bottom centre: Chicken In Gravy, page 85
Right: Chicken And Chutney, page 85

Margo's Rosemary Chicken

This dish has such a wonderful flavour and aroma.

Boneless, skinless chicken breast halves (about 2 1/2 lbs., 1.1 kg)	10	10
Cooking oil	2 tsp.	10 mL
Water	1 cup	250 mL
White (or alcohol-free white) wine	1 cup	250 mL
Red wine vinegar	1/3 cup	75 mL
Cornstarch	1 tbsp.	15 mL
Ketchup	1/4 cup	60 mL
Grated onion	2 tbsp.	30 mL
Garlic clove, minced	1	1
Brown sugar, packed	2 tbsp.	30 mL
Dried rosemary	1 tsp.	5 mL
Dried whole oregano	1 tsp.	5 mL
Dill weed	1 tsp.	5 mL
Chicken bouillon powder	1 tsp.	5 mL
Salt	1 tsp.	5 mL
Soy sauce	1 tsp.	5 mL
Worcestershire sauce	1 tsp.	5 mL
Paprika	1/2 tsp.	2 mL

Sauté chicken quickly in cooking oil in non-stick frying pan to brown both sides. Transfer to ungreased 2 1/2 quart (2.5 L) casserole.

Combine remaining 16 ingredients in medium saucepan. Heat and stir until boiling. Pour over chicken. Cover. Bake in 350°F (175°C) oven for about 1 hour until tender. Serves 10.

1 serving: 186 Calories; 28 g Protein; 2.5 g Total Fat; 6 g Carbohydrate; 543 mg Sodium; trace Dietary Fibre

Note: If desired, thicken sauce with a mixture of 1 1/2 tbsp. (25 mL) cornstarch and 3 tbsp. (50 mL) water. Boil gently until thickened.

Pictured on front cover.

Chicken In Gravy

Rich, full-bodied flavour in a dark brown gravy. Serve with broad noodles or mashed potatoes.

Hard margarine (or butter)	1 tbsp.	15 mL
Boneless, skinless chicken breast halves (about 1 1/2 lbs., 680 g)	6	6
Sliced fresh mushrooms	2 cups	500 mL
Chili sauce	2 tbsp.	30 mL
Skim evaporated milk (or light cream)	1/2 cup	125 mL
Chicken bouillon powder	1 tbsp.	15 mL
Sherry (or alcohol-free sherry)	1 tbsp.	15 mL
Envelope onion gravy mix	1 x 1 oz.	1 x 28 g
Water	1 1/4 cups	300 mL

Melt margarine in non-stick frying pan. Add chicken. Brown well on both sides. Transfer to ungreased 2 quart (2 L) casserole.

Sauté mushrooms in same frying pan. Scatter over chicken.

Measure remaining 6 ingredients into frying pan. Heat and stir to remove any browned bits. Pour over all, making sure mushrooms are covered with sauce. Cover. Bake in 350°F (175°C) oven for about 1 hour until chicken is tender. Makes about 1 1/2 cups (375 mL) gravy. Serves 6.

1 serving: 198 Calories; 30 g Protein; 4 g Total Fat; 9 g Carbohydrate; 724 mg Sodium; 1 g Dietary Fibre

Pictured on page 84.

Chicken And Chutney

The chutney adds subtle sweetness. Ready in 30 minutes.

Boneless, skinless chicken breast halves (about 1 1/2 lbs., 680 g), cut into 1/2 inch (12 mm) cubes	6	6
Hard margarine (or butter)	1 tbsp.	15 mL
Salt, sprinkle		
Pepper, sprinkle		
Skim evaporated milk	13 1/2 oz.	385 mL
Mango chutney (or other), finely chopped	1/4 cup	60 mL

Sauté chicken in margarine in non-stick frying pan until browned. Sprinkle with salt and pepper.

Add evaporated milk and chutney. Stir until boiling and slightly thickened. Serves 6.

1 serving: 213 Calories; 33 g Protein; 3.6 g Total Fat; 11 g Carbohydrate; 180 mg Sodium; trace Dietary Fibre

Pictured on page 84.

Brandied Chicken

Fried chicken with a saucy mushroom topping.

Cooking oil	2 tsp.	10 mL
Boneless, skinless chicken breast halves (about 1 1/2 lbs., 680 g)	6	6
Salt, sprinkle		
Pepper, sprinkle		
Sliced fresh mushrooms	2 cups	500 mL
Skim evaporated milk	1/2 cup	125 mL
Brandy	1 tsp.	5 mL

Heat cooking oil in non-stick frying pan. Add chicken. Cook both sides until chicken is no longer pink. Sprinkle with salt and pepper. Remove chicken to warmed platter. Cover to keep warm.

Add mushrooms to same frying pan. Sauté quickly until golden and moisture is evaporated.

Add evaporated milk and brandy. Stir until hot, loosening any browned bits in pan. Spoon over chicken. Serves 6.

1 serving: 169 Calories; 29 g Protein; 3.2 g Total Fat; 4 g Carbohydrate; 104 mg Sodium; trace Dietary Fibre

Pictured below.

Bottom left: Brandied Chicken, above
Top centre: Whimsical Chicken, this page
Top right: Reverse Cordon Bleu, page 87
Bottom right: Mustard Chicken, page 87

Whimsical Chicken

Chicken covered with a piquant mustard sauce bakes slowly to tender goodness.

Hard margarine (or butter), melted	1/3 cup	75 mL
Salad dressing (or mayonnaise)	1/3 cup	75 mL
Prepared mustard	1 1/2 tbsp.	25 mL
Paprika	1 tsp.	5 mL
Parsley flakes	1 tsp.	5 mL
Salt	3/4 tsp.	4 mL
Pepper	1/4 tsp.	1 mL
Boneless, skinless chicken breast halves (about 2 lbs., 900 g), pounded flat	8	8
Fine dry bread crumbs	1 cup	250 mL

Mix first 7 ingredients in small bowl.

Dip chicken into salad dressing mixture, then roll in bread crumbs being sure to coat well. Place in single layer on ungreased baking sheet. Bake in 325°F (160°C) oven for about 1 1/2 hours until tender. Serves 8.

1 serving: 307 Calories; 29 g Protein; 14.8 g Total Fat; 12 g Carbohydrate; 626 mg Sodium; trace Dietary Fibre

Pictured below.

Mustard Chicken

Coated, then oven-baked, for very tender chicken.

Fine dry bread crumbs	3 tbsp.	50 mL
Grated Parmesan cheese	1/4 cup	60 mL
Dry mustard	1 tsp.	5 mL
Ground rosemary	1/2 tsp.	2 mL
Salt (optional)	1/2 tsp.	2 mL
Pepper	1/4 tsp.	1 mL
Boneless, skinless chicken breast halves (about 1 1/2 lbs., 680 g)	6	6
Hot water	1/4 cup	60 mL
Chicken bouillon powder	2 tsp.	10 mL
Light sour cream	3/4 cup	175 mL
Paprika, sprinkle		

Measure first 6 ingredients into small bowl. Mix well.

Dip chicken into Parmesan cheese mixture to coat. Place on greased baking sheet with sides.

Combine hot water and bouillon powder in separate small bowl. Stir well. Add sour cream. Mix until smooth. Spoon over chicken being sure to cover each piece.

Sprinkle with paprika. Bake in 350°F (175°C) oven for about 40 minutes until tender. Serves 6.

1 serving: 197 Calories; 31 g Protein; 5.4 g Total Fat; 5 g Carbohydrate; 415 mg Sodium; trace Dietary Fibre

Pictured on pages 86/87.

Reverse Cordon Bleu

You get the familiar flavour of the traditional cordon bleu, but with a lot less effort.

Hard margarine (or butter)	1 tbsp.	15 mL
Boneless, skinless chicken breast halves (about 1 1/2 lbs., 680 g)	6	6
Apple juice	1 cup	250 mL
Large cooked ham slices (about 8 oz., 225 g)	6	6
Swiss cheese, thinly sliced	9 oz.	255 g
SAUCE		
Granulated sugar	4 tsp.	20 mL
All-purpose flour	1 tbsp.	15 mL
Dry mustard	1/2 tsp.	2 mL
Salt	1/4 tsp.	1 mL
Reserved juice, plus water if needed to make	1 cup	250 mL
White vinegar	4 tsp.	20 mL
Skim evaporated milk (or light cream)	1/4 cup	60 mL
Green onions, chopped	3	3

Melt margarine in non-stick frying pan. Add chicken. Quickly brown both sides.

Add apple juice. Cover. Simmer for about 15 minutes until chicken is no longer pink. Transfer chicken to large plate. Reserve juice.

Lay ham slices on working surface. Lay 1/2 of cheese on centre of each piece of ham. Set 1 chicken breast half on each slice of cheese. Cover with second 1/2 of cheese. Fold ham edges over top. Lay folded side down in ungreased shallow 2 quart (2 L) casserole. Cover. Bake in 350°F (175°C) oven for about 8 minutes until cheese is melted.

Sauce: Stir sugar, flour, dry mustard and salt in small saucepan.

Mix in reserved juice until smooth. Add vinegar and evaporated milk. Heat and stir until boiling and thickened.

Stir in green onion. Pour over chicken. Serves 6.

1 serving: 423 Calories; 47 g Protein; 19.2 g Total Fat; 13 g Carbohydrate; 832 mg Sodium; trace Dietary Fibre

Pictured on this page.

Chicken With Ginger

Excellent served as-is or with a peanut or chili sauce for dipping.

Soy sauce	1/2 cup	125 mL
Liquid honey	1/3 cup	75 mL
White vinegar	3 tbsp.	50 mL
Garlic powder (or 2 cloves, minced)	1/2 tsp.	2 mL
Grated fresh gingerroot	1 tbsp.	15 mL
Boneless, skinless chicken breast halves (about 2 lbs., 900 g), cut bite-size	8	8

Stir first 5 ingredients in small bowl.

Add chicken. Stir. Cover tightly. Marinate in refrigerator for about 3 hours, stirring occasionally.

Arrange chicken with marinade on greased baking sheet. Bake in 375°F (190°C) oven for about 25 minutes, stirring once or twice. Serves 8.

1 serving: 188 Calories; 29 g Protein; 1.5 g Total Fat; 14 g Carbohydrate; 1165 mg Sodium; trace Dietary Fibre

Variation: Soak eight 10 inch (25 cm) bamboo skewers in water for 10 minutes. Pound chicken flat. Cut into long strips. Marinate as above. Thread chicken strips onto skewers. Discard marinade. Arrange skewers on greased baking sheet. Bake in 375°F (190°C) oven for about 25 minutes. Makes 8 skewers.

Pictured on page 89.

Glazed Chicken

Great eye appeal! For easier cleanup, line dish with foil.

Chicken parts, skin removed	3 lbs.	1.4 kg
Salad dressing (or mayonnaise)	2/3 cup	150 mL
Chili sauce	2 tbsp.	30 mL
Sweet pickle relish	1 tbsp.	15 mL
Lemon juice	1 tbsp.	15 mL
Worcestershire sauce	1 tsp.	5 mL
Envelope dry onion soup mix	1 x 1.4 oz.	1 x 38 g
Apricot jam	1/2 cup	125 mL
Brown sugar, packed	1 tbsp.	15 mL

Arrange chicken in greased 3 quart (3 L) casserole or small roaster.

Mix salad dressing, chili sauce, pickle relish, lemon juice and Worcestershire sauce in small bowl. Stir in soup mix, jam and brown sugar. Spoon over chicken being sure to get some on every piece. Bake, uncovered, in 350°F (175°C) oven for about 1 hour until tender. Baste chicken at halftime. Serves 4 to 6.

1/4 recipe: 737 Calories; 57 g Protein; 35 g Total Fat; 47 g Carbohydrate; 1515 mg Sodium; 1 g Dietary Fibre

Pictured on page 89.

Chicken Breasts Supreme

Crispy, golden-brown, flavourful coating.

Boneless, skinless chicken breast halves (about 1 1/2 lbs., 680 g)	6	6
Non-fat sour cream	1 cup	250 mL
Lemon juice	2 tbsp.	30 mL
Worcestershire sauce	1 tsp.	5 mL
Garlic powder (or 1 clove, minced)	1/4 tsp.	1 mL
Celery salt	1 tsp.	5 mL
Paprika	1 tsp.	5 mL
Salt	1 tsp.	5 mL
Pepper	1/4 tsp.	1 mL
Coarsely crushed cornflakes cereal (not crumbs)	1 3/4 cups	425 mL
Hard margarine (or butter), melted	3 tbsp.	50 mL

Put chicken into medium bowl or sealable plastic bag.

Stir next 8 ingredients in small bowl. Pour over chicken. Stir lightly to coat each piece. Cover or seal. Marinate in refrigerator for 6 hours or overnight.

Coat 1 piece of chicken at a time with crushed cereal. Arrange on greased baking sheet. Refrigerate for 1 to 2 hours to make a crispier coating if desired.

Drizzle with margarine. Bake in 350°F (175°C) oven for about 1 hour until tender. Serves 6.

1 serving: 225 Calories; 29 g Protein; 6.9 g Total Fat; 10 g Carbohydrate; 931 mg Sodium; trace Dietary Fibre

Pictured on page 89.

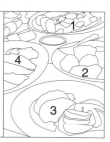

1. Chicken With Ginger on skewers, this page
2. Glazed Chicken, this page
3. Continental Chicken, page 90
4. Chicken Breasts Supreme, this page

Continental Chicken

Looks delicious with cranberries and a gravy-type sauce.

Boneless, skinless chicken breast halves (about 3 lbs., 1.4 kg)	12	12
Whole cranberry sauce	1 1/4 cups	300 mL
Envelope dry onion soup mix (stir before dividing)	1/2 × 1.4 oz.	1/2 × 38 g
French dressing	1/2 cup	125 mL
Granulated sugar	1 tbsp.	15 mL
Pepper	1/8 tsp.	0.5 mL

Arrange chicken in 5 quart (5 L) slow cooker. Mix remaining 5 ingredients in small bowl. Spoon over chicken. Cover. Cook on Low for 8 to 10 hours or on High for 4 to 5 hours. Serves 12.

1 serving: 224 Calories; 27 g Protein; 5.9 g Total Fat; 15 g Carbohydrate; 415 mg Sodium; trace Dietary Fibre

Pictured on page 89.

Note: This may be baked, covered, in ungreased 4 quart (4 L) casserole in 325°F (160°C) oven for 1 1/2 to 2 hours.

Elegant Chicken Phyllo

This recipe makes one pouch. Multiply as needed.

Phyllo pastry sheets	2	2
Hard margarine (or butter), melted	1 tbsp.	15 mL
Light spreadable cream cheese, mashed with fork to soften	1 tbsp.	15 mL
Chopped pimiento	1 1/2 tsp.	7 mL
Boneless, skinless chicken breast half (about 1/4 lb., 113 g), pounded flat and cut into thin strips	1	1
Salt, sprinkle		
Pepper, sprinkle		
Medium fresh mushroom, sliced	1	1

Lay 1 sheet of pastry on working surface. Brush with melted margarine. Fold in half crosswise. Repeat with second pastry sheet. Place second sheet on top of first sheet in opposite direction.

Spread cream cheese, 4 inches (10 cm) in diameter, in centre of pastry. Sprinkle with pimiento. Lay strips of chicken over top. Sprinkle with salt and pepper. Arrange mushroom slices over chicken. Gather up pastry on top. Press together to seal. Frill edges outward. Place on greased baking sheet. Bake in 350°F (175°C) oven for about 30 minutes until browned and crisp. Serve immediately to prevent sogginess. Makes 1 pouch.

1 pouch: 409 Calories; 33 g Protein; 15.8 g Total Fat; 32 g Carbohydrate; 619 mg Sodium; 1 g Dietary Fibre

Pictured on this page.

Top: Ham And Chicken En Croûte, below
Bottom: Elegant Chicken Phyllo, this page

Ham And Chicken En Croûte

These packets may also be cooked in puff pastry. Brush with beaten egg before baking. Similar to, but easier than, chicken cordon bleu.

Hard margarine (or butter)	1 tbsp.	15 mL
Dried thyme	1/4 tsp.	1 mL
Boneless, skinless chicken breast halves (about 1 1/2 lbs., 680 g)	6	6
Salt, sprinkle		
Pepper, sprinkle		
Pie crust pastry, enough for 2 crust pie		
Cooked ham slices	6	6
Slices of Gruyère (or Brie or Swiss) cheese	6	6

Combine margarine and thyme in non-stick frying pan. Add chicken. Sauté until no longer pink. Sprinkle with salt and pepper. Cool.

Divide pastry into 2 portions. Roll out 1 portion into 8 × 18 inch (20 × 45 cm) rectangle. Cut rectangle into 3 equal rectangles. Cut ham slices same size as chicken. Lay 1 ham slice near short edge of pastry. Place cheese and chicken on top of ham. Fold pastry over and roll up to cover. Dampen edges of side and top. Seal. Cut slits in top. Repeat, to make 6 packets. Arrange on ungreased baking sheet. Bake in 400°F (205°C) oven for 25 to 30 minutes until browned. Serves 6.

1 serving: 595 Calories; 43 g Protein; 33.7 g Total Fat; 28 g Carbohydrate; 1001 mg Sodium; 1 g Dietary Fibre

Pictured above.

Condiments

It wasn't until the 1906 edition of Fannie Farmer's cookbook that we saw a larger selection of butters and spreads. Today there are incredible choices of condiments available, including chutneys, compotes, salsas and relishes, to enhance our meals. The five recipes in this section are classics that you will be able to pass on in your family for generations to come.

Spiced Plums

An old family recipe. Especially good with baked ham or cold beef. Also good served over cream cheese, cottage cheese or just to eat a spoonful.

Prune plums	3 1/2 lbs.	1.6 kg
Granulated sugar	6 cups	1.5 L
Ground cinnamon	1 tbsp.	15 mL
Ground cloves	1 1/2 tsp.	7 mL
Salt	1/2 tsp.	2 mL
White vinegar	1 1/2 cups	375 mL

Cut plums in half. Remove stones. If you don't have a food processor, cut each plum half into at least 8 pieces. If you do have a food processor or blender, cut each half into 3 or 4 pieces. You will need to process later. Place in large pot or Dutch oven.

Add remaining 5 ingredients. Stir over medium-high until sugar is dissolved. Bring to a boil. Boil, stirring occasionally, for about 5 minutes until plums are mushy. Cool. Pour into food processor or blender in batches. Process. Some bits of skin should show. Return to pot. Bring to a boil. Boil, stirring often, until desired thickness. Pour into hot sterile jars to within 1/4 inch (6 mm) of top. Place sterile metal lids on jars and screw metal bands on securely. For added assurance against spoilage, you may choose to process in a boiling water bath for 10 minutes. Makes 5 1/2 pints (11 cups, 2.75 L) plums.

1/2 cup (125 mL) plums: 261 Calories; 1 g Protein; 0.5 g Total Fat; 67 g Carbohydrate; 63 mg Sodium; 1 g Dietary Fibre

Pictured on this page.

Curried Fruit Compote

Mild curry flavour. Serve hot or cold. Delicious over ice cream or served as a side dish with beef, chicken or pork.

Canned sliced peaches, juice reserved	14 oz.	398 mL
Canned pears, each half cut into 3 pieces, juice reserved	14 oz.	398 mL
Canned pineapple tidbits, juice reserved	14 oz.	398 mL
Canned mandarin orange segments, discard juice	12 oz.	341 mL
Maraschino cherries	20	20
Brown sugar, packed	3/4 cup	175 mL
Cornstarch	3 tbsp.	50 mL
Curry powder	1 1/2 tsp.	7 mL
All reserved juice, approximately	2 cups	500 mL

Place peaches, pears, pineapple, orange segments and cherries in 3 1/2 quart (3.5 L) slow cooker.

Mix brown sugar, cornstarch and curry powder in small saucepan. Add reserved juice. Heat and stir until boiling and thickened. Pour over fruit. Cover. Cook on Low for 3 hours. Makes 6 1/4 cups (1.55 L) fruit.

1/2 cup (125 mL) fruit: 32 Calories, trace Protein, trace Total Fat, 8 g Carbohydrate, 2 mg Sodium; trace Dietary Fibre

Pictured below.

Note: This may be baked, covered, in ungreased 2 quart (2 L) casserole in 350°F (175°C) oven for 30 to 40 minutes until hot.

Spiced Plums, this page

Curried Fruit Compote, above

Top: Old-Time Butter, this page
Centre right: Chow Chow Maritime, below
Bottom: Pickled Peaches, this page

HEIRLOOM RECIPE

Chow Chow Maritime

*Triple this old recipe so you have some for family and friends.
Especially good with meats served with gravy.*

Medium green tomatoes, stem ends and cores removed, sliced	5 1/3 lbs.	2.5 kg
Onions, cut up	1 1/2 lbs.	680 g
Coarse (pickling) salt	1/3 cup	75 mL
Granulated sugar	3 1/3 cups	825 mL
Mixed pickling spice, tied in double layer of cheesecloth	4 1/2 tbsp.	67 mL
Turmeric	2 tsp.	10 mL
White vinegar	2 cups	500 mL

Layer tomato, onion and salt in large saucepan. Cover and let stand on counter overnight. Drain.

Add remaining 4 ingredients. Vinegar should be just a bit visible. Too much will make excessive juice. Heat and stir until sugar is dissolved. Bring to a boil. Simmer, uncovered, stirring occasionally, for 2 hours. More turmeric can be added for colour and more sugar can be added for taste. In order to obtain an accurate taste, cool a spoonful and then sample. Discard cheesecloth bag. Pour into hot sterile pint jars to within 1/2 inch (12 mm) of top. Place sterile metal lids on jars and screw metal bands on securely. For added assurance against spoilage, you may choose to process in a boiling water bath for 5 minutes. Makes 4 pints (8 cups, 2 L) preserves.

1/2 cup (125 mL) preserves: 232 Calories; 2 g Protein; 0.4 g Total Fat; 58 g Carbohydrate; 1183 mg Sodium; 3 g Dietary Fibre

Pictured above.

Pickled Peaches

Serve hot or cold with baked ham, beef or pork.

Granulated sugar	1 1/3 cups	325 mL
White vinegar	1/2 cup	125 mL
Cinnamon sticks (3 inches, 7.5 cm, each), broken up (see Note)	3	3
Whole cloves	10	10
Fresh (or frozen) peaches, sliced (about 2 1/2 cups, 625 mL)	1 1/2 lbs.	680 g

Measure sugar and vinegar into medium saucepan. Tie cinnamon and cloves in small cheesecloth bag. Add to saucepan. Stir.

Add peaches. Heat, stirring occasionally, until peaches are tender. Discard cheesecloth bag. Cool. Refrigerate. When ready to serve, drain, reserving juice to store leftover peaches. Makes 2 1/2 cups (625 mL) peaches.

1/2 cup (125 mL) peaches: 153 Calories; 1 g Protein; 0.1 g Total Fat; 40 g Carbohydrate; trace Sodium; 2 g Dietary Fibre

Pictured on this page.

Note: Put cinnamon sticks into plastic bag. Break up with bottom of glass.

Old-Time Butter

Butter-making is almost a lost art. Have kids and adults gather 'round while you make some from sweet pasteurized cream. In days gone by, unpasteurized soured cream was used.

Whipping cream, chilled	2 cups	500 mL
Lots of cold water		
Salt	1/8 tsp.	0.5 mL

Beat whipping cream on high in large bowl until thickened. Notice you now have whipped cream. Continue to beat until the smooth shiny appearance changes to a grainy look. Keep beating until cream starts to separate into little goblets and liquid. Stop beating occasionally to see if little particles can be pushed together with spoon or collected by gathering with spoon. When it becomes lumpy, use slotted spoon to remove lumps to small bowl, or strain liquid through sieve. The liquid is buttermilk. The lumps are butter.

Work butter lumps into 1 lump. Pour cold water over butter. Work with spoon until water is milky looking. Drain. Repeat until water runs clear. This will take at least 4 rinses. Work more to release all water from butter.

Sprinkle with salt. Work in. Press in, or pipe butter into, small dish. Makes 3/4 cup (175 mL) butter.

2 tsp. (10 mL) butter: 46 Calories; trace Protein; 5.2 g Total Fat; 0 g Carbohydrate; 53 mg Sodium; 0 g Dietary Fibre

Pictured on this page.

Cookies

Cookies

In the days when ovens could not be relied on for regular, even heat, many batches of cookies burned or were unevenly browned. In 1920, gas ranges started to phase out coal, wood and petroleum stoves. The evolution of the oven had a great deal to do with the kinds of cookies that were baked. Hermits, macaroons, sugar cookies, molasses cookies and gingersnaps were just a few of the cookie recipes that appeared repeatedly in late nineteenth century cookbooks and are still made today. When electric ranges were popular in homes in the 1930s, baking cookies became common practice until butter and sugar rationing during the Second World War. After the war, many people turned to baking a wider variety of cookies. And with convenience cooking and baking the preference in the busy latter half of the century, cookie mixes and refrigerated, slice-and-bake cookie dough emerged. Serve a plateful of memories with Soft Molasses Drops (page 96), Wartime Cookies (page 96) and Hermits (page 97).

1. Oatmeal Macaroons, this page
2. Chocolate Oatmeal Cookies, this page
3. Circus Cookies, page 95

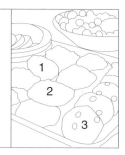

Chocolate Oatmeal Cookies

Soft on the inside and crunchy on the outside.
Balanced flavours of chocolate and oatmeal.

Hard margarine (or butter), softened	1/2 cup	125 mL
Granulated sugar	1 cup	250 mL
Large egg	1	1
Milk	1/4 cup	60 mL
Vanilla	1 tsp.	5 mL
Unsweetened chocolate baking squares, cut up	2 x 1 oz.	2 x 28 g
Quick-cooking rolled oats (not instant)	1 1/2 cups	375 mL
All-purpose flour	1 cup	250 mL
Baking powder	2 tsp.	10 mL
Salt	1/8 tsp.	0.5 mL

Cream margarine and sugar together in large bowl. Beat in egg. Add milk and vanilla. Beat.

Place chocolate in small saucepan over low. Heat, stirring often, until melted. Add to batter. Stir.

Add rolled oats, flour, baking powder and salt. Mix well. Drop by tablespoonfuls onto greased cookie sheet. Bake in 350°F (175°C) oven for 12 to 15 minutes. Makes about 3 dozen cookies.

1 cookie: 85 Calories; 1 g Protein; 4 g Total Fat; 12 g Carbohydrate; 46 mg Sodium; 1 g Dietary Fibre

Pictured on page 93.

Oatmeal Macaroons

Crunchy oatmeal but with the distinctive coconut taste.
Look more like macaroons than oatmeal cookies.

Hard margarine (or butter), softened	2 tbsp.	30 mL
Granulated sugar	1/2 cup	125 mL
Large eggs	2	2
cornflakes cereal	2 cups	500 mL
Quick-cooking rolled oats (not instant)	3/4 cup	175 mL
Medium (or flake) coconut	2/3 cup	150 mL
Baking powder	1/2 tsp.	2 mL
Salt	1/2 tsp.	2 mL

Beat margarine, sugar and eggs in medium bowl until smooth and increased in volume.

Mix in remaining 5 ingredients. Drop by tablespoonfuls onto greased cookie sheet. Bake in 350°F (175°C) oven for 13 to 15 minutes. Makes 2 dozen cookies.

1 cookie: 69 Calories; 1 g Protein; 3.3 g Total Fat; 9 g Carbohydrate; 99 mg Sodium; trace Dietary Fibre

Pictured on page 93.

Circus Cookies

Crispy outside and soft inside. Colourful candies add the circus touch.

Hard margarine (or butter), softened	1 cup	250 mL
Brown sugar, packed	2 cups	500 mL
Large eggs	2	2
Vanilla	1 tsp.	5 mL
All-purpose flour	2 cups	500 mL
Baking powder	1 tsp.	5 mL
Baking soda	1/2 tsp.	2 mL
Salt	1/2 tsp.	2 mL
Quick-cooking rolled oats (not instant)	2 cups	500 mL
Chopped walnuts (or pecans)	1/2 cup	125 mL
Candy-coated chocolate bits (about 3 oz., 85 g)	1/3 cup	75 mL

Cream margarine and brown sugar together in large bowl. Beat in eggs, 1 at a time. Add vanilla. Mix.

Stir next 6 ingredients together in medium bowl. Add to batter. Mix in. Drop by tablespoonfuls onto greased cookie sheet.

Press candy pieces into dough. Bake in 400°F (205°C) oven for 10 to 12 minutes. Makes about 4 1/2 dozen cookies.

1 cookie: 113 Calories; 2 g Protein; 5.1 g Total Fat; 16 g Carbohydrate; 87 mg Sodium; 1 g Dietary Fibre

Pictured on page 93.

Oatmeal Crisps

Chewy while warm; crispy when cooled.

Hard margarine (or butter), softened	1 cup	250 mL
Brown sugar, packed	1 1/2 cups	375 mL
Large egg	1	1
Corn syrup	1/2 cup	125 mL
Fancy molasses	1/4 cup	60 mL
Vanilla	1 tsp.	5 mL
Quick-cooking rolled oats (not instant)	2 1/2 cups	625 mL
All-purpose flour	2 1/2 cups	625 mL
Baking soda	2 tsp.	10 mL
Ground cinnamon	1 tsp.	5 mL
Ground nutmeg	1 tsp.	5 mL
Ground allspice	1 tsp.	5 mL

Cream margarine, brown sugar and egg together in large bowl. Mix in corn syrup, molasses and vanilla.

Add remaining 6 ingredients. Mix well. Shape into 1 inch (2.5 cm) balls. Arrange on greased cookie sheet. Flatten with floured fork. Bake in 375°F (190°C) oven for 8 to 10 minutes until lightly browned. Makes about 5 dozen cookies.

1 cookie: 98 Calories; 1 g Protein; 3.6 g Total Fat; 15 g Carbohydrate; 89 mg Sodium; 1 g Dietary Fibre

Pictured on this page.

Oatmeal Cookies

Cinnamon, walnuts and raisins combine to make this a nutritious and delicious cookie.

Hard margarine (or butter), softened	1 cup	250 mL
Brown sugar, packed	1 cup	250 mL
Granulated sugar	1/2 cup	125 mL
Large eggs	2	2
Vanilla	1 tsp.	5 mL
Quick-cooking rolled oats (not instant)	2 cups	500 mL
All-purpose flour	2 1/2 cups	625 mL
Baking soda	1 tsp.	5 mL
Ground cinnamon	1 tsp.	5 mL
Chopped walnuts	1 cup	250 mL
Dark raisins	2 cups	500 mL
Golden raisins	1 cup	250 mL

Cream margarine and both sugars together in large bowl. Beat in eggs, 1 at a time. Add vanilla. Mix.

Stir in rolled oats.

Add flour, baking soda and cinnamon. Mix well.

Add walnuts and both raisins. Mix well. Drop by rounded tablespoonfuls onto greased cookie sheet about 1 inch (2.5 cm) apart. Bake in 375°F (190°C) oven for 12 to 15 minutes. Makes about 4 1/2 dozen cookies.

1 cookie: 133 Calories; 2 g Protein; 5.5 g Total Fat; 20 g Carbohydrate; 71 mg Sodium; 1 g Dietary Fibre

Pictured below.

Oatmeal Crisps, this page

Oatmeal Cookies, above

Soft Molasses Drops

An old-time recipe that Mom used to bake. Moist and spicy.

All-purpose flour	3 1/2 cups	875 mL
Granulated sugar	3/4 cup	175 mL
Ground ginger	1 tsp.	5 mL
Ground cinnamon	1 tsp.	5 mL
Salt	1/2 tsp.	2 mL
Fancy molasses	3/4 cup	175 mL
Hard margarine (or butter), softened	3/4 cup	175 mL
Large egg	1	1
Baking soda	1 1/2 tsp.	7 mL
Hot prepared coffee (or hot milk)	1/2 cup	125 mL

Measure first 8 ingredients into large bowl. Mix well.

Stir baking soda into hot prepared coffee in small cup. Add to dough. Beat well until blended. Drop by tablespoonfuls onto greased cookie sheet. Bake in 375°F (190°C) oven for 10 to 12 minutes. Makes 5 dozen cookies.

1 cookie: 72 Calories; 1 g Protein; 2.5 g Total Fat; 11 g Carbohydrate; 86 mg Sodium; trace Dietary Fibre

Pictured on page 97.

Snappy Gingersnaps

Great with tea, and even better for dunking in a glass of milk.

All-purpose flour	3 cups	750 mL
Baking powder	1 tsp.	5 mL
Baking soda	1/2 tsp.	2 mL
Ground ginger	1 tsp.	5 mL
Ground cinnamon	1/2 tsp.	2 mL
Salt	1/2 tsp.	2 mL
Cayenne pepper, just a pinch		
Hard margarine (or butter), softened	1/2 cup	125 mL
Granulated sugar	1/2 cup	125 mL
Fancy molasses	1/2 cup	125 mL
Cold prepared tea	2 tbsp.	30 mL

Measure first 7 ingredients into medium bowl. Stir well.

Cream margarine and sugar together in large bowl. Add molasses and prepared tea. Mix well. Add flour mixture. Mix well. Cover. Refrigerate for several hours or overnight. Roll out on lightly floured surface about 1/8 inch (3 mm) thick. Cut into 2 1/2 inch (6.4 cm) circles. Place on greased cookie sheet. Bake in 375°F (190°C) oven for 10 to 12 minutes. Makes 4 1/2 dozen cookies.

1 cookie: 59 Calories; 1 g Protein; 1.9 g Total Fat; 10 g Carbohydrate; 60 mg Sodium; trace Dietary Fibre

Pictured on this page.

Snappy Gingersnaps, this page   Wartime Cookies, below

Wartime Cookies

During the Second World War when sugar was scarce, people were in luck if pudding powders were available. Today, this is still a favourite.

Butterscotch (or caramel) pudding powder (not instant), 6 serving size	1	1
Hard margarine (or butter), softened	3/4 cup	175 mL
Granulated sugar	1 tbsp.	15 mL
All-purpose flour	1 cup	250 mL
Quick-cooking rolled oats (not instant)	1 1/2 cups	375 mL
Baking powder	1/4 tsp.	1 mL
Baking soda	1/4 tsp.	1 mL
Salt	1/8 tsp.	0.5 mL
Vanilla	1 tsp.	5 mL
Large egg	1	1

Measure all 10 ingredients into large bowl. Mix well. Roll into balls, 1 to 1 1/4 inches (2.5 to 3 cm) in diameter. Place on greased cookie sheet. Press with fork. Bake in 375°F (190°C) oven for 10 to 15 minutes. Makes about 3 dozen cookies.

1 cookie: 79 Calories; 1 g Protein; 4.5 g Total Fat; 9 g Carbohydrate; 79 mg Sodium; trace Dietary Fibre

Pictured above.

Top: Soft Molasses Drops, page 96

Bottom centre: Nutri Cookies, below

Right: Hermits, below

Nutri Cookies

Tell the kids they can have cookies for breakfast. They'll love it.

Hard margarine (or butter), softened	1/2 cup	125 mL
Smooth peanut butter	1/2 cup	125 mL
Liquid honey	1 cup	250 mL
Large eggs	2	2
Vanilla	1 tsp.	5 mL
All-purpose flour	1 1/2 cups	375 mL
Quick-cooking rolled oats (not instant)	3 cups	750 mL
Medium coconut	1 cup	250 mL
Natural bran	3/4 cup	175 mL
Sunflower seeds	1/2 cup	125 mL
Baking soda	1 tsp.	5 mL
Salt	1 tsp.	5 mL
Raisins	1 cup	250 mL
Chopped walnuts (or your choice of nuts)	1/2 cup	125 mL

Beat margarine and peanut butter in large bowl until blended. Add honey, eggs and vanilla. Beat slowly until blended.

Add remaining 9 ingredients. Mix well. Shape into balls using 1 tbsp. (15 mL) each. Flatten between your palms. Arrange on ungreased cookie sheet. Bake in 375°F (190°C) oven for about 12 minutes. Makes 8 dozen small cookies.

1 cookie: 69 Calories; 2 g Protein; 3.5 g Total Fat; 9 g Carbohydrate; 64 mg Sodium; 1 g Dietary Fibre

Pictured above.

Variation: Omit sunflower seeds. Add 1/4 cup (60 mL) wheat germ.

Hermits

One of the best known drop cookies.
Mom kept our cookie jar filled with these.

Hard margarine (or butter), softened	1 cup	250 mL
Brown sugar, packed	1 1/2 cups	375 mL
Large eggs	3	3
Vanilla	1 tsp.	5 mL
All-purpose flour	3 cups	750 mL
Baking powder	1 tsp.	5 mL
Baking soda	1 tsp.	5 mL
Salt	1/2 tsp.	2 mL
Ground cinnamon	1 tsp.	5 mL
Ground nutmeg	1/2 tsp.	2 mL
Ground allspice	1/4 tsp.	1 mL
Raisins	1 cup	250 mL
Chopped dates	1 cup	250 mL
Chopped nuts	2/3 cup	150 mL

Cream margarine and brown sugar together in large bowl. Beat in eggs, 1 at a time. Add vanilla.

Add remaining 10 ingredients. Mix well. Drop by tablespoonfuls onto greased cookie sheet. Bake in 375°F (190°C) oven for 6 to 8 minutes. Makes 4 1/2 dozen cookies.

1 cookie: 115 Calories; 2 g Protein; 5 g Total Fat; 17 g Carbohydrate; 99 mg Sodium; 1 g Dietary Fibre

Pictured above.

Brown Sugar Cookies

An old-fashioned cookie taste. Not too sweet, with little bits of almond crunch.

Hard margarine (or butter), softened	1 cup	250 mL
Brown sugar, packed	1 1/3 cups	325 mL
Large eggs	2	2
Vanilla	1/2 tsp.	2 mL
All-purpose flour	3 1/4 cups	810 mL
Baking soda	1 1/4 tsp.	6 mL
Ground cinnamon	3/4 tsp.	4 mL
Salt	1/4 tsp.	1 mL
Chopped almonds	1/3 cup	75 mL

Cream margarine and brown sugar together in large bowl. Beat in eggs, 1 at a time. Add vanilla. Mix.

Stir in remaining 5 ingredients. Form into 2 rolls, 2 inches (5 cm) in diameter. Cover. Refrigerate overnight. Slice 1/4 inch (6 mm) thick. Arrange on ungreased cookie sheet. Bake in 375°F (190°C) oven for 10 to 12 minutes until browned. Makes 3 1/2 dozen cookies.

1 cookie: 117 Calories; 2 g Protein; 5.6 g Total Fat; 15 g Carbohydrate; 117 mg Sodium; 1 g Dietary Fibre

Pictured below.

Pan Shortbread

This recipe came from one of Mom's friends. A favourite recipe for shortbread that always turns out.

Icing (confectioner's) sugar	1/2 cup	125 mL
All-purpose flour	2 cups	500 mL
Butter (not margarine)	1 cup	250 mL

Combine sugar and flour in large bowl. Cut in butter until mixture is mealy. Using your hands, mix until you get a smooth ball. Press flat in ungreased 9 x 9 inch (22 x 22 cm) pan. Poke all over with fork right through to the bottom. Bake in 300°F (150°C) oven for 50 to 60 minutes until set and very lightly golden. Cut into 36 squares while warm.

1 square: 81 Calories; 1 g Protein; 5.5 g Total Fat; 7 g Carbohydrate; 55 mg Sodium; trace Dietary Fibre

Pictured below.

Brown Sugar Cookies, above

Pan Shortbread, above

Desserts

Our obsession with the sweet taste of dessert dates back through the centuries. Puddings, pies, ice cream and sauces were enjoyed throughout the 1800s. Custards, steamed puddings and whips were often served, along with ice cream desserts such as baked Alaska, and a variety of dishes using fresh fruits and berries. Chocolate desserts did not become popular until the twentieth century when chocolate became more widely available and was more reasonably priced. As kitchens were modernized with gas and electric ranges, electric mixers, blenders and food processors, the variety and complexity of desserts changed. With the introduction of flavoured jelly powders, packaged puddings and toppings, frozen puff pastry and phyllo after the Second World War, desserts now can be as simple as Fruit in Jelly (page 107) or as elaborate as Turtle Cheesecake (page 100).

Chocolate Raspberry Dessert

A rich, creamy dessert. Garnish with whipped topping.

CRUST		
Hard margarine (or butter)	1/2 cup	125 mL
Graham cracker crumbs	1 1/2 cups	375 mL
Finely chopped pecans	1/3 cup	75 mL
FILLING		
Hard margarine (or butter), softened	1/2 cup	125 mL
Icing (confectioner's) sugar	1 1/2 cups	375 mL
Light cream cheese, softened	4 oz.	125 g
Unsweetened chocolate baking squares, cut up	2 x 1 oz.	2 x 28 g
Raspberry jam	1/2 cup	125 mL
Envelope unflavoured gelatin	1 x 1/4 oz.	1 x 7 g
Water	1/4 cup	60 mL
Envelope dessert topping (prepared according to package directions), or 1 cup (250 mL) whipping cream, whipped	1	1
Frozen raspberries in syrup, thawed, drained and syrup reserved	15 oz.	425 g
RASPBERRY SAUCE		
Cornstarch	1 1/2 tbsp.	25 mL
Reserved raspberry syrup, plus water to make	1 1/4 cups	300 mL

Crust: Melt margarine in small saucepan. Stir in graham crumbs and pecans. Press in ungreased 9 inch (22 cm) springform pan. Bake in 350°F (175°C) oven for 10 minutes. Cool.

Filling: Cream margarine, icing sugar and cream cheese together in medium bowl.

Combine chocolate and jam in small saucepan. Heat and stir over low until chocolate is melted.

Sprinkle gelatin over water in small bowl. Let stand for 1 minute. Add to chocolate mixture in saucepan. Stir until gelatin is dissolved. Chill until syrupy. Beat into cream cheese mixture.

Fold in dessert topping and raspberries. Pour over crust. Chill. Transfer to large serving plate.

Raspberry Sauce: Stir cornstarch into reserved raspberry syrup in small saucepan. Heat and stir until boiling and thickened. Cool thoroughly. Spoon over top of dessert. Cuts into 12 wedges.

1 wedge: 438 Calories; 5 g Protein; 26.1 g Total Fat; 51 g Carbohydrate; 399 mg Sodium; 3 g Dietary Fibre

Pictured on page 101.

Cool Lime Soufflé

Present this in a soufflé dish for a lasting impression.
Garnish with whipped topping and lime peel.

Envelope unflavoured gelatin	1 x 1/4 oz.	1 x 7 g
Cold water	1/3 cup	75 mL
Granulated sugar	1/2 cup	125 mL
Lime juice	1/2 cup	125 mL
Egg yolks (large)	4	4
Salt, sprinkle		
Finely grated lime peel	1 1/2 tsp.	7 mL
Drops of green food colouring	4	4
Egg whites (large), room temperature	4	4
Granulated sugar	1/2 cup	125 mL
Envelope dessert topping (not prepared)	1	1
Milk	1/2 cup	125 mL

Sprinkle gelatin over cold water in small bowl. Let stand while making custard.

Combine next 4 ingredients in top of double boiler. Cook over slowly boiling water, stirring constantly, until thickened enough to coat back of spoon. Add gelatin mixture. Stir until dissolved.

Add lime peel and food colouring. Chill, stirring and scraping down sides occasionally, until cool and beginning to gel.

Beat egg whites in medium bowl until soft peaks form. Gradually add second amount of sugar while beating until stiff and glossy.

Using same beaters, beat dessert topping and milk on low in small bowl. Beat on medium until stiff. Fold egg whites into gelatin mixture. Add whipped topping. Gently fold in until no white streaks remain. Tie waxed paper collar, about 3 inches (7.5 cm) high, around top of ungreased 4 cup (1 L) soufflé dish or 6 individual ramekins. Turn mixture into soufflé dish or divide evenly among ramekins. Chill well. Remove collar before serving. Serves 6.

1 serving: 244 Calories; 6 g Protein; 6.4 g Total Fat; 42 g Carbohydrate; 63 mg Sodium; trace Dietary Fibre

Pictured on page 101.

Rhubarb Cobbler

A cobbler with a pinwheel design topping.
Scrumptious any time of the year.

Cut up fresh (or frozen) rhubarb (1/2 inch, 12 mm, lengths)	6 cups	1.5 L
Minute tapioca	3 tbsp.	50 mL
Granulated sugar	1 1/2 cups	375 mL
Water	1/3 cup	75 mL
Lemon juice	1 tbsp.	15 mL
TOPPING		
All-purpose flour	2 cups	500 mL
Granulated sugar	1 1/2 tbsp.	25 mL
Baking powder	4 tsp.	20 mL
Salt	1/2 tsp.	2 mL
Milk	2/3 cup	150 mL
Cooking oil	3 tbsp.	50 mL
Hard margarine (or butter), softened	1/2 tbsp.	7 mL
Grated peel of 1 large lemon		
Granulated sugar	1/4 cup	60 mL

Stir rhubarb, tapioca, sugar, water and lemon juice in large saucepan. Heat, stirring occasionally, until boiling. Turn into ungreased 3 quart (3 L) casserole. Bake, uncovered, in 450°F (230°C) oven for about 20 minutes.

Topping: Measure first 4 ingredients into medium bowl. Stir.

Add milk and cooking oil. Stir to make soft ball. Turn out onto lightly floured surface. Knead 8 times. Roll out into 1/2 inch (12 mm) thick rectangle about 10 inches (25 cm) long.

Brush margarine over surface.

Stir lemon peel and sugar in small cup. Sprinkle 1/2 of mixture over margarine. Roll up like jelly roll from 10 inch (25 cm) side. Cut into 14 slices. Arrange over rhubarb, cut side down. Sprinkle remaining lemon peel mixture on top. Bake for another 25 minutes. Serves 8.

1 serving: 404 Calories; 5 g Protein; 6.6 g Total Fat; 83 g Carbohydrate; 202 mg Sodium; 3 g Dietary Fibre

Pictured on page 101.

Quick Date Pudding

Serve with a scoop of ice cream for the ultimate finish.

All-purpose flour	1 cup	250 mL
Granulated sugar	2/3 cup	150 mL
Baking powder	2 tsp.	10 mL
Salt	1/4 tsp.	1 mL
Milk	1/2 cup	125 mL
Hard margarine (or butter), melted	2 tbsp.	30 mL
Chopped dates	1 cup	250 mL
Chopped walnuts	1/2 cup	125 mL
Brown sugar, packed	1 cup	250 mL
Hard margarine (or butter), softened	1 tbsp.	15 mL
Vanilla	1 tsp.	5 mL
Boiling water	2 cups	500 mL

Measure first 8 ingredients into medium bowl. Mix well. Turn into greased 8 inch (20 cm) round casserole.

Stir remaining 4 ingredients in separate medium bowl. Pour carefully over batter. Do not stir. Bake, uncovered, in 350°F (175°C) oven for 30 to 35 minutes until top crust is firm to touch. Serves 6.

1 serving: 522 Calories; 5 g Protein; 13.2 g Total Fat; 100 g Carbohydrate; 212 mg Sodium; 4 g Dietary Fibre

Pictured on this page.

Tapioca Pudding

*A creamy blend of orange and pineapple.
Quite a refreshing dessert.*

Water	1 2/3 cups	400 mL
Tapioca pudding powder (not Instant), 6 serving size (see Note)	1	1
Orange-flavoured gelatin (jelly powder)	1 x 3 oz.	1 x 85 g
Envelope dessert topping (prepared according to package directions)	1	1
Canned crushed pineapple, drained	8 oz.	227 mL
Canned mandarin orange segments, drained	12 oz.	341 mL

Gradually mix water into pudding powder in medium saucepan. Heat and stir until boiling and thickened.

Add gelatin. Stir until dissolved. Chill, stirring and scraping down sides occasionally, until thickened.

Fold in dessert topping. Fold in pineapple and orange segments. Chill for several hours. Makes 4 cups (1 L) pudding.

2/3 cup (150 mL) pudding: 208 Calories; 2 g Protein; 3.3 g Total Fat; 44 g Carbohydrate; 122 mg Sodium; 1 g Dietary Fibre

Pictured on this page.

Note: If you can't find tapioca pudding powder, substitute coconut or vanilla pudding powder.

Hazelnut Dip

Tastes like European chocolate spread. Serve separately as fruit dip, or arrange the fruit on each plate with large dollops of dip in centre.

Sliced hazelnuts (filberts), toasted in 350°F (175°C) oven for 5 to 8 minutes	3 1/2 oz.	100 g
Vanilla	1 tsp.	5 mL
Water	1/2 cup	125 mL
Envelope dessert topping (not prepared)	1	1
Milk	1/3 cup	75 mL
Brown sugar, packed	2 tbsp.	30 mL
Amaretto (or Frangelico) liqueur	4 tsp.	20 mL
Chocolate syrup (optional)	2 tsp.	10 mL

Combine first 3 ingredients in blender. Process until smooth.

Stir dessert topping and milk in medium bowl. Beat until stiff.

Beat in remaining 3 ingredients. Fold in hazelnut mixture. Makes 2 1/2 cups (625 mL) dip.

2 tbsp. (30 mL) dip: 53 Calories; 1 g Protein; 3.9 g Total Fat; 4 g Carbohydrate; 51 mg Sodium; trace Dietary Fibre

Pictured below.

Top: Hazelnut Dip, above
Bottom left: Quick Date Pudding, this page
Bottom right: Tapioca Pudding, this page

Top left: Strawberries And Cream, below
Top right and centre: Choco Peanut Dessert Topping, this page
Bottom: Creamy Blueberry Dessert, this page

Strawberries And Cream

Rich and wonderful without being too sweet.

Sweetened condensed milk	11 oz.	300 mL
Water	1 1/2 cups	375 mL
Instant vanilla pudding powder (4 serving size)	1	1
Frozen whipped topping (in a tub), thawed	4 cups	1 L
Frozen pound cake, cut into 1/2 inch (12 mm) cubes (about 5 cups, 1.25 L)	10 1/2 oz.	298 g
Sliced fresh strawberries	4 cups	1 L
Slivered almonds, toasted in 350°F (175°C) oven for 5 to 8 minutes	1/4 cup	60 mL

Beat condensed milk and water in medium bowl until blended. Add pudding powder. Beat until smooth. Chill until set.

Stir pudding mixture. Fold in whipped topping.

Pour 2 cups pudding mixture into bottom of glass bowl. Spread with 1/2 of cake cubes and 1/2 of strawberries. Spoon 1/2 of remaining pudding mixture over strawberries. Cover with second 1/2 of cake cubes and second 1/2 of strawberries. Spoon remaining pudding mixture over top. Sprinkle with almonds. Serves 12.

1 serving: 355 Calories; 5 g Protein; 15.7 g Total Fat; 50 g Carbohydrate; 120 mg Sodium; 1 g Dietary Fibre

Pictured above.

Creamy Blueberry Dessert

*This is a great dessert to make ahead.
Tastes even better the second day.*

CRUST		
Hard margarine (or butter), softened	1/2 cup	125 mL
Brown sugar, packed	1/4 cup	60 mL
All-purpose flour	1 cup	250 mL
FILLING		
Hard margarine (or butter), softened	1/2 cup	125 mL
Non-fat spreadable cream cheese	4 oz.	125 g
Icing (confectioner's) sugar	1 cup	250 mL
Canned blueberry pie filling	19 oz.	540 mL
Chopped pecans	1/2 cup	125 mL
Frozen whipped topping (in a tub), thawed	2 cups	500 mL

Crust: Mix margarine, brown sugar and flour in small bowl until crumbly. Press in ungreased 9 x 9 inch (22 x 22 cm) pan. Bake in 350°F (175°C) oven for 10 minutes. Cool.

Filling: Cream margarine, cream cheese and icing sugar together well in small bowl. Spread over crust.

Spread pie filling over top. Sprinkle with pecans.

Put dabs of whipped topping here and there over top of pie filling. Spread to cover. Chill. Cuts into 12 pieces.

1 piece: 386 Calories; 3 g Protein; 23.4 g Total Fat; 43 g Carbohydrate; 196 mg Sodium; 1 g Dietary Fibre

Pictured on this page.

Choco Peanut Dessert Topping

*Spoon this warm topping over vanilla ice cream.
Not too sweet. Garnish with crushed peanuts.*

Chocolate pudding powder (not instant), 6 serving size	1	1
Water	1 1/3 cups	325 mL
Corn syrup	1 cup	250 mL
Smooth peanut butter	3/4 cup	175 mL

Stir pudding powder and water in medium saucepan. Heat and stir until boiling and thickened. Remove from heat.

Add corn syrup and peanut butter. Stir until smooth. Makes 2 cups (500 mL) topping.

1/4 cup (60 mL) topping: 352 Calories; 7 g Protein; 13.1 g Total Fat; 57 g Carbohydrate; 246 mg Sodium; 2 g Dietary Fibre

Pictured on this page.

Steamed Ginger Pudding

This recipe was passed down from Gram to Mom and then to me. Mom would serve this with applesauce or whipped cream. Or serve with Brown Sugar Sauce, this page.

All-purpose flour	2 cups	500 mL
Granulated sugar	2 tbsp.	30 mL
Ground ginger	1 tsp.	5 mL
Hard margarine (or butter), softened	1/4 cup	60 mL
Raisins	1/2 cup	125 mL
Baking soda	1 tsp.	5 mL
Milk	1 cup	250 mL
Fancy molasses	2 tbsp.	30 mL

Measure flour, sugar and ginger into medium bowl. Add margarine. Mix until crumbly. Stir in raisins to coat with flour mixture.

Mix baking soda and milk in small bowl. Add to flour mixture. Add molasses. Stir to mix. Turn into greased 1 1/2 quart (1.5 L) pudding pan. Cover with double square greased foil, tying sides down with string. Place in steamer with boiling water 2/3 up side of pan. Steam for 2 hours, adding more boiling water as needed to keep level up. Serves 6.

1 serving (without sauce): 325 Calories; 6 g Protein; 9.2 g Total Fat; 55 g Carbohydrate; 350 mg Sodium; 2 g Dietary Fibre

Pictured below.

Brown Sugar Sauce

The finishing touch for all steamed and cottage fruit puddings.

Brown sugar, packed	1 cup	250 mL
All-purpose flour	1/4 cup	60 mL
Salt	1/2 tsp.	2 mL
Water	2 cups	500 mL
Vanilla	1 tsp.	5 mL

Mix brown sugar, flour and salt well in medium saucepan. This allows water to be mixed in with no lumps.

Stir in water and vanilla. Heat over medium, stirring constantly, until boiling and thickened. Makes about 2 1/2 cups (625 mL) sauce.

2 tbsp. (30 mL) sauce: 48 Calories; trace Protein; trace Total Fat; 12 g Carbohydrate; 69 mg Sodium; trace Dietary Fibre

Pictured below and on page 106.

Steamed Ginger Pudding with Brown Sugar Sauce, above

Brown Betty

Good hot or cold. Serve with cream or ice cream.

Cooking apples, peeled and sliced	6 cups	1.5 L
Granulated sugar	3/4 cup	175 mL
TOPPING		
All-purpose flour	1 1/4 cups	300 mL
Brown sugar, packed	3/4 cup	175 mL
Hard margarine (or butter)	1/2 cup	125 mL
Salt	1/2 tsp.	2 mL

Fill greased 10 inch (25 cm) round casserole with apples about 2 to 3 inches (5 to 7.5 cm) deep. Sprinkle sugar over top.

Topping: Mix flour, brown sugar, margarine and salt until crumbly. Scatter over apples. Pat down lightly with hand. Bake, uncovered, in 375°F (190°C) oven for about 40 minutes until apples are tender. Serves 8 generously.

1 serving: 392 Calories; 2 g Protein; 12.7 g Total Fat; 70 g Carbohydrate; 320 mg Sodium; 2 g Dietary Fibre

Pictured on this page.

Carrot Pudding

Fruity, dark and moist. Ice cream makes a good addition.
Serve with Brown Sugar Sauce, page 105.

Grated carrot	1 cup	250 mL
Grated potato	1 cup	250 mL
Ground suet	1 cup	250 mL
Granulated sugar	1 cup	250 mL
Raisins	1 cup	250 mL
Currants	1/4 cup	60 mL
All-purpose flour	1 1/2 cups	375 mL
Baking powder	1 tsp.	5 mL
Baking soda	1 tsp.	5 mL
Ground cinnamon	1 tsp.	5 mL
Ground allspice	1/2 tsp.	2 mL

Measure all 11 ingredients into large bowl. Stir together well. Pack in greased 10 cup (2.5 L) pudding pan. If you don't have a pudding pan, you can use sealer jars, vegetable or juice cans or even a bowl, filling 2/3 full. Cover with double square greased foil, tying side down with string. Place in steamer with boiling water 2/3 up side of pan. Steam for at least 3 hours, adding more boiling water as needed to keep level up. Serves 15.

1 serving: 282 Calories; 2 g Protein; 14.7 g Total Fat; 37 g Carbohydrate; 98 mg Sodium; 1 g Dietary Fibre

Pictured on this page.

Fruit Cobbler

A pretty cobbler that makes and bakes quickly.

Frozen raspberries in syrup, thawed, drained and syrup reserved	15 oz.	425 g
Canned pears, drained and juice reserved, cut up	14 oz.	398 mL
Granulated sugar	1/3 cup	75 mL
All-purpose flour	1 1/2 tbsp.	25 mL
Ground cinnamon	1/4 tsp.	1 mL
Reserved raspberry syrup, plus pear juice to make	3/4 cup	175 mL
TOPPING		
Large egg	1	1
Hard margarine (or butter), melted	1/4 cup	60 mL
Milk	1/3 cup	75 mL
All-purpose flour	1 cup	250 mL
Granulated sugar	1/4 cup	60 mL
Baking powder	1 1/2 tsp.	7 mL
Salt	1/4 tsp.	1 mL

Layer raspberries and pears in ungreased 2 quart (2 L) casserole.

Combine sugar, flour and cinnamon in small saucepan. Add reserved juices. Mix well. Heat and stir until boiling and thickened. Pour over fruit. Stir. Place in 425°F (220°C) oven to heat while preparing topping.

Topping: Beat egg in medium bowl. Stir in margarine. Add milk. Stir.

Add remaining 4 ingredients. Stir just to moisten. Drop by tablespoonfuls over fruit mixture. Return to oven. Bake, uncovered, for about 20 minutes until risen and browned. Serves 6.

1 serving: 340 Calories; 5 g Protein; 8.9 g Total Fat; 62 g Carbohydrate; 227 mg Sodium; 4 g Dietary Fibre

Pictured on page 107.

Top and centre left: Carrot Pudding, this page
Right: Brown Sugar Sauce, page 105
Bottom: Brown Betty, this page

Nothing Dessert, below   Fruit Cobbler, page 106   Fruit In Jelly, below

Nothing Dessert
So light, it's like eating nothing.

Large marshmallows (8 oz., 250 g)	32	32
Milk	1/3 cup	75 mL
Envelopes dessert topping (not prepared)	2	2
Milk	1 cup	250 mL
Vanilla	1 tsp.	5 mL
Fresh blueberries (or frozen, thawed and dried with paper towel)	2 cups	500 mL
Graham cracker crumbs	1 – 2 tbsp.	15 – 30 mL

Combine marshmallows and first amount of milk in large saucepan. Heat, stirring often, until marshmallows are melted. Transfer to large bowl. Cool, stirring often, until thickened.

Combine dessert topping, second amount of milk and vanilla in medium bowl. Beat until stiff. Fold into marshmallow mixture.

Reserve about 1/4 cup (60 mL) blueberries for garnish. Add remaining blueberries to marshmallow mixture. Fold in lightly. Turn into serving bowl.

Sprinkle with graham crumbs and reserved blueberries. Chill. Makes 6 cups (1.5 L) dessert.

1/2 cup (125 mL) dessert: 137 Calories; 2 g Protein; 3.3 g Total Fat; 26 g Carbohydrate; 47 mg Sodium; 1 g Dietary Fibre

Pictured above.

Fruit In Jelly
A fast and easy favourite dessert for longer than can be remembered. It was served in a wide shallow bowl so that everyone got fruit and cream.

Raspberry-flavoured gelatin (jelly powder), see Note	2 x 3 oz.	2 x 85 g
Boiling water	2 cups	500 mL
Cold water	2 cups	500 mL
Medium banana, sliced	1	1
Frozen whipped topping (in a tub), thawed	2 cups	500 mL

Stir gelatin into boiling water in medium bowl. Stir well until dissolved. Stir in cold water. Cool to room temperature on counter or put into refrigerator. When jelly gets syrupy but before it begins to set, lay banana slices on top to cover. Push down into jelly to coat. Chill.

Spread with whipped topping. Serves 8.

1 serving: 155 Calories; 2 g Protein; 5.1 g Total Fat; 27 g Carbohydrate; 66 mg Sodium; trace Dietary Fibre

Pictured above.

Note: Any flavour of jelly powder can be used. Pair with other fruits like diced apple or pear, peach or strawberry slices, or raspberries. Miniature marshmallows and chopped nuts are nice additions, too.

Fish & Seafood

In the 1940s, we were told that every homemaker should replace meat courses with fish at least twice a week. Today the benefits of including more fish in our diets are well documented. Fish and seafood are also more popular now because of the availability of recipes for varied preparation. You will have every member of the family enjoying the dishes in this section. Fish Sticks (right) remain a classic favourite among children and Lobster Newburg (page 112) is an elegant dish to serve for a special adult occasion.

Fish Sticks

Serve with tartar sauce or ketchup.
Every member of the family will love these!

All-purpose flour	1/3 cup	75 mL
Large eggs	2	2
Water	4 tsp.	20 mL
Fine dry bread crumbs	1 cup	250 mL
Salt	1 tsp.	5 mL
Pepper	1/4 tsp.	1 mL
Paprika	1 tsp.	5 mL
Cod fish fillets, skin removed, cut 3 1/2 x 1 inch (9 x 2.5 cm)	1 lb.	454 g
Hard margarine (or butter)	2 tbsp.	30 mL

Put flour into small bowl.

Beat eggs and water in separate small bowl.

Stir bread crumbs, salt, pepper and paprika in separate small bowl.

Dip each fish piece into flour to coat, then dip into egg mixture, then into bread crumb mixture. Set on large plate.

Melt margarine in non-stick frying pan. Add fish sticks. Brown both sides until medium to medium-dark and fish flakes easily when tested with fork. Makes about 20 fish sticks.

3 fish sticks: 202 Calories; 17 g Protein; 6.4 g Total Fat; 18 g Carbohydrate; 631 mg Sodium; 1 g Dietary Fibre

Pictured below.

Fish Sticks, above

Finnan Haddie, page 109

Finnan Haddie

*This smoked and salted haddock is a member
of the cod family. It's very popular in
Scotland and Atlantic Canada.*

Finnan haddie, cut into serving-size pieces	2 lbs.	900 g
Water, to cover		
Hard margarine (or butter)	3 tbsp.	50 mL
All-purpose flour	3 tbsp.	50 mL
Salt	1/2 tsp.	2 mL
Pepper	1/8 tsp.	0.5 mL
Milk	1 1/2 cups	375 mL
Parsley flakes (optional)	1/2 tsp.	2 mL

Put fish into medium saucepan. Cover with water. Bring to a boil. Simmer slowly for 5 to 8 minutes to poach until fish flakes easily when tested with fork. Drain. Keep warm.

Melt margarine in small saucepan. Mix in flour, salt and pepper. Stir in milk and parsley until boiling and thickened. Cover fish with sauce in serving bowl. Serves 5 to 6.

1/5 recipe: 322 Calories; 49 g Protein; 9.6 g Total Fat; 7 g Carbohydrate; 1766 mg Sodium; trace Dietary Fibre

Pictured on page 108.

Fish And Sauce

*Sauce complements fish well. A good mushroom flavour. If
making sauce ahead, add a bit of milk when reheating to thin.*

MUSHROOM SAUCE		
Hard margarine (or butter)	2 tsp.	10 mL
Chopped onion	1/2 cup	125 mL
Sliced fresh mushrooms	2 cups	500 mL
All-purpose flour	1 tbsp.	15 mL
Salt	1/4 tsp.	1 mL
Pepper	1/16 tsp.	0.5 mL
Parsley flakes	1/2 tsp.	2 mL
Milk	1/2 cup	125 mL
FISH		
Hard margarine (or butter)	2 tsp.	10 mL
Fish fillets (such as cod, perch, jack fish or haddock)	1 1/4 lbs.	560 g
Lemon juice	1 tsp.	5 mL
Salt	1/4 tsp.	1 mL
Pepper, sprinkle		

Mushroom Sauce: Melt margarine in non-stick frying pan. Add onion and mushrooms. Sauté until onion is soft and mushrooms are golden.

Mix in flour, salt, pepper and parsley. Stir in milk until boiling and thickened. Makes 1 1/4 cups (300 mL) sauce.

Fish: Melt margarine in non-stick frying pan. Add fish fillets. Brown both sides. Drizzle with lemon juice. Sprinkle with salt and pepper. Cook for about 8 minutes until fish flakes when tested with fork. Place on platter or individual plates. Spoon sauce over top. Serves 4.

1 serving: 188 Calories; 27 g Protein; 5.4 g Total Fat; 7 g Carbohydrate; 479 mg Sodium; 1 g Dietary Fibre

Pictured on pages 108/109.

> *"It was difficult to get fresh fish during the war.
> Fridays (and eventually Tuesdays) were designated as
> 'fish only' days. The stores weren't allowed to sell
> meat on those days, even if they had it."*
>
> Jean Paré

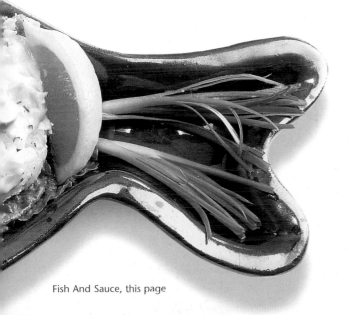

Fish And Sauce, this page

Left: Salmon Pasta Dish, below   Bottom right: Baked Fish Fillets, below   Top right: Salmon Casserole, page 111

Salmon Pasta Dish

A homey dish. Appearance is best when using red salmon.
Peas, carrots and corn show their colours too.

Elbow macaroni (about 4 oz.,113 g)	1 cup	250 mL
Diced (or chopped) carrot	1/2 cup	125 mL
Chopped onion	1/2 cup	125 mL
Boiling water	2 qts.	2 L
Cooking oil (optional)	2 tsp.	10 mL
Salt	2 tsp.	10 mL
Condensed cream of celery soup	10 oz.	284 mL
Reserved liquid from salmon	1/3 cup	75 mL
Worcestershire sauce	1/2 tsp.	2 mL
Canned salmon, drained, liquid reserved, skin and round bones removed	7 1/2 oz.	213 g
Frozen peas	1/2 cup	125 mL
Frozen kernel corn	1/3 cup	75 mL
Salt	1/2 tsp.	2 mL
Pepper	1/8 tsp.	0.5 mL

Combine first 6 ingredients in large pot or Dutch oven. Cook, uncovered, for 5 to 7 minutes, stirring occasionally, until macaroni is tender but firm. Drain. Return to pot.

Stir soup, reserved salmon liquid and Worcestershire sauce together well in large bowl. Add macaroni mixture. Stir.

Break up salmon. Add to macaroni mixture. Add remaining 4 ingredients. Stir lightly. Turn into ungreased 2 quart (2 L) casserole. Bake, uncovered, in 350°F (175°C) oven for about 30 minutes. Serves 4.

1 serving: 272 Calories; 15 g Protein; 8 g Total Fat; 35 g Carbohydrate; 1194 mg Sodium; 3 g Dietary Fibre

Pictured above.

Baked Fish Fillets

This recipe will turn hesitant fish eaters into fish lovers.
Delicious. Serve with lemon wedges.

Thick fish fillets (your favourite), cut bite-size	1 1/2 lbs.	680 g
Milk	1 1/4 cups	300 mL
All-purpose flour	3 tbsp.	50 mL
Dill weed	1/2 tsp.	2 mL
Salt	1/2 tsp.	2 mL
Pepper	1/8 tsp.	0.5 mL
TOPPING		
Hard margarine (or butter)	2 tbsp.	30 mL
Dry bread crumbs	1/2 cup	125 mL
Poultry seasoning	1/4 tsp.	1 mL
Parsley flakes	1 tsp.	5 mL
Onion powder	1/2 tsp.	2 mL
Pepper	1/8 tsp.	0.5 mL

Place fish pieces in ungreased shallow 2 quart (2 L) casserole.

Whisk milk into flour in small saucepan until no lumps remain. Add dill weed, salt and pepper. Heat and stir until boiling and thickened. Pour over fish.

Topping: Melt margarine in small saucepan. Mix in remaining 5 ingredients. Sprinkle over sauce. Bake, uncovered, in 400°F (205°C) oven for about 40 minutes until fish flakes when tested with fork. Serves 6.

1 serving: 204 Calories; 24 g Protein; 5.7 g Total Fat; 13 g Carbohydrate; 431 mg Sodium; trace Dietary Fibre

Pictured above.

Salmon Casserole

Nothing could be easier and quicker to prepare.

Canned salmon, drained, skin and round bones removed	7 1/2 oz.	213 g
Dry bread crumbs	1/2 cup	125 mL
SAUCE		
Hard margarine (or butter)	6 tbsp.	100 mL
All-purpose flour	6 tbsp.	100 mL
Salt	3/4 tsp.	4 mL
Pepper	1/4 tsp.	1 mL
Milk	3 1/3 cups	825 mL
Canned salmon, drained, skin and round bones removed	7 1/2 oz.	213 g
Dry bread crumbs	1/2 cup	125 mL

Crumble first amount of salmon into ungreased 1 1/2 quart (1.5 L) casserole. Sprinkle first amount of bread crumbs over top.

Sauce: Melt margarine in medium saucepan. Mix in flour, salt and pepper. Stir in milk. Heat, stirring constantly, until boiling and thickened. A whisk works really well to prevent lumps. Pour 1/3 of sauce over bread crumbs in casserole.

Crumble second amount of salmon over top. Sprinkle second amount of bread crumbs over salmon. Pour remaining sauce over top layer of crumbs. Use a knife to poke holes here and there to allow a bit of sauce to sink to bottom. Bake, uncovered, in 350°F (175°C) oven for 30 minutes until hot and bubbly. Serves 6.

1 serving: 359 Calories; 19 g Protein; 19.1 g Total Fat; 27 g Carbohydrate; 1001 mg Sodium; 1 g Dietary Fibre

Pictured on page 110.

Salmon Loaf

When few households had refrigerators, canned goods came in handy. An old standby. Serve with or without sauce.

Canned salmon (red is best for colour), drained, skin and round bones removed	2 x 7 1/2 oz.	2 x 213 g
Large eggs, fork-beaten	2	2
Dry bread crumbs	2 cups	500 mL
Finely chopped onion	1/2 cup	125 mL
Lemon juice	2 tbsp.	30 mL
Milk	1/2 cup	125 mL
Salt	1/4 tsp.	1 mL
Dill weed	1/4 tsp.	1 mL
DILL SAUCE		
Salad dressing (or mayonnaise)	1/2 cup	125 mL
Sour cream	1/4 cup	60 mL
Lemon juice	2 tsp.	10 mL
Dill weed	1 tsp.	5 mL

Mix first 8 ingredients in medium bowl. Round bones of salmon may be added if mashed well. Pack in greased 8 x 4 x 3 inch (20 x 10 x 7.5 cm) loaf pan. Bake in 350°F (175°C) oven for 30 to 40 minutes.

Dill Sauce: Mix all 4 ingredients in small bowl. Put a dollop on each slice of loaf. Serves 6.

1 serving (with sauce): 400 Calories; 19 g Protein; 20.2 g Total Fat; 34 g Carbohydrate; 874 mg Sodium; 1 g Dietary Fibre

Pictured below.

Salmon Loaf, this page

Top: Peanut-Sauced Pasta, below
Centre left: Pasta And Mushrooms, page 113
Centre right and bottom: Four Cheese Lasagne, this page

Peanut-Sauced Pasta

Peanut butter flavour is mild enough to allow the soy sauce flavour to come through. Serve as an accompaniment to spicy chicken or skewered beef.

PEANUT SAUCE		
Smooth (or chunky) peanut butter	1/3 cup	75 mL
Cooking oil	1 tbsp.	15 mL
Soy sauce	2 tbsp.	30 mL
White vinegar	1 tbsp.	15 mL
Garlic powder	1/4 tsp.	1 mL
Granulated sugar	1/2 tsp.	2 mL
Water	1/4 cup	60 mL
Hot pepper sauce	1/4 tsp.	1 mL
Linguine pasta	8 oz.	225 g
Boiling water	2 qts.	2 L
Cooking oil (optional)	1 tbsp.	15 mL
Salt	2 tsp.	10 mL
Chopped green onion	1 tbsp.	15 mL

Peanut Sauce: Mix first 8 ingredients in small bowl.

Cook pasta in boiling water, cooking oil and salt in large uncovered pot or Dutch oven until tender but firm. Drain. Return pasta to pot. Add sauce. Toss. Turn into serving bowl.

Sprinkle with green onion. Makes 4 cups (1 L).

1 cup (250 mL): 403 Calories; 14 g Protein; 15.7 g Total Fat; 53 g Carbohydrate; 634 mg Sodium; 3 g Dietary Fibre

Pictured above.

Four Cheese Lasagne

Layers of four varieties of white cheese keep this light coloured. Reminds you of Swiss fondue! Very rich, so serve small portions with a nice green salad.

Lasagna noodles (about 12 oz., 340 g)	16	16
Boiling water	3 qts.	3 L
Cooking oil (optional)	1 tbsp.	15 mL
Salt	2 tsp.	10 mL
SAUCE		
Hard margarine (or butter)	1/3 cup	75 mL
All-purpose flour	1/3 cup	75 mL
Salt	1 tsp.	5 mL
Pepper	1/4 tsp.	1 mL
Milk	3 cups	750 mL
Sherry (or alcohol-free sherry)	3 tbsp.	50 mL
Ground nutmeg	1/4 tsp.	1 mL
Garlic powder	1/16 tsp.	0.5 mL
Cayenne pepper	1/16 tsp.	0.5 mL
Grated Gruyère cheese	3/4 cup	175 mL
Grated white Cheddar (or Havarti) cheese	1 cup	250 mL
Freshly grated Parmesan cheese	1/2 cup	125 mL
Grated mozzarella cheese	1 cup	250 mL

Cook noodles in boiling water, cooking oil and salt in large uncovered pot or Dutch oven for 14 to 16 minutes until tender but firm. Drain. Rinse with cold water. Drain.

Sauce: Melt margarine in medium saucepan. Mix in flour, salt and pepper. Stir in milk, sherry, nutmeg, garlic powder and cayenne pepper until boiling and thickened.

Assemble in greased 9 x 13 inch (22 x 33 cm) pan in layers as follows:

1. 4 lasagna noodles
2. All Gruyère cheese
3. 3/4 cup (175 mL) sauce
4. 4 lasagna noodles
5. All white Cheddar cheese
6. 3/4 cup (175 mL) sauce
7. 4 lasagna noodles
8. All Parmesan cheese
9. 3/4 cup (175 mL) sauce
10. 4 lasagna noodles
11. Remaining sauce
12. All mozzarella cheese

Bake, uncovered, in 325°F (160°C) oven for 30 to 40 minutes until hot and cheese is melted. Let stand for 10 minutes before cutting. Serve immediately. Cuts into 12 pieces.

1 piece: 318 Calories; 11 g Protein; 13.3 g Total Fat; 28 g Carbohydrate; 524 mg Sodium; 1 g Dietary Fibre

Pictured on this page.

Garden Pasta

Crispy vegetables with pasta. Serve this colourful dish warm.

Radiatore pasta	8 oz.	225 g
Boiling water	3 qts.	3 L
Cooking oil (optional)	1 tbsp.	15 mL
Salt	1 tbsp.	15 mL
Fresh pea pods (small handful)		
Fresh (or frozen) peas	1/2 cup	125 mL
Broccoli florets	1 cup	250 mL
Sliced small zucchini, with peel	1 cup	250 mL
White (or alcohol-free white) wine	3/4 cup	175 mL
Dried sweet basil	1 tsp.	5 mL
Pepper	1/16 tsp.	0.5 mL
Garlic clove, minced (or 1/4 tsp., 1 mL, powder)	1	1
Sliced fresh mushrooms	3/4 cup	175 mL
Grated carrot	1/4 cup	60 mL
Light cream cheese, cut up	4 oz.	125 g
Cherry tomatoes, halved	8	8
Chopped fresh parsley	1/4 cup	60 mL
Grated Parmesan cheese	2 tbsp.	30 mL

Cook pasta in boiling water, cooking oil and salt in large uncovered pot or Dutch oven for 6 minutes. Pasta will be undercooked.

Add next 4 ingredients. Stir. Return to a boil. Boil for 2 minutes. Drain. Return pasta and vegetables to pot. Cover to keep warm.

Combine next 6 ingredients in small saucepan. Bring to a simmer. Simmer until vegetables are tender.

Add cream cheese. Stir until melted. Add to pasta mixture.

Add tomatoes, parsley and Parmesan cheese. Toss. Serve immediately. Makes 8 cups (2 L).

1 cup (250 mL): 184 Calories; 8 g Protein; 3.5 g Total Fat; 27 g Carbohydrate; 188 mg Sodium; 3 g Dietary Fibre

Pictured on page 117.

> *"Pasta was fairly common when I was growing up, but it was just things like macaroni and cheese or spaghetti and meatballs. Nothing like the variety we have today."*
>
> Jean Paré

One-Pot Noodles

Easy to prepare and a perfect accompaniment to any meal.

Hard margarine (or butter)	1 tbsp.	15 mL
Chopped onion	1/2 cup	125 mL
Canned sliced mushrooms, drained	10 oz.	284 mL
Beef bouillon cubes	5 x 1/5 oz.	5 x 6 g
Boiling water	2 1/2 cups	625 mL
Fusilli pasta	8 oz.	225 g
Pine nuts (or almonds), toasted in 350°F (175°C) oven for 5 to 8 minutes (optional)	1/2 cup	125 mL

Melt margarine in large pot or Dutch oven. Add onion and mushrooms. Sauté until onion is soft.

Dissolve bouillon cubes in boiling water in small bowl. Add to mushroom mixture.

Add pasta. Bring to a boil. Cover. Simmer slowly for about 10 minutes until pasta is tender and liquid is absorbed. Add a bit more boiling water if needed during cooking. If mixture boils too fast pasta won't have time to cook before liquid is absorbed.

Sprinkle with nuts. Makes 6 cups (1.5 L).

1 cup (250 mL): 195 Calories; 7 g Protein; 3.1 g Total Fat; 35 g Carbohydrate; 668 mg Sodium; 2 g Dietary Fibre

Pictured on page 116.

Noodles With Herbs

A tasty combination of herbs.

Broad noodles	8 oz.	225 g
Boiling water	2 qts.	2 L
Cooking oil (optional)	1 tbsp.	15 mL
Salt	2 tsp.	10 mL
Olive (or cooking) oil	1 tbsp.	15 mL
Hard margarine (or butter)	1 tbsp.	15 mL
Garlic cloves, minced	2	2
Chopped fresh parsley	1/2 cup	125 mL
Dried sweet basil	1 tsp.	5 mL
Salt	1/2 tsp.	2 mL
Dried crushed chilies	1/4 tsp.	1 mL

Grated Parmesan cheese, sprinkle

Cook noodles in boiling water, cooking oil and first amount of salt in large uncovered pot or Dutch oven for 5 to 7 minutes until tender but firm. Drain. Return noodles to pot.

Heat olive oil and margarine in non-stick frying pan. Add next 5 ingredients. Sauté until garlic is soft. Add to noodles. Mix.

Sprinkle with Parmesan cheese. Makes about 3 1/2 cups (875 mL).

1 cup (250 mL): 337 Calories; 10 g Protein; 8.5 g Total Fat; 55 g Carbohydrate; 438 mg Sodium; 2 g Dietary Fibre

Pictured on page 117.

Casserole Lasagne

A jumbled lasagne with a cheesy top.

Lean ground beef	1 lb.	454 g
Canned stewed tomatoes, with juice	14 oz.	398 mL
Envelope spaghetti sauce mix	1 x 1 1/2 oz.	1 x 43 g
Frozen peas	2 cups	500 mL
Creamed cottage cheese	1 cup	250 mL
Large egg, fork-beaten	1	1
Medium egg noodles (about 3 1/3 cups, 825 mL)	8 oz.	225 g
Boiling water	2 1/2 qts.	2.5 L
Cooking oil (optional)	1 tbsp.	15 mL
Salt	2 tsp.	10 mL
Grated Parmesan cheese	1/4 cup	60 mL
Grated part-skim mozzarella cheese	3/4 cup	175 mL

Scramble-fry ground beef in non-stick frying pan until no longer pink. Drain.

Add tomatoes with juice and spaghetti sauce mix. Stir well. Add peas, cottage cheese and egg. Stir. Turn into ungreased 3 quart (3 L) casserole.

Cook noodles in boiling water, cooking oil and salt in large uncovered pot or Dutch oven for 5 to 7 minutes until tender but firm. Drain. Add to casserole. Stir lightly.

Sprinkle with both cheeses. Bake, uncovered, in 350°F (175°C) oven for about 45 minutes. Serves 8.

1 serving: 325 Calories; 25 g Protein; 9.9 g Total Fat; 33 g Carbohydrate; 903 mg Sodium; 3 g Dietary Fibre

Pictured on page 117.

1. Noodles With Herbs, page 115
2. Garden Pasta, page 115
3. Casserole Lasagne, above
4. One-Pot Noodles, page 115

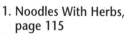

Perogies

When you have some extra time, make these savoury potato and cheese-filled perogies. Serve with sour cream, diced cooked bacon and fried onion.

DOUGH
All-purpose flour	2 1/3 cups	575 mL
Cooking oil	2 tbsp.	30 mL
Water (or more if needed)	3/4 cup	175 mL
Salt	1/2 tsp.	2 mL

FILLING
Warm mashed potatoes	2 cups	500 mL
Grated medium Cheddar cheese	1 cup	250 mL
Hard margarine (or butter)	2 tbsp.	30 mL
Onion flakes, crushed	2 tsp.	10 mL
Salt	1/2 tsp.	2 mL
Pepper	1/8 tsp.	0.5 mL
Boiling water	4 qts.	4 L

Hard margarine (or butter), melted (optional)

Dough: Mix all 4 ingredients well in medium bowl. Knead on lightly floured surface until smooth. Return to bowl. Let rest for 20 minutes.

Filling: Mix first 6 ingredients well in separate medium bowl. Turn out dough onto lightly floured surface. Roll out about 1/16 inch (1.5 mm) thin. Cut into 2 1/2 inch (6.4 cm) circles. Place rounded teaspoonful of filling in centre of each. Fold dough over, pressing edges together to seal. Transfer to lightly floured baking sheet. Cover to prevent drying out until all are made.

Drop by batches into large pot of boiling water. Stir with wooden spoon to keep from sticking to bottom. Boil for 3 to 4 minutes. They will float to top and be puffed up when cooked.

Remove with slotted spoon to large bowl. Add melted margarine. Toss gently so they won't stick together. Cover. Keep hot while rest are cooking. Makes about 7 dozen perogies.

4 perogies: 121 Calories; 3 g Protein; 4.5 g Total Fat; 17 g Carbohydrate; 179 mg Sodium; 1 g Dietary Fibre

Pictured on page 119.

Note: These may be frozen, uncooked, individually on trays, then bagged. Cook from frozen state.

Red Pepper Sauce

Citric acid enhances the flavour and adds zip! Makes a fairly thin sauce. Best with a shaped pasta such as radiatore or fusilli.

Chopped red pepper	2 cups	500 mL
Water	1/2 cup	125 mL
Chicken bouillon powder	1 tbsp.	15 mL
Skim evaporated milk	1 cup	250 mL
Salt	1/4 tsp.	1 mL
Pepper, light sprinkle		
Onion powder	1/4 tsp.	1 mL
Citric acid (available at drug stores), optional	1/8 tsp.	0.5 mL

Put red pepper, water and bouillon powder into medium saucepan. Cover. Simmer until tender. Do not drain. Cool slightly. Turn into blender. Process until smooth.

Combine evaporated milk, salt, pepper, onion powder and citric acid in small saucepan. Bring to a boil. Add red pepper mixture. Return to a boil. Makes about 2 cups (500 mL) sauce.

1/2 cup (125 mL) sauce: 76 Calories; 6 g Protein; 0.6 g Total Fat; 12 g Carbohydrate; 736 mg Sodium; 1 g Dietary Fibre

Pictured below.

Note: For a thicker sauce, mix 2 tsp. (10 mL) cornstarch and 2 tsp. (10 mL) water. Stir into boiling sauce until thickened.

Red Pepper Sauce, above

Top left: Perogies, page 118   Bottom left: Cheesy Manicotti, below   Right: Armenian Pilaf, below

Cheesy Manicotti

An attractive dish. Very filling.

MEAT SAUCE

Lean ground beef	1/2 lb.	225 g
Chopped onion	1/2 cup	125 mL
Chopped fresh mushrooms	1 cup	250 mL
Garlic clove, minced (or 1/4 tsp., 1 mL, powder)	1	1
Tomato paste	5 1/2 oz.	156 mL
Water	1 1/2 cups	375 mL
Salt	1/2 tsp.	2 mL
Pepper	1/8 tsp.	0.5 mL
Manicotti shells	8	8
Boiling water	3 qts.	3 L
Cooking oil (optional)	1 tbsp.	15 mL
Salt	2 tsp.	10 mL

CHEESE FILLING

Large egg	1	1
Creamed cottage cheese	3/4 cup	175 mL
Grated part-skim mozzarella cheese	3/4 cup	175 mL
Grated Parmesan cheese	1/4 cup	60 mL
Parsley flakes	1 1/2 tsp.	7 mL

Meat Sauce: Scramble-fry ground beef, onion, mushrooms and garlic in non-stick frying pan until beef is no longer pink. Drain.

Add next 4 ingredients. Stir. Spoon enough sauce into ungreased 9 x 9 inch (22 x 22) pan or shallow casserole to rest manicotti on.

Cook manicotti shells in boiling water, cooking oil and salt in large uncovered pot or Dutch oven for 6 to 7 minutes until tender but firm. Drain. Rinse with cold water. Drain.

Cheese Filling: Stir all 5 ingredients together in small bowl. Spoon filling into each shell. Lay all shells in single layer over sauce in pan. Spoon remaining sauce over top. Cover. Bake in 350°F (175°C) oven for about 40 minutes. Serves 4.

1 serving: 351 Calories; 31 g Protein; 12.9 g Total Fat; 28 g Carbohydrate; 827 mg Sodium; 3 g Dietary Fibre

Pictured above.

Armenian Pilaf

Both a pasta and rice dish. The perfect accompaniment to beef, chicken, fish or pork.

Hard margarine (or butter)	2 tbsp.	30 mL
Uncooked vermicelli (or angel hair) pasta, broken up	1/2 cup	125 mL
Long grain white rice	1 1/2 cups	375 mL
Water	3 cups	750 mL
Chicken bouillon powder	2 tbsp.	30 mL
Salt	1/2 tsp.	2 mL
Pepper	1/4 tsp.	1 mL

Melt margarine in large saucepan. Add vermicelli. Stir occasionally as pasta browns.

Add remaining 5 ingredients. Stir. Cover. Simmer for 15 to 20 minutes until rice and pasta are tender. Makes 5 cups (1.25 L).

3/4 cup (175 mL): 223 Calories; 4 g Protein; 4.4 g Total Fat; 40 g Carbohydrate; 835 mg Sodium; 1 g Dietary Fibre

Pictured above.

Blue Banana Pie, this page

Working Man's Pie

Anyone would work all day for this. The pie forms a natural nest to accommodate whipped topping.

Brown sugar, packed	3/4 cup	175 mL
Maple syrup	3/4 cup	175 mL
Evaporated milk (or light cream)	1/3 cup	75 mL
Hard margarine (or butter)	3 tbsp.	50 mL
Egg yolks (large)	3	3
Egg whites (large), room temperature	3	3
Ground nutmeg, sprinkle		
Unbaked deep 9 inch (22 cm) pie shell	1	1
Envelope dessert topping (prepared according to package directions), or 1 cup (250 mL) whipping cream, whipped	1	1

Whisk first 5 ingredients together in small saucepan. Heat, stirring constantly, until hot and slightly thickened. Remove from heat.

Beat egg whites in medium bowl until stiff. Sprinkle with nutmeg. Gradually fold in hot mixture.

Pour into pie shell. Bake on bottom rack in 350°F (175°C) oven for 40 to 50 minutes until browned. Cool. Filling will collapse in centre.

Fill centre of pie with dessert topping. Cuts into 8 wedges.

1 wedge: 387 Calories; 5 g Protein; 16.4 g Total Fat; 56 g Carbohydrate; 249 mg Sodium; trace Dietary Fibre

Pictured on page 123.

Blue Banana Pie

Actually with blueberries, not blue bananas. A natural combination. Very showy. Garnish with whipped topping.

Small bananas, sliced	2	2
Baked deep 9 inch (22 cm) pie shell	1	1
Cream cheese, softened	8 oz.	250 g
Granulated sugar	3/4 cup	175 mL
Envelope dessert topping (prepared according to package directions)	1	1
Canned blueberry pie filling	19 oz.	540 mL

Lay banana slices over bottom of pie shell to cover.

Beat cream cheese and sugar in medium bowl until smooth. Fold in dessert topping. Spoon over banana.

Place dabs of pie filling here and there over top. Spread as best you can. Chill well. Cuts into 8 wedges.

1 wedge: 442 Calories; 5 g Protein; 22 g Total Fat; 59 g Carbohydrate; 258 mg Sodium; 1 g Dietary Fibre

Pictured on this page.

Cherry Cream Pie

A creamy cheesecake layer tops a red cherry layer. Lovely contrast.

Pastry for deep 9 inch (22 cm) pie shell (your own or a mix)		
Canned cherry pie filling	19 oz.	540 mL
TOPPING		
Light cream cheese	8 oz.	250 g
Large eggs	2	2
Granulated sugar	2/3 cup	150 mL
All-purpose flour	3 tbsp.	50 mL
Vanilla	1 tsp.	5 mL
Frozen whipped topping (in a tub), thawed	1 cup	250 mL

Roll out pastry on lightly floured surface. Fit into ungreased pie plate. Crimp and trim edge.

Spread pie filling in pie shell. Bake on bottom rack in 425°F (220°C) oven for 15 minutes.

Topping: Beat cream cheese, eggs, sugar, flour and vanilla in medium bowl until smooth. Spoon dabs over cherry filling. Smooth. Reduce heat to 350°F (175°C). Bake for about 30 minutes. Chill.

Garnish with whipped topping. Cuts into 8 wedges.

1 wedge: 392 Calories; 7 g Protein; 16.7 g Total Fat; 55 g Carbohydrate; 454 mg Sodium; 1 g Dietary Fibre

Pictured on page 120.

Oatmeal Pie

Rich like pecan pie. You would never know oatmeal is in the pie. Scrumptious!

Hard margarine (or butter), softened	6 tbsp.	100 mL
Granulated sugar	1 cup	250 mL
Large eggs	2	2
Golden corn syrup	3/4 cup	175 mL
Vanilla	1 tsp.	5 mL
Quick-cooking rolled oats (not instant)	1 cup	250 mL
Unbaked 9 inch (22 cm) pie shell	1	1

Cream margarine and sugar together in medium bowl. Beat in eggs, 1 at a time. Add corn syrup and vanilla. Mix.

Stir in rolled oats.

Pour into pie shell. Bake on bottom rack in 350°F (175°C) oven for 40 to 50 minutes until set. Lay a piece of foil over pie if crust browns too much. Cuts into 8 wedges.

1 wedge: 449 Calories; 5 g Protein; 18.2 g Total Fat; 68 g Carbohydrate; 280 mg Sodium; 1 g Dietary Fibre

Pictured below.

Glazed Fresh Raspberry Pie

Garnish with whipped cream for the final touch.

Water	1 1/2 cups	375 mL
Granulated sugar	3/4 cup	175 mL
Cornstarch	2 tbsp.	30 mL
Raspberry-flavoured gelatin (jelly powder)	1 x 3 oz.	1 x 85 g
Fresh raspberries	4 cups	1 L
Baked 9 inch (22 cm) pie shell	1	1

Mix water, sugar and cornstarch in small saucepan over medium. Stir until boiling and thickened.

Add gelatin. Stir until dissolved. Cool for 30 minutes.

Pile raspberries evenly in pie shell. Pour gelatin mixture over berries. Chill until set. Cuts into 8 wedges.

1 wedge: 267 Calories; 3 g Protein; 7.9 g Total Fat; 48 g Carbohydrate; 168 mg Sodium; 3 g Dietary Fibre

Pictured below.

Top left: Oatmeal Pie, above   Top right and bottom left: Working Man's Pie, page 122   Bottom right: Glazed Fresh Raspberry Pie, above

Top: Butter Date Pie, this page   Bottom: Frozen Peanut Butter Pie, below

Frozen Peanut Butter Pie

What could be more convenient and more tempting than a frozen pie waiting in the freezer? Serve with whipped topping or chocolate syrup, or both!

CHOCOLATE CRUMB CRUST

Hard margarine (or butter)	1/3 cup	75 mL
Chocolate wafer crumbs	1 1/3 cups	325 mL
Granulated sugar	1/4 cup	60 mL

FILLING

Vanilla ice cream	3 cups	750 mL
Smooth (or chunky) peanut butter	1/2 cup	125 mL
Unsalted peanuts, crushed or ground	1/4 cup	60 mL
Envelope dessert topping (not prepared)	1	1
Milk	1/2 cup	125 mL
Unsalted peanuts, crushed or ground	2 tbsp.	30 mL

Chocolate Crumb Crust: Melt margarine in small saucepan. Stir in wafer crumbs and sugar. Press in ungreased 9 inch (22 cm) pie plate. Bake in 350°F (175°C) oven for 10 minutes. Cool well.

Filling: Stir ice cream, peanut butter and first amount of peanuts in medium bowl until well mixed.

Beat dessert topping and milk in small bowl until stiff. Fold into ice cream mixture. Pour into pie shell.

Sprinkle with second amount of peanuts. Freeze. Remove from freezer about 10 minutes before cutting. Cuts into 8 wedges.

1 wedge: 468 Calories; 10 g Protein; 31.1 g Total Fat; 42 g Carbohydrate; 263 mg Sodium; 2 g Dietary Fibre

Pictured above.

Butter Date Pie

Delicious and incredibly good. Garnish with whipped topping.

Pastry for 9 inch (22 cm) pie shell (your own or a mix)		
Hard margarine (or butter)	1/2 cup	125 mL
Brown sugar, packed	1/2 cup	125 mL
Granulated sugar	1/2 cup	125 mL
Egg yolks (large)	2	2
Vanilla	1/2 tsp.	2 mL
White vinegar	1 tbsp.	15 mL
Chopped pecans (or walnuts)	3/4 cup	175 mL
Chopped dates	1 cup	250 mL
Egg whites (large), room temperature	2	2

Roll out pastry on lightly floured surface. Fit into ungreased pie plate. Crimp and trim edge.

Cream margarine, both sugars, egg yolks and vanilla together in medium bowl until smooth.

Stir in vinegar, pecans and dates.

Beat egg whites in small bowl until stiff. Fold into date mixture. Turn into pie shell. Bake in 350°F (175°C) oven for 45 to 55 minutes. Cuts into 8 wedges.

1 wedge: 477 Calories; 4 g Protein; 29 g Total Fat; 54 g Carbohydrate; 302 mg Sodium; 3 g Dietary Fibre

Pictured on this page.

Lemon Cheese Pie

Delicate lemon flavour with a smooth texture.

Granulated sugar	1 1/4 cups	300 mL
Cornstarch	1/4 cup	60 mL
Hot water	1 cup	250 mL
Lemon juice	1/3 cup	75 mL
Finely grated lemon peel	1 tsp.	5 mL
Large egg, fork-beaten	1	1
Cream cheese, cut up	8 oz.	250 g
Envelope dessert topping (prepared according to package directions)	1	1
Baked 9 inch (22 cm) pie shell	1	1

Stir sugar and cornstarch together in medium saucepan. Add hot water and mix. Add lemon juice, lemon peel and egg. Heat and stir over medium until boiling and thickened.

Add cream cheese. Stir until melted and mixture is smooth. Cool completely.

Fold dessert topping into lemon filling.

Pour into pie shell. Chill. Cuts into 8 wedges.

1 wedge: 406 Calories; 5 g Protein; 20.6 g Total Fat; 52 g Carbohydrate; 243 mg Sodium; trace Dietary Fibre

Pictured on page 125.

Lemon Cheese Pie, page 124

Mock Mince Pie, below

Mock Mince Pie

*During the Depression, this was an economical
way to still have a mince-flavoured pie.*

Granulated sugar	1 cup	250 mL
Ground cinnamon	1/2 tsp.	2 mL
Ground nutmeg	1/4 tsp.	1 mL
Ground cloves	1/4 tsp.	1 mL
Salt	1/4 tsp.	1 mL
Raisins	1 cup	250 mL
Sour cream	1 cup	250 mL
Egg yolks (large), see Note	3	3
Unbaked 9 inch (22 cm) pie shell	1	1
MERINGUE		
Egg whites (large), room temperature	3	3
Cream of tartar	1/4 tsp.	1 mL
Granulated sugar	6 tbsp.	100 mL

Measure first 5 ingredients into medium bowl. Stir well.

Mix in raisins, sour cream and egg yolks.

Pour into pie shell. Bake on bottom rack in 425°F (220°C) oven for 10 minutes. Reduce heat to 350°F (175°C). Bake for about 50 minutes until set.

Meringue: Beat egg whites and cream of tartar in medium bowl until almost stiff. Gradually beat in sugar until stiff and sugar is dissolved. Spread over hot pie. Return to oven for about 15 minutes until browned. Cuts into 8 wedges.

1 wedge: 383 Calories; 5 g Protein; 13.8 g Total Fat; 62 g Carbohydrate; 273 mg Sodium; 1 g Dietary Fibre

Pictured above.

Note: To make pie without meringue, use 2 whole eggs in filling instead of 3 egg yolks.

Strawberry Pie

A delicious, double-crust red pie that Mom made.
Glazed pies had not been "invented" yet.
Serve with whipped cream.

Pastry, enough for 2 crust pie (your own or a mix)		
Fresh strawberries, halved (quartered if large)	4 cups	1 L
Granulated sugar	1 cup	250 mL
Minute tapioca	3 tbsp.	50 mL
Granulated sugar	1/4 – 1/2 tsp.	1 – 2 mL

Roll out pastry on lightly floured surface. Fit into ungreased 9 inch (22 cm) pie plate. Roll out top crust.

Place strawberries, first amount of sugar and tapioca in large bowl. Mix. Let stand for 15 minutes. Stir. Pour into pie shell. Dampen edge of pastry. Cover with top crust. Trim and crimp to seal. Cut vents in top.

Sprinkle with second amount of sugar. Bake on bottom rack in 350°F (175°C) oven for about 45 minutes until cooked. Cuts into 8 wedges.

1 wedge: 361 Calories; 3 g Protein; 15.3 g Total Fat; 54 g Carbohydrate; 277 mg Sodium; 2 g Dietary Fibre

Pictured below.

Marmalade Tarts, page 127

"We would always make five or six pies on Saturday.
What we didn't use Sunday for company,
we would eat the rest of the week."

Jean Paré

Strawberry Pie, above

Kahlúa Pie, below

Marmalade Tarts

Even though this is such an odd mixture, you will be pleasantly surprised by the tasty results.

Pastry, enough for 2 crust pie
    (your own or a mix)

Orange marmalade	3/4 cup	175 mL
Grated sharp Cheddar cheese	3/4 cup	175 mL
Granulated sugar	1/4 – 1/2 tsp.	1 – 2 mL

Roll out pastry on lightly floured surface. Cut out 24 circles, 3 inches (7.5 cm) in diameter. Fit into 24 greased muffin cups. Roll remaining pastry and cut out 24 decorative tops.

Combine marmalade and cheese in small bowl. Divide among tart shells. Top with pastry cut-outs.

Sprinkle each with a pinch of sugar. Bake in 450°F (230°C) oven for 12 to 15 minutes until golden. Makes 24 tarts.

1 tart: 117 Calories; 2 g Protein; 6.3 g Total Fat; 14 g Carbohydrate; 117 mg Sodium; 1 g Dietary Fibre

Pictured on page 126 and on this page.

Kahlúa Pie

Incredibly good! Garnish with chocolate curls and/or whipped topping.

CHOCOLATE GRAHAM CRUMB CRUST

Hard margarine (or butter)	6 tbsp.	100 mL
Graham cracker crumbs	1 1/4 cups	300 mL
Cocoa	1 tbsp.	15 mL
Granulated sugar	2 tbsp.	30 mL

FILLING

Large marshmallows	30	30
Milk	1/4 cup	60 mL
Prepared coffee	1/4 cup	60 mL
Kahlúa liqueur	1/2 cup	125 mL
Envelope dessert topping (prepared according to package directions)	1	1

Chocolate Graham Crumb Crust: Melt margarine in small saucepan. Stir in graham crumbs, cocoa and sugar. Press in ungreased 9 inch (22 cm) pie plate. Bake in 350°F (175°C) oven for 10 minutes. Cool completely.

Filling: Heat marshmallows, milk and prepared coffee in large saucepan, stirring often, until marshmallows are melted.

Stir in Kahlúa. Chill, stirring occasionally, until starting to thicken.

Fold in dessert topping. Turn into pie crust. Chill. Cuts into 8 wedges.

1 wedge: 347 Calories; 3 g Protein; 13.3 g Total Fat; 48 g Carbohydrate; 267 mg Sodium; 1 g Dietary Fibre

Pictured above.

Carrot Pie, below

Vinegar Pie, below

Carrot Pie

From the period of the Depression. Tastes like pumpkin pie.

Large eggs	2	2
Granulated sugar	1/2 cup	125 mL
Ground cinnamon	3/4 tsp.	4 mL
Ground nutmeg	1/2 tsp.	2 mL
Ground ginger	1/2 tsp.	2 mL
Ground cloves	1/8 tsp.	0.5 mL
Cooked mashed carrot	1 cup	250 mL
Milk	1 1/2 cups	375 mL
Fancy molasses (optional, but good)	1 tbsp.	15 mL
Unbaked 10 inch (25 cm) pie shell	1	1
Envelope dessert topping (prepared according to package directions)	1	1

Beat eggs lightly in medium bowl. Add and mix in next 8 ingredients in order given.

Pour into pie shell. Bake on bottom rack in 450°F (230°C) oven for 10 minutes. Reduce heat to 350°F (175°C). Bake for about 45 minutes until knife inserted in centre comes out clean. Cool.

Smooth dessert topping over pie. Cuts into 8 wedges.

1 wedge: 269 Calories; 6 g Protein; 12.8 g Total Fat; 33 g Carbohydrate; 226 mg Sodium; 1 g Dietary Fibre

Pictured above.

Note: An unbaked 9 inch (22 cm) pie shell may be used. There will be about 2/3 cup (150 mL) filling left over that will need to be baked in a small greased baking dish.

Vinegar Pie

When grocery stores were far away and fresh lemons were scarce, this pie was a good substitute. Tastes like lemon pie.

White vinegar	1/3 cup	75 mL
Granulated sugar	1/2 cup	125 mL
Water	1 3/4 cups	425 mL
Granulated sugar	1/2 cup	125 mL
All-purpose flour	6 tbsp.	100 mL
Egg yolks (large)	3	3
Water	1/4 cup	60 mL
Lemon flavouring	1 tsp.	5 mL
Baked 9 inch (22 cm) pie shell	1	1
MERINGUE		
Egg whites (large), room temperature	3	3
White vinegar	1/2 tsp.	2 mL
Granulated sugar	6 tbsp.	100 mL

Measure vinegar and first amounts of sugar and water into medium saucepan. Stir. Bring to a boil over medium.

Mix next 5 ingredients in small bowl. Stir into boiling mixture until boiling and thickened.

Pour into pie shell.

Meringue: Beat egg whites and vinegar in small bowl until a stiff froth. Gradually add sugar, beating until stiff and sugar is dissolved. Spread over pie, sealing well to crust. Bake in 350°F (175°C) oven for about 10 minutes until browned. Cuts into 8 wedges.

1 wedge: 301 Calories; 4 g Protein; 9.5 g Total Fat; 51 g Carbohydrate; 162 mg Sodium; trace Dietary Fibre

Pictured above.

Custard Pie Without Crust

(old recipe)

This recipe is from an 1886 cookbook lent to me by a friend. An interesting way to make a crustless pie. The amount of milk will vary depending on the cook's interpretation of "fill the pie pan."

Custard Pie Without Crust

Three eggs, 3 tablespoons sugar, 1/2 cup Graham flour, salt and flavour. The flour settles to the bottom and forms a good crust. Fill the pie-pan with milk, mixing a part of it with the other ingredients first.

Impossible Pie

(new recipe)

This has evolved from a plain custard pie to one with coconut, added for flavour. The recipe's also a bit larger, to suit today's pie plate. Serve with a dab of jam on each slice.

Large eggs	3	3
Milk	2 cups	500 mL
Granulated sugar	3 tbsp.	50 mL
All-purpose flour	1/2 cup	125 mL
Vanilla	1 tsp.	5 mL
Salt	1/4 tsp.	1 mL
Medium coconut	1 cup	250 mL

Measure first 6 ingredients into blender. Process until smooth. If you don't have a blender, simply beat together in medium bowl.

Sprinkle coconut in bottom of greased 9 inch (22 cm) pie plate. Pour blender contents over coconut. Bake on bottom rack in 350°F (175°C) oven for 45 to 55 minutes until knife inserted in centre comes out clean. Cuts into 8 wedges.

1 wedge: 184 Calories; 6 g Protein; 10.3 g Total Fat; 17 g Carbohydrate; 145 mg Sodium; 1 g Dietary Fibre

Pictured below.

Impossible Pie, above

Pork

Pork roasts, pork chops, pork tenderloin and bacon have been served at the table for centuries. With the luxury of refrigeration and freezers in today's modern society, we have the opportunity to stock up on pork and plan a few weeks of meals in advance. As far back as can be remembered, applesauce has been a favourite to serve with pork and this is still the trend today. But once you try the distinctive flavours of Blackberry Ribs (below) and our Ham and Chicken Loaf (page 133), we know they'll become favourites too.

Blackberry Ribs

Tangy sweet when glazed. Broil or barbecue.

Pork spareribs, cut into 2 or 3 rib sections	3 1/2 lbs.	1.6 kg
Water, to cover		
Salt	1 tsp.	5 mL
BLACKBERRY GLAZE		
Blackberry jam (or jelly)	1/2 cup	125 mL
Ketchup	1/3 cup	75 mL
Steak sauce	1 tbsp.	15 mL
Dry mustard	1/2 tsp.	2 mL
Garlic powder	1/8 tsp.	0.5 mL

Boil spareribs in water and salt in large saucepan for about 1 hour until very tender. Drain. Arrange on greased baking sheet with sides. Line with greased foil for easy cleanup.

Blackberry Glaze: Mix all 5 ingredients in small saucepan. Heat, stirring often, until boiling. Simmer for 5 to 10 minutes. Makes 1 cup (250 mL) glaze. Brush on hot ribs. Broil or barbecue for about 5 minutes per side. Serves 4.

1 serving: 611 Calories; 37 g Protein; 35.8 g Total Fat; 35 g Carbohydrate; 761 mg Sodium; 1 g Dietary Fibre

Pictured on page 131.

BLACKBERRY CHICKEN: Cook about 3 lbs. (1.4 kg) chicken parts in water and salt for about 40 minutes. Brush with glaze and broil or barbecue.

Sweet And Sour Ribs

Sweet, sour, spicy and tender. All this in one roaster!

Pork spareribs, cut into 2 or 3 rib sections	5 lbs.	2.3 kg
Water, to cover		
SMOKY SWEET AND SOUR SAUCE		
Brown sugar, packed	3/4 cup	175 mL
Chili powder	1/2 tsp.	2 mL
Apple cider vinegar	3/4 cup	175 mL
Ketchup	1/2 cup	125 mL
Small onion, chopped	1	1
Worcestershire sauce	2 tbsp.	30 mL
Water	1/2 cup	125 mL
Salt	1/2 tsp.	2 mL
Cornstarch	1 tbsp.	15 mL
Dry mustard	1 tsp.	5 mL
Liquid smoke	1/8 tsp.	0.5 mL
Liquid gravy browner	1/8 tsp.	0.5 mL

Boil ribs in water in large uncovered pot or Dutch oven for 15 minutes. Drain. Arrange ribs in small roaster.

Smoky Sweet And Sour Sauce: Mix all 12 ingredients in medium bowl. Pour over ribs. Cover. Bake in 350°F (175°C) oven for 1 to 1 1/2 hours until pork is falling-off-the-bone tender. Serves 6.

1 serving: 607 Calories; 35 g Protein; 34.3 g Total Fat; 39 g Carbohydrate; 714 mg Sodium; 1 g Dietary Fibre

Pictured on page 131.

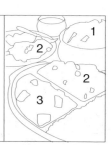

1. Sweet And Sour Ribs, above
2. Blackberry Ribs, this page
3. Sweet And Sour Pork, page 131

Sweet And Sour Pork

This is all meat, which makes it so easy to serve over rice.

Lean boneless pork steaks, trimmed of fat, cut into 1 1/2 inch (3.8 cm) cubes	3 lbs.	1.4 kg
Water, to cover		
SWEET AND SOUR SAUCE		
Reserved stock	1 cup	250 mL
Brown sugar, packed	2/3 cup	150 mL
White vinegar	1/2 cup	125 mL
Ketchup	1/2 cup	125 mL

Cook pork cubes in water in large uncovered pot or Dutch oven for 1 to 1 1/2 hours. Drain stock, reserving 1 cup (250 mL).

Sweet And Sour Sauce: Stir all 4 ingredients in small bowl. Pour over pork. Simmer slowly, stirring occasionally, for 30 minutes. Serves 8.

1 serving: 259 Calories; 25 g Protein; 6.6 g Total Fat; 24 g Carbohydrate; 315 mg Sodium; trace Dietary Fibre

Pictured on this page.

Ham Cauliflower Bake,
below

Ham Cauliflower Bake

*This is a dish the whole family will enjoy.
Cheesy and delicious.*

Cauliflower pieces	5 cups	1.25 L
Water, to cover		
Condensed cream of chicken soup	10 oz.	284 mL
Light sour cream	1/3 cup	75 mL
Canned whole mushrooms, drained	10 oz.	284 mL
Chopped green onion	1/4 cup	60 mL
Grated medium Cheddar cheese	1/2 cup	125 mL
Cubed cooked ham (3/4 inch, 2 cm)	2 cups	500 mL
Grated medium Cheddar cheese	3/4 cup	175 mL

Cook cauliflower in water in large saucepan until tender-crisp. Drain.

Mix next 6 ingredients in medium bowl. Stir in cauliflower. Turn into ungreased 2 quart (2 L) casserole.

Sprinkle with second amount of cheese. Bake, uncovered, in 350°F (175°C) oven for 30 to 40 minutes. Makes 4 generous servings.

1 serving: 432 Calories; 30 g Protein; 26.9 g Total Fat; 20 g Carbohydrate; 2024 mg Sodium; 6 g Dietary Fibre

Pictured above.

Quick Ham Bake

Once the tiny onions are peeled, this is in the oven in a flash.

Tiny white pearl onions, peeled (see Note)	24	24
Water, to cover		
Milk	1 cup	250 mL
All-purpose flour	2 tbsp.	30 mL
Salt	1/2 tsp.	2 mL
Pepper	1/8 tsp.	0.5 mL
Boneless ham steak	1 lb.	454 g
Thin process cheese slices	6	6

Cook onions in water in large uncovered saucepan until tender. Drain.

Gradually whisk milk into flour in medium saucepan until smooth. Add salt and pepper. Heat and stir until boiling and thickened. Add onions. Stir.

Brown ham quickly in non-stick frying pan. Lay ham slice in ungreased shallow 2 quart (2 L) casserole. Cover with cheese. Spoon creamed onions over top. Bake, uncovered, in 350°F (175°C) oven for 25 to 30 minutes until bubbly hot. Serves 4.

1 serving: 343 Calories; 33 g Protein; 15.5 g Total Fat; 17 g Carbohydrate; 2262 mg Sodium; 2 g Dietary Fibre

Pictured on page 133.

Note: To peel onions easily, blanch first in boiling water for about 2 minutes.

Super Sauerkraut Supper

The perfect Oktoberfest meal.

Hard margarine (or butter)	2 tsp.	10 mL
Large onion, thinly sliced	1	1
Jar of sauerkraut, drained	17 1/2 oz.	500 mL
Water	3/4 cup	175 mL
Brown sugar, packed	2 tsp.	10 mL
Chicken bouillon powder	1 tsp.	5 mL
Bay leaf	1	1
Dijon mustard	1 tbsp.	15 mL
New baby potatoes, with peel, halved	1 lb.	454 g
Salt	1/4 tsp.	1 mL
Pepper	1/16 tsp.	0.5 mL
Lean ham garlic sausage (kielbasa), sliced	12 oz.	340 g

Heat margarine in non-stick frying pan. Add onion. Sauté until soft.

Add next 5 ingredients. Stir. Bring to a boil. Cover. Simmer for 10 minutes.

Stir in remaining 5 ingredients. Cover. Cook for about 30 minutes until potato is tender. Discard bay leaf. Serves 4.

1 serving: 430 Calories; 16 g Protein; 27.7 g Total Fat; 31 g Carbohydrate; 2014 mg Sodium; 5 g Dietary Fibre

Pictured on page 133.

Ham Loaf

A layer of browned pineapple rings adds lots of flavour.
Topped with a sweet and sour glaze.

Large eggs	2	2
Milk	1/2 cup	125 mL
Pepper	1/4 tsp.	1 mL
Prepared horseradish	1 tsp.	5 mL
Sweet pickle relish	1 tbsp.	15 mL
Dry bread crumbs	1 cup	250 mL
Brown sugar, packed	2 tbsp.	30 mL
White vinegar	1 tbsp.	15 mL
Cooked ham, ground	2 lbs.	900 g
Hard margarine (or butter)	2 tsp.	10 mL
Granulated sugar	2 tbsp.	30 mL
Canned pineapple slices, drained, juice reserved	14 oz.	398 mL

TOPPING

Brown sugar, packed	1/3 cup	75 mL
Prepared mustard	2 tsp.	10 mL
Reserved pineapple juice	1 tbsp.	15 mL

Beat eggs in large bowl until smooth. Add next 7 ingredients. Stir.

Add ground ham. Mix well. Pack 1/2 of ham mixture in greased 9 x 5 x 3 inch (22 x 12.5 x 7.5 cm) loaf pan. It is easy to remove loaf if you line pan with foil.

Melt margarine in non-stick frying pan. Sprinkle with granulated sugar. Lay pineapple slices over top. Brown both sides. Arrange over ham mixture in loaf pan. Cover with second 1/2 of ham mixture.

Topping: Stir brown sugar, prepared mustard and pineapple juice in small bowl. Spread over top of loaf. Bake in 350°F (175°C) oven for 1 1/2 hours. Cuts into 8 slices.

1 slice: 391 Calories; 24 g Protein; 15.1 g Total Fat; 40 g Carbohydrate; 1655 mg Sodium; 1 g Dietary Fibre

Pictured below.

Ham And Chicken Loaf

Flavours of both ham and chicken come through in this loaf.
Gravy browner may be used for colour.

Large eggs, fork-beaten	2	2
Milk	2/3 cup	150 mL
Prepared mustard	1 tbsp.	15 mL
Finely chopped onion	1/3 cup	75 mL
Salt	1/4 tsp.	1 mL
Pepper	1/4 tsp.	1 mL
Ground thyme	1/8 tsp.	0.5 mL
Coarsely crushed cornflakes cereal (not crumbs)	1 cup	250 mL
Liquid gravy browner, as needed for colour (optional)		
Ground chicken	1 lb.	454 g
Ground ham (see Note)	2 cups	500 mL

Combine first 9 ingredients in large bowl. Mix well.

Add ground chicken and ground ham. Mix well. Pack in greased 9 x 5 x 3 inch (22 x 12.5 x 7.5 cm) loaf pan. Cover. Bake in 350°F (175°C) oven for 1 hour. Cuts into 8 slices.

1 slice: 180 Calories; 20 g Protein; 4.7 g Total Fat; 13 g Carbohydrate; 822 mg Sodium; 1 g Dietary Fibre

Pictured below.

Note: A food processor works well for grinding.

Top left: Ham Loaf, above
Bottom left: Ham And Chicken Loaf, this page

Top right: Super Sauerkraut Supper, page 132
Bottom right: Quick Ham Bake, page 132

Apple Pork Chops

Dark brown, rich-looking dish.

Cooking oil	2 tsp.	10 mL
Pork chops, trimmed of fat (about 2 1/4 lbs.,1 kg)	6	6
Medium cooking apples, peeled and sliced (McIntosh is good)	3	3
Brown sugar, packed	1/4 cup	60 mL
Ground cinnamon	1/2 tsp.	2 mL

Heat cooking oil in non-stick frying pan. Add pork chops. Brown both sides. Transfer to ungreased 2 quart (2 L) casserole or small roaster.

Layer apple over each chop.

Mix brown sugar and cinnamon in small cup. Sprinkle over apple. Cover. Bake in 350°F (175°C) oven for 1 to 1 1/4 hours. Serves 6.

1 serving: 243 Calories; 24 g Protein; 8 g Total Fat; 19 g Carbohydrate; 70 mg Sodium; 1 g Dietary Fibre

Pictured below.

Top: Breaded Pork Cutlets, this page
Centre: Apple Pork Chops, above
Bottom: Baked Chops And Stuffing, this page

Breaded Pork Cutlets

A slight taste of wine clings to these moist, tender cutlets.

Large egg, fork-beaten	1	1
Fine dry bread crumbs	1/2 cup	125 mL
Pork cutlets (about 1 1/4 lbs., 568 g)	4	4
Cooking oil	1 tbsp.	15 mL
Salt, sprinkle		
Pepper, sprinkle		
Chicken bouillon powder	2 tsp.	10 mL
Hot water	1/2 cup	125 mL
Red (or alcohol-free red) wine	1/2 cup	125 mL

Place egg and bread crumbs in separate small dishes. Dip pork cutlets into egg, then into bread crumbs to coat.

Brown pork in cooking oil in non-stick frying pan. Sprinkle with salt and pepper.

Stir bouillon powder into hot water in small cup. Add wine. Stir. Pour over pork cutlets. Cover. Simmer for 50 to 60 minutes until tender and most of liquid is evaporated. Serves 4.

1 serving: 339 Calories; 35 g Protein; 13.8 g Total Fat; 12 g Carbohydrate; 537 mg Sodium; trace Dietary Fibre

Pictured on this page.

Baked Chops And Stuffing

Pre-browning is not required. Just lay chops in pan, cover with stuffing mixture and bake. Very easy.

Pork chops, trimmed of fat (about 2 1/4 lbs.,1 kg)	6	6
Salt, sprinkle		
Pepper, sprinkle		
Condensed cream of mushroom soup	10 oz.	284 mL
Seasoned stuffing mix	1 cup	250 mL
Canned cream-style corn	14 oz.	398 mL
Chopped celery	1/2 cup	125 mL
Chopped onion	1/2 cup	125 mL

Lay pork chops in ungreased baking pan large enough to hold in single layer. Sprinkle with salt and pepper.

Mix remaining 5 ingredients in medium bowl. Spoon over pork chops. Bake, uncovered, in 325°F (160°C) oven for about 1 1/2 hours until tender. Serves 6.

1 serving: 314 Calories; 28 g Protein; 10.9 g Total Fat; 27 g Carbohydrate; 853 mg Sodium; 2 g Dietary Fibre

Pictured on this page.

Salads

Pesto-Sauced Salad, page 136

Salads

Prior to the twentieth century, a wedge of iceberg lettuce with seasoned cream poured over top, or some leftover meat with lettuce or fruit, was about the extent of a "served salad." Molded salads were first made with calf's foot jelly, later with sheet gelatin, and then finally with the new granulated gelatin. The advent of flavoured jelly powders made molded salads appealing as desserts as well. After the Second World War, North Americans travelling abroad began to discover other varieties of lettuce. Herb gardens and flavoured oils became fashionable, and new exotic vegetables added a delicious touch. Now our own imaginations are the only limits on the kinds of salads we're able to create. Try the Pesto-Sauced Salad (this page) or the Sweet Wheat Salad (page 140) for two unique options.

Pesto-Sauced Salad

Pesto (PEH-stoh) is a rich sauce made from fresh sweet basil. It is available in supermarkets and Italian stores. A real Italian salad.

Fusilli pasta	1 lb.	454 g
Boiling water	4 qts.	4 L
Cooking oil (optional)	1 tbsp.	15 mL
Salt	4 tsp.	20 mL
Broccoli, cut up and cooked tender crisp	2 cups	500 mL
Cauliflower, cut up and cooked tender crisp	2 cups	500 mL
Pea pods, cooked tender crisp	2 cups	500 mL
Sliced carrot, cooked tender crisp	1 1/2 cups	375 mL
Sliced fresh mushrooms	1 cup	250 mL
PESTO DRESSING		
Commercial basil pesto	3/4 cup	175 mL
White vinegar	1/3 cup	75 mL
Olive oil	2/3 cup	150 mL
Grated Parmesan cheese	1/2 cup	125 mL
Salt	1 tsp.	5 mL

Cook pasta in boiling water, cooking oil and salt in large uncovered pot or Dutch oven for 8 to 10 minutes until tender but firm. Drain. Rinse with cold water. Drain. Return to pot.

Add broccoli, cauliflower, pea pods, carrot and mushrooms.

Pesto Dressing: Mix all 5 ingredients in small bowl. Pour over pasta mixture. Toss to coat. Serves 8.

1 serving: 529 Calories; 14 g Protein; 29.5 g Total Fat; 54 g Carbohydrate; 501 mg Sodium; 5 g Dietary Fibre

Pictured on page 135.

Pasta Salad Oriental

Add some crusty dinner rolls and you have a complete meal. Refreshing and delicious.

Vermicelli (or angel hair) pasta	12 oz.	340 g
Boiling water	2 1/2 qts.	2.5 L
Cooking oil	1 tbsp.	15 mL
Salt	1 tbsp.	15 mL
Sesame (or cooking) oil	1 tbsp.	15 mL
Julienned English cucumber	2 cups	500 mL
Julienned carrot	1 1/2 cups	375 mL
Diced cooked chicken (or 2 cans, 6 1/2 oz., 184 g, each, chicken flakes, drained)	2 cups	500 mL
Sliced green onion	1/2 cup	125 mL
DRESSING		
Boiling water	1/2 cup	125 mL
Chicken bouillon powder	1 tsp.	5 mL
Cooking oil	2 tbsp.	30 mL
Soy sauce	1/4 cup	60 mL
White vinegar	2 tbsp.	30 mL
Granulated sugar	1 tbsp.	15 mL
Pepper	1/8 tsp.	0.5 mL
Toasted sesame seeds	1/4 cup	60 mL

Cook pasta in boiling water, cooking oil and salt in large uncovered pot or Dutch oven for 4 to 6 minutes until tender but firm. Drain. Rinse with cold water. Drain well. Transfer to large bowl.

Add sesame oil. Toss well to coat.

Add cucumber, carrot, chicken and green onion. Toss.

Dressing: Stir boiling water and bouillon powder in small bowl.

Add remaining 6 ingredients. Stir. Pour over pasta mixture. Toss together well. Makes about 10 cups (2.5 L) salad.

1 cup (250 mL) salad: 258 Calories; 15 g Protein; 7.8 g Total Fat; 31 g Carbohydrate; 516 mg Sodium; 2 g Dietary Fibre

Pictured on page 137.

Broccoli Salad

This is one you'll serve often. Very colourful.

Broccoli florets	5 cups	1.25 L
Diced red onion	1/2 cup	125 mL
Grated medium Cheddar cheese	1/2 cup	125 mL
Roasted and salted sunflower seeds (optional, but good)	1/4 cup	60 mL
Bacon slices, diced	6	6
DRESSING		
Granulated sugar	2 tbsp.	30 mL
White vinegar	2 tbsp.	30 mL
Light salad dressing (or mayonnaise)	6 tbsp.	100 mL

Combine broccoli, red onion, cheese and sunflower seeds in large bowl.

Cook bacon in non-stick frying pan. Drain well. Cool. Add to broccoli mixture.

Dressing: Mix all 3 ingredients well in small bowl. Add to broccoli mixture just before serving. Toss together. Makes 5 cups (1.25 L) salad.

1 cup (250 mL) salad: 180 Calories; 7 g Protein; 12.4 g Total Fat; 12 g Carbohydrate; 344 mg Sodium; 1 g Dietary Fibre

Pictured below and on front cover.

BROCCOLI SLAW: Substitute 1 bag 16 oz., 454 g, broccoli slaw for the broccoli florets. Colour will be lighter

Top: Pasta Salad Oriental, page 136
Bottom: Broccoli Salad, above

Bean Salad, below

Bean Salad

Pineapple makes this different from the usual bean salad. Dressing has a good bite to it.

Canned kidney beans, drained	14 oz.	398 mL
Canned pinto (or white) beans, drained	14 oz.	398 mL
Canned cut green beans, drained	14 oz.	398 mL
Sliced celery	1 cup	250 mL
Canned pineapple chunks, drained, juice reserved	14 oz.	398 mL
DRESSING		
Cornstarch	1 tbsp.	15 mL
Reserved pineapple juice		
Lemon juice	1 tsp.	5 mL
Red wine vinegar	1/4 cup	60 mL
Cooking oil	2 tbsp.	30 mL
Water	2 tbsp.	30 mL
Dry mustard	2 tsp.	10 mL
Granulated sugar	2 tsp.	10 mL
Dill weed	1/2 tsp.	2 mL
Salt	1/2 tsp.	2 mL
Pepper	1/4 tsp.	1 mL
Dried whole oregano	1/4 tsp.	1 mL
Garlic powder	1/4 tsp.	1 mL
Onion powder	1/4 tsp.	1 mL

Combine first 5 ingredients in large bowl.

Dressing: Mix cornstarch, reserved pineapple juice and lemon juice in small saucepan.

Add remaining 11 ingredients. Heat and stir until boiling and slightly thickened. Pour over vegetables in bowl. Stir. Cover. Refrigerate for 24 hours, stirring occasionally. Makes 6 cups (1.5 L) salad.

1 cup (250 mL) salad: 208 Calories; 7 g Protein; 5.4 g Total Fat; 35 g Carbohydrate; 493 mg Sodium; 6 g Dietary Fibre

Pictured above.

Top: Bacon And Pea Salad, this page
Bottom: Noodle Slaw, below

Noodle Slaw

A good way to doctor a store-bought salad.

Bag of shredded cabbage with carrot	1 lb.	454 g
Instant Chinese noodles with chicken-flavoured packet, crumbled, chicken-flavoured packet reserved	3 oz.	85 g
DRESSING		
Reserved chicken-flavoured packet	1	1
Soy sauce	2 tbsp.	30 mL
Cooking oil	2 tsp.	10 mL
Granulated sugar	2 tsp.	10 mL
Pepper	1/4 tsp.	1 mL
Toasted sesame seeds	4 tsp.	20 mL

Combine cabbage mixture and Chinese noodles in large bowl.

Dressing: Stir all 6 ingredients together in small bowl. Just before serving, pour over salad. Toss together well. Makes 7 1/2 cups (1.9 L) salad.

1 cup (250 mL) salad: 87 Calories; 3 g Protein; 2.4 g Total Fat; 14 g Carbohydrate; 379 mg Sodium; 2 g Dietary Fibre

Pictured above.

Bacon And Pea Salad

A good addition to a lunch whether eating inside or out. Garnish with slices of red pepper.

Bacon slices, diced	5	5
Frozen peas, thawed	3 cups	750 mL
Green onions, sliced	4	4
Light sour cream	1/3 cup	75 mL
Dill weed	1/4 tsp.	1 mL
Salt	1/2 tsp.	2 mL
Pepper, sprinkle		

Cook bacon in non-stick frying pan. Drain. Transfer to medium bowl.

Add remaining 6 ingredients. Stir. Chill until serving time. Makes 3 1/4 cups (800 mL) salad.

1/2 cup (125 mL) salad: 94 Calories; 6 g Protein; 3.5 g Total Fat; 10 g Carbohydrate; 371 mg Sodium; 3 g Dietary Fibre

Pictured on this page.

Variation: Omit green onions and add 1/4 cup (60 mL) slivered red onion.

Dilled Onions

Make your own quantity according to how much pickle juice you have.

Medium onions, thinly sliced and separated into rings	2	2
Dill pickle juice	1 cup	250 mL
Light sour cream	1/2 cup	125 mL
Celery seed	1/8 tsp.	0.5 mL

Combine onion rings and dill pickle juice in medium bowl. Cover and marinate in the refrigerator for at least 2 days. Drain well.

Add sour cream to onion rings. Mix well. Sprinkle with celery seed. Makes 2 1/2 cups (625 mL).

1/2 cup (125 mL) onion: 39 Calories; 1 g Protein; 1.8 g Total Fat; 5 g Carbohydrate; 419 mg Sodium; 1 g Dietary Fibre

Pictured on page 139.

"Salads were mostly a summer dish. Lettuce just couldn't survive the cold winter temperatures."

"We made fruit salads (fruit cocktail) and jellied salads with fruit."

Jean Paré

Left: Spinach Mushroom Salad, below

Top right: Dilled Onions, page 138
Bottom right: Tomato Mushroom Salad, below

Spinach Mushroom Salad

Salad and dressing can be made ahead of time and tossed together at the last minute. Dressing is tangy.

Bunch of fresh spinach leaves	1	1
Sliced fresh mushrooms	2 cups	500 mL
Sliced green onion	1/3 cup	75 mL
Bacon slices, cooked crisp and crumbled	6	6
DRESSING		
Cooking oil	2 tbsp.	30 mL
Lemon juice	2 tbsp.	30 mL
Egg yolk (large)	1	1
Salt	3/4 tsp.	4 mL
Pepper	1/8 tsp.	0.5 mL
Granulated sugar	1/2 tsp.	2 mL

Combine first 4 ingredients in large bowl. Cover. Refrigerate until ready.

Dressing: Whisk all 6 ingredients together in small bowl. Pour over spinach mixture. Toss to coat. Serves 8.

1 serving: 84 Calories; 4 g Protein; 6.7 g Total Fat; 4 g Carbohydrate; 372 mg Sodium; 2 g Dietary Fibre

Pictured above.

Tomato Mushroom Salad

A terrific blend of flavours. A brightly coloured salad.

Firm medium tomatoes, cut into 8 wedges each	3	3
Thickly sliced fresh mushrooms	3 cups	750 mL
Medium red onion, thinly sliced	1	1
Slivered green pepper (optional)	1/2 cup	125 mL
DRESSING		
Cooking oil	1/4 cup	60 mL
Red wine vinegar	1/4 cup	60 mL
Granulated sugar	1 1/2 tsp.	7 mL
Salt	1 tsp.	5 mL
Parsley flakes	1/2 tsp.	2 mL
Dried sweet basil	1/2 tsp.	2 mL
Lemon pepper	1/4 tsp.	1 mL
Garlic powder	1/8 tsp.	0.5 mL

Put tomato wedges, mushrooms, red onion and green pepper into large bowl.

Dressing: Stir all 8 ingredients in small bowl until sugar is dissolved. Pour over tomato mixture. Stir well. Let stand for at least 1 hour before serving. Makes 8 cups (2 L) salad.

1 cup (250 mL) salad: 91 Calories; 1 g Protein; 7.6 g Total Fat; 6 g Carbohydrate; 315 mg Sodium; 1 g Dietary Fibre

Pictured above.

Potato Raita

Pronounced RI-tah. This potato salad has a different taste than most. The yogurt, ginger paste and coriander give this its East Indian flavour.

Medium potatoes, with peel	4	4
Boiling water, to cover		
Plain yogurt	1/2 cup	125 mL
Lemon juice	1 tsp.	5 mL
Granulated sugar	1/2 tsp.	2 mL
Salt	1/2 tsp.	2 mL
Ginger paste (available in Asian section of grocery stores)	1/4 tsp.	1 mL
Chopped fresh coriander (cilantro)	1 tbsp.	15 mL

Cook potatoes in boiling water in medium uncovered saucepan until tender. Drain and cool. Remove peel, if desired. Dice into 3/8 inch (1 cm) cubes.

Mix remaining 6 ingredients in small bowl. Add to potato. Stir well. Makes a generous 4 cups (1 L).

1 cup (250 mL) salad: 141 Calories; 4 g Protein; 0.6 g Total Fat; 30 g Carbohydrate; 368 mg Sodium; 2 g Dietary Fibre

Pictured on this page and on front cover.

Sweet Wheat Salad

Fruit, grain and dairy—all this in a mouth-watering salad. Also makes a good dessert.

Wheat (available at grocery and health food stores)	1 cup	250 mL
Boiling water, to cover		
Cream cheese, softened	8 oz.	250 g
Canned crushed pineapple, with juice	14 oz.	398 mL
Instant vanilla pudding powder (4 serving size)	1	1
Lemon juice	2 tbsp.	30 mL
Frozen whipped topping (in a tub), thawed	4 cups	1 L
Maraschino cherries, for garnish		

Cook wheat in boiling water in small saucepan for 1 hour until tender. Drain. Cool.

Beat cream cheese and pineapple with juice in medium bowl until mixed.

Beat in pudding powder and lemon juice. Add wheat. Stir.

Fold in whipped topping. Turn into serving bowl.

Garnish with cherries. Makes 8 cups (2 L) salad.

1/2 cup (125 mL) salad: 196 Calories; 3 g Protein; 10.7 g Total Fat; 24 g Carbohydrate; 71 mg Sodium; 2 g Dietary Fibre.

Pictured on this page.

Orange Lettuce Salad

Most attractive. A hint of both sweet and sour in the dressing.

Mixture of cut or torn greens, lightly packed	6 cups	1.5 L
Canned mandarin orange segments, drained (use all or part)	10 oz.	284 mL
Sliced almonds, toasted in 350°F (175°C) oven for 5 to 8 minutes	1/4 cup	60 mL
Bacon slices, cooked crisp and crumbled (optional)	6	6
DRESSING		
White vinegar	3 tbsp.	50 mL
Granulated sugar	1/4 cup	60 mL
Prepared mustard	1/2 tsp.	2 mL
Paprika	1/2 tsp.	2 mL
Cooking oil	1 tbsp.	15 mL

Place first 4 ingredients in large bowl.

Dressing: Stir vinegar, sugar, prepared mustard and paprika together well in small bowl until sugar dissolves.

Drizzle cooking oil over greens mixture. Toss well. Add dressing. Toss again. Makes 8 cups (2 L) salad.

1 cup (250 mL) salad: 73 Calories; 1 g Protein; 3.5 g Total Fat; 11 g Carbohydrate; 10 mg Sodium; 1 g Dietary Fibre

Pictured below.

Top: Potato Raita, this page
Bottom: Sweet Wheat Salad, this page

Centre: Orange Lettuce Salad, above

Caesar-Dressed Salad

Contains extras such as bacon, green onion and tomato.

Large head of romaine lettuce, cut or torn	1	1
Bacon slices, cooked crisp and crumbled	5	5
Chopped green onion	3 tbsp.	50 mL
Grated Parmesan cheese	3 tbsp.	50 mL
Croutons	1/2 cup	125 mL
Pepper	1/4 tsp.	1 mL
Dried whole oregano	1/8 tsp.	0.5 mL
Creamy Caesar salad dressing	2/3 cup	150 mL
Medium tomatoes, cut into 6 wedges each	2	2

Combine first 7 ingredients in large bowl.

Add dressing shortly before serving. Toss.

Set tomato wedges on top. Serves 6.

1 serving: 193 Calories; 5 g Protein; 14.1 g Total Fat; 11 g Carbohydrate; 371 mg Sodium; 2 g Dietary Fibre

Pictured on this page.

Caesar-Dressed Salad, this page

Poppy Seed Salad, this page

Poppy Seed Salad

Have dressing made ahead and waiting in the refrigerator. Toss together at the last minute.

DRESSING		
Granulated sugar	1/2 cup	125 mL
White vinegar	6 tbsp.	100 mL
Cooking oil	2 1/2 tbsp.	37 mL
Onion flakes	1 tsp.	5 mL
Dry mustard	1/2 tsp.	2 mL
Salt	1/2 tsp.	2 mL
Paprika	1/4 tsp.	1 mL
Poppy seeds	2 1/2 tsp.	12 mL
Head of lettuce, chopped (about 8 cups, 2 L)	1	1
Green onions, sliced	3	3
Radishes, sliced	8	8
Green pepper strips	1/3 cup	75 mL

Dressing: Measure all 8 ingredients into small bowl. Beat together well. Let stand in refrigerator overnight. Makes about 2/3 cup (150 mL) dressing.

Combine remaining 4 ingredients in large bowl. Pour dressing over top. Toss well. Serves 8.

1 serving: 108 Calories; 1 g Protein; 4.9 g Total Fat; 16 g Carbohydrate; 178 mg Sodium; 1 g Dietary Fibre

Pictured on this page.

Springtime Salad

Actually, delicious in all four seasons.

Fresh spinach (or romaine) leaves, torn and lightly packed	4 cups	1 L
Medium red pepper, slivered	1/2	1/2
Small red onion, thinly sliced and separated into rings	1/2	1/2
Croutons	1/2 cup	125 mL
Sunflower seeds	1/4 cup	60 mL
Italian dressing	1/3 cup	75 mL

Combine spinach, red pepper and onion in large bowl. Cover. Refrigerate until ready.

Add croutons, sunflower seeds and Italian dressing just before serving. Toss well. Serves 4.

1 serving: 222 Calories; 5 g Protein; 19.4 g Total Fat; 10 g Carbohydrate; 410 mg Sodium; 3 g Dietary Fibre

Pictured on page 144 and on front cover.

FIDDLEHEAD SALAD: Cook and drain 10 oz (284 g) frozen fiddleheads. Cool. Add to salad along with more dressing if needed.

Cherry Cola Salad

Cola adds flavour, yet it doesn't taste like cola. A dusty rose-coloured jellied salad. Garnish with whipped topping.

Envelope unflavoured gelatin	1 x 1/4 oz.	1 x 7 g
Water	1/4 cup	60 mL
Cherry-flavoured gelatin (jelly powder)	1 x 3 oz.	1 x 85 g
Canned crushed pineapple, with juice	8 oz.	227 mL
Light cream cheese, diced	4 oz.	125 g
Cola soft drink	1 1/2 cups	375 mL
Finely chopped walnuts (or pecans)	1/4 cup	60 mL

Sprinkle gelatin over water in medium saucepan. Let stand for 1 minute.

Add cherry gelatin and pineapple with juice. Heat and stir until both gelatins are dissolved.

Add cream cheese. Stir, whisking if needed, until cream cheese is melted and smooth. Remove from heat.

Add soft drink and walnuts. Stir. Pour into 4 cup (1 L) mold that has been lightly sprayed with cooking spray. Chill until firm. Stir occasionally as it becomes syrupy so walnuts are evenly distributed. Unmold onto serving plate. Makes 3 1/2 cups (875 mL) salad.

1/2 cup (125 mL) salad: 191 Calories; 6 g Protein; 8.3 g Total Fat; 25 g Carbohydrate; 345 mg Sodium; 1 g Dietary Fibre

Pictured below.

Top: Cherry Cola Salad, above   Bottom: Egg Salad Mold, this page

Egg Salad Mold

A pretty yellow colour. Especially good served with cold cuts and buns. Garnish with salad dressing and parsley.

Boiling water	1 cup	250 mL
Lemon-flavoured gelatin (jelly powder)	1 x 3 oz.	1 x 85 g
Light salad dressing (or mayonnaise)	2/3 cup	150 mL
White vinegar	1 tbsp.	15 mL
Finely chopped celery	1/2 cup	125 mL
Chopped green onion	1/4 cup	60 mL
Salt	1/2 tsp.	2 mL
Large hard-boiled eggs, mashed with fork	2	2

Stir boiling water into gelatin in medium bowl until dissolved. Chill until syrupy. Stir and scrape down sides often until beginning to thicken.

Fold in salad dressing. Add remaining 5 ingredients. Stir. Turn into 3 cup (750 mL) mold. Chill for at least 2 1/2 hours until firm. Unmold onto serving plate. Makes 2 2/3 cups (650 mL) salad.

1/2 cup (125 mL) salad: 182 Calories; 4 g Protein; 10 g Total Fat; 20 g Carbohydrate; 575 mg Sodium; trace Dietary Fibre

Pictured on this page.

Avocado Mold

A smooth texture with a pleasing tang. Best served same day.

Envelope unflavoured gelatin	1 x 1 1/4 oz.	1 x 7 g
Lime-flavoured gelatin (jelly powder)	1 x 3 oz.	1 x 85 g
Boiling water	1 cup	250 mL
Mashed avocado (about 1 large)	1 cup	250 mL
Sour cream	1 cup	250 mL
Mayonnaise	1 cup	250 mL
Salt	1/2 tsp.	2 mL
Onion powder	1/4 tsp.	1 mL
Mayonnaise, for garnish	2 tbsp.	30 mL
Paprika, sprinkle, for garnish		

Stir both gelatins in medium bowl. Stir in boiling water until dissolved.

Add next 5 ingredients. Whisk until smooth. Turn into 4 cup (1 L) mold. Chill until firm.

Unmold salad onto serving plate. Put dollop of second amount of mayonnaise on top in centre. Sprinkle paprika over mayonnaise. Makes 4 cups (1 L) salad.

1/2 cup (125 mL) salad: 291 Calories; 4 g Protein; 24.1 g Total Fat; 17 g Carbohydrate; 411 mg Sodium; 1 g Dietary Fibre

Pictured on page 143.

Cranberry Jelly Salad,
below

Cranberry Jelly Salad

Three fruits combine to make this jellied salad.
Excellent with turkey.

Envelope unflavoured gelatin	1 x 1/4 oz.	1 x 7 g
Cherry-flavoured gelatin (jelly powder)	1 x 3 oz.	1 x 85 g
Boiling water	1 1/4 cups	300 mL
Canned crushed pineapple, with juice	14 oz.	398 mL
Canned whole cranberry sauce	14 oz.	398 mL
Finely diced red apple, with peel	1/2 cup	125 mL

Stir both gelatins in medium bowl. Stir in boiling water until dissolved.

Stir in pineapple with juice, cranberry sauce and apple. Chill, stirring occasionally, until syrupy. Pour into 4 1/2 to 5 cup (1.1 to 1.25 L) mold. Chill for 2 to 3 hours until firm. Makes 4 1/2 cups (1.1 L) salad.

1/2 cup (125 mL) salad: 148 Calories; 2 g Protein; 0.1 g Total Fat; 37 g Carbohydrate; 43 mg Sodium; 1 g Dietary Fibre

Pictured above.

Avocado Mold,
page 142

"I used to iron clothes and sheets with an iron that had to be heated on the wood stove. The iron had two bases, but only one handle that fit into each of them. While one base would be heating, I ironed with the other. When it cooled, I'd put it back on the stove and move the handle to the hot one."

Jean Paré

1. Springtime Salad, page 141
2. Pecan Dressing, page 145
3. Cooked Salad Dressing, page 145
4. Sunny Dressing, page 145
5. Coleslaw Dressing, page 145
6. Tomato Relish Dressing, page 145

Pecan Dressing

Fast and fabulous for yogurt lovers. Use regular or low-fat yogurt. Serve with fruit salads.

Mayonnaise	1/3 cup	75 mL
White corn syrup	1/4 cup	60 mL
Chopped pecans, toasted in 350°F (175°C) oven for 8 to 10 minutes	1/3 cup	75 mL
Vanilla yogurt	1 cup	250 mL

Stir mayonnaise, corn syrup and pecans well in small bowl.

Fold in yogurt. Cover and chill. Makes 1 2/3 cups (400 mL) dressing.

2 tbsp. (30 mL) dressing: 67 Calories; 1 g Protein; 3.8 g Total Fat; 7 g Carbohydrate; 63 mg Sodium; trace Dietary Fibre

Pictured on page 144.

Sunny Dressing

So smooth and special drizzled over a fresh fruit salad.

Cream cheese, softened	8 oz.	250 g
Prepared orange juice	1/4 cup	60 mL
Granulated sugar	1/4 cup	60 mL

Beat all 3 ingredients together in small bowl until creamy. Makes about 1 1/3 cups (325 mL) dressing.

2 tbsp. (30 mL) dressing: 100 Calories; 2 g Protein; 7.9 g Total Fat; 6 g Carbohydrate; 67 mg Sodium; trace Dietary Fibre

Pictured on page 144.

FLUFFY DIP: Thaw 2 cups (500 mL) frozen whipped topping. Fold into Sunny Dressing.

Coleslaw Dressing

Just like you get in a fast-food outlet. Keeps well in the refrigerator for several weeks.

Cooking oil	1/2 cup	125 mL
White vinegar	2/3 cup	150 mL
Salad dressing (or mayonnaise)	2 1/4 cups	550 mL
Granulated sugar	3/4 cup	175 mL
Salt	2 tsp.	10 mL
Minced onion	1/3 cup	75 mL
Drops of green food colouring, enough to make pale green		

Measure all 7 ingredients into blender. Process until smooth. Makes 4 cups (1 L) dressing.

2 tbsp. (30 mL) dressing: 133 Calories; trace Protein; 11.7 g Total Fat; 7 g Carbohydrate; 268 mg Sodium; trace Dietary Fibre

Pictured on page 144.

Cooked Salad Dressing

From way, way back. This has a lot of zip to it. A little goes a long way.

Granulated sugar	1/2 cup	125 mL
All-purpose flour	2 tbsp.	30 mL
Dry mustard	1 tbsp.	15 mL
Salt	1 tsp.	5 mL
Large eggs	3	3
Milk	1 cup	250 mL
White vinegar	1/2 cup	125 mL
Water	1/2 cup	125 mL

Put sugar, flour, dry mustard and salt in top of double boiler. Stir until flour is mixed in well. Beat in eggs, 1 at a time.

Stir in milk, vinegar and water. Cook over boiling water, stirring often, until thickened. Pour into container. Cover and refrigerate. Makes about 2 1/2 cups (625 mL) dressing.

2 tbsp. (30 mL) dressing: 41 Calories; 2 g Protein; 1 g Total Fat; 7 g Carbohydrate; 146 mg Sodium; trace Dietary Fibre

Pictured on page 144.

Tomato Relish Dressing

This will remind you of a well-known salad dressing.

Hard margarine (or butter)	1/4 cup	60 mL
All-purpose flour	1/4 cup	60 mL
Water	1 cup	250 mL
Ketchup	1 cup	250 mL
White vinegar	1/2 cup	125 mL
Granulated sugar	1 cup	250 mL
Celery salt	1 tsp.	5 mL
Onion powder	1 tsp.	5 mL
Salt	1 tbsp.	15 mL
Pepper	1/2 tsp.	2 ml
Sweet pickle relish	1/2 cup	125 mL

Melt margarine in medium saucepan. Add flour. Mix.

Stir in water, ketchup and vinegar until boiling and thickened.

Add remaining 6 ingredients. Stir until sugar is dissolved. Makes 4 cups (1 L) dressing.

2 tbsp. (30 mL) dressing: 54 Calories; trace Protein; 1.5 g Total Fat; 10 g Carbohydrate; 421 mg Sodium; trace Dietary Fibre

Pictured on page 144.

Variation: For a less sweet dressing, omit ketchup. Add 5 1/2 oz. (156 mL) tomato paste.

Soups

Once upon a time, our grandmothers and great-grandmothers had farms and vegetable gardens to create fresh and hearty soups. The arrival of quick and convenient canned, frozen, dried and freeze-dried soups was not until the mid-twentieth century. Today many of us rely on the good old can opener to provide us with an instant, warm meal. Some of the recipes that follow use the convenience of canned goods, while others employ fresh ingredients for that homemade touch.

Top: Lentil Spinach Soup, this page   Bottom: Garbanzo Soup, this page

Garbanzo Soup

A soft yellow-coloured broth with diced potato, ham and chickpeas. Hearty.

Lean meaty ham bone (about 2 cups, 500 mL, meat), see Note	1	1
Water, to cover, approximately	6 cups	1.5 L
Medium onion, finely chopped	1	1
Garlic clove, minced (or 1/4 tsp., 1 mL, powder)	1	1
Bay leaves	2	2
Medium potatoes, diced	2	2
Paprika	1/2 tsp.	2 mL
Salt	1/4 tsp.	1 mL
Pepper	1/4 tsp.	1 mL
Canned chickpeas (garbanzo beans), with liquid, slightly mashed	19 oz.	540 mL

Combine first 5 ingredients in large pot or Dutch oven. Cover. Boil for about 2 hours. Discard bay leaves. Remove ham bone. Chop ham and return to pot. Discard bone.

Add remaining 5 ingredients. Cover. Cook until potato is tender. Makes 7 1/2 cups (1.8 L) soup.

1 cup (250 mL) soup: 228 Calories; 13 g Protein; 9.3 g Total Fat; 23 g Carbohydrate; 734 mg Sodium; 3 g Dietary Fibre

Pictured on this page.

Note: If there is not much meat on the bone, add one 6.5 oz. (184 g) can of flaked ham, drained and broken up.

Lentil Spinach Soup

Full-bodied soup. Freezes well. May be halved if desired.

Water	10 cups	2.5 L
Green lentils	2 cups	500 mL
Medium onion, chopped	1	1
Celery ribs, chopped	2	2
Chicken bouillon powder	1/4 cup	60 mL
Pepper	1/4 tsp.	1 mL
Frozen chopped spinach, thawed and chopped more	10 oz.	300 g
Grated medium Cheddar cheese, for garnish		

Combine first 6 ingredients in large pot or Dutch oven. Cover. Simmer for about 45 minutes until lentils are soft.

Add spinach. Cook for 5 minutes. Taste for salt, adding a bit if needed.

Sprinkle cheese over each serving. Makes 12 cups (3 L) soup.

1 cup (250 mL) soup: 61 Calories; 5 g Protein; 0.7 g Total Fat; 10 g Carbohydrate; 676 mg Sodium; 2 g Dietary Fibre

Pictured on this page.

Onion Soup

With just enough red wine to taste.

Halved and thinly sliced onion	3 cups	750 mL
All-purpose flour	2 tbsp.	30 mL
Granulated sugar	1 tsp.	5 mL
Hard margarine (or butter)	2 tbsp.	30 mL
Water	4 cups	1 L
Liquid beef bouillon	1/4 cup	60 mL
Red (or alcohol-free red) wine	1/2 cup	125 mL
Worcestershire sauce	1/2 tsp.	2 mL
Salt, sprinkle		
Pepper, sprinkle		
Baguette, cut into 1 inch (2.5 cm) thick slices	1/2	1/2
Grated mozzarella cheese	1 cup	250 mL
Grated Swiss cheese	1 cup	250 mL
Grated Parmesan cheese	2 tbsp.	30 mL

Toss onion, flour and sugar together well in medium bowl.

Melt margarine in large saucepan. Add onion mixture. Cook, stirring often, for 15 to 20 minutes until onion is very soft and starting to brown.

Add next 6 ingredients. Cover. Simmer over medium-low for 20 minutes.

To make croutons, cut each baguette slice into quarters. Spread in ungreased 9 x 13 inch (22 x 33 cm) pan. Broil in centre of oven, stirring twice, until dried and golden.

Combine mozzarella cheese and Swiss cheese in medium bowl. Sprinkle evenly over croutons. Broil until cheese is melted. Ladle soup into 6 bowls. Top with cheese croutons.

Sprinkle 1 tsp. (5 mL) Parmesan cheese over each. Serves 6.

1 serving: 363 Calories; 16 g Protein; 16.4 g Total Fat; 34 g Carbohydrate; 1658 mg Sodium; 2 g Dietary Fibre

Pictured below.

Note: If you have ovenproof bowls, top each soup serving with croutons. Sprinkle with cheeses. Bake in 450°F (230°C) oven until cheese is melted and golden.

Onion Soup, above

Potato Soup

Creamy and cheesy. Good soup.

Hard margarine (or butter)	1 tbsp.	15 mL
Chopped onion	1 cup	250 mL
All-purpose flour	2 tbsp.	30 mL
Chicken bouillon powder	1 1/2 tbsp.	25 mL
Water	4 cups	1 L
Bay leaf	1	1
Salt	1/2 tsp.	2 mL
Pepper	1/4 tsp.	1 mL
Diced potato	4 cups	1 L
Half-and-half cream	1 cup	250 mL
Grated sharp Cheddar cheese	1 cup	250 mL

Melt margarine in non-stick frying pan. Add onion. Sauté until soft.

Mix in flour and bouillon powder. Stir in water until boiling and slightly thickened.

Add remaining 6 ingredients. Cover. Simmer for about 30 minutes until potato is cooked. Discard bay leaf. Run whole mixture through blender. Reheat if needed. Makes 6 cups (1.5 L) soup.

1 cup (250 mL) soup: 259 Calories; 9 g Protein; 13.4 g Total Fat; 26 g Carbohydrate; 885 mg Sodium; 2 g Dietary Fibre

Pictured on page 149.

Cream Of Garlic Soup

A creamy, foolproof version. Add as many garlic cloves as you dare. Garnish with chopped chives.

Garlic cloves, minced	4 – 8	4 – 8
Hard margarine (or butter)	3 tbsp.	50 mL
All-purpose flour	3 tbsp.	50 mL
Condensed chicken broth	2 x 10 oz.	2 x 284 mL
Soup cans of milk	2 x 10 oz.	2 x 284 mL
Paprika	1/2 tsp.	2 mL

Sauté garlic in margarine in medium saucepan until golden.

Mix in flour. Add chicken broth, stirring until boiling and thickened. Add milk and paprika. Gently simmer for about 5 minutes until garlic is cooked. Makes about 4 1/2 cups (1.1 L) soup.

1 cup (250 mL) soup: 190 Calories; 11 g Protein; 10.7 g Total Fat; 12 g Carbohydrate; 996 mg Sodium; trace Dietary Fibre

Pictured on page 149.

Pumpkin Soup

A thick, hearty soup. Delicious served with a fresh dinner roll.

Chopped onion	1 cup	250 mL
Green onions, chopped	4	4
Hard margarine (or butter)	1/4 cup	60 mL
All-purpose flour	2 tbsp.	30 mL
Salt	1/2 tsp.	2 mL
Pepper	1/8 tsp.	0.5 mL
Ground ginger	1/4 tsp.	1 mL
Chicken stock	1 cup	250 mL
Chicken stock	3 cups	750 mL
Canned pumpkin, without spices	14 oz.	398 mL
Light cream	1/2 cup	125 mL

Sauté onion and green onion in margarine in large saucepan. Sauté until soft.

Mix in flour, salt, pepper and ginger. Add first amount of chicken stock, stirring until boiling and thickened. Process in blender until smooth.

Stir in second amount of chicken stock, pumpkin and cream. Heat through. Makes a generous 6 cups (1.5 L) soup.

1 cup (250 mL) soup: 171 Calories; 6 g Protein; 11.6 g Total Fat; 12 g Carbohydrate; 883 mg Sodium; 2 g Dietary Fibre

Pictured below.

Avocado Cucumber Soup

Medium thickness. Serve small portions of this elegant cold soup.

Medium very ripe avocados, peeled and cut into chunks	2	2
Medium English cucumber, peeled	1	1
Condensed chicken broth	10 oz.	284 mL
Light sour cream	1/2 cup	125 mL
Lemon juice	1 tbsp.	15 mL
Onion powder	1/16 tsp.	0.5 mL
Cayenne pepper	1/16 tsp.	0.5 mL
Chopped fresh parsley (or chives), for garnish		

Put avocado into blender.

Cut cucumber in half lengthwise. Remove seeds. Cut into chunks. Put into blender with avocado.

Add next 5 ingredients. Process until smooth. Chill.

Garnish with parsley. Makes about 4 1/4 cups (1 L) soup.

3/4 cup (175 mL) soup: 159 Calories; 5 g Protein; 13 g Total Fat; 9 g Carbohydrate; 352 mg Sodium; 2 g Dietary Fibre

Pictured below.

Crab Bisque

An elegant first course. Doubles easily.

Condensed cream of tomato soup	10 oz.	284 mL
Condensed pea soup	10 oz.	284 mL
Condensed beef consommé	10 oz.	284 mL
Skim evaporated milk	1 cup	250 mL
Cooked fresh (or frozen or imitation) crab, broken up fine	1/2 lb.	225 g
Sherry (or alcohol-free sherry or white wine)	2 tbsp.	30 mL

Empty all 3 soups into large saucepan.

Add evaporated milk, crab and sherry. Heat, stirring often, until very hot but not boiling. Makes 6 cups (1.5 L) soup.

3/4 cup (175 mL) soup: 180 Calories; 15 g Protein; 2.4 g Total Fat; 24 g Carbohydrate; 1188 mg Sodium; 2 g Dietary Fibre

Pictured on page 150.

Top left: Pumpkin Soup, page 148
Top right: Potato Soup, page 148
Bottom right: Cream Of Garlic Soup, page 148
Bottom centre: Avocado Cucumber Soup, this page

Fresh Pea Soup, below

Cream Of Mushroom Soup

Creamy with lots of mushrooms. Just like it should be. Garnish with fresh parsley and sliced fresh mushrooms.

Hard margarine (or butter)	1 tbsp.	15 mL
Chopped fresh mushrooms	4 1/2 cups	1.1 L
Chopped onion	1/2 cup	125 mL
Water	1 cup	250 mL
All-purpose flour	6 tbsp.	100 mL
Condensed chicken broth	2 x 10 oz.	2 x 284 mL
Pepper	1/8 tsp.	0.5 mL
Paprika, sprinkle		
Skim evaporated milk	13 1/2 oz.	385 mL

Melt margarine in non-stick frying pan. Add mushrooms and onion. Sauté until onion is soft and moisture is evaporated. This may need to be done in 2 batches. Turn into large saucepan.

Whisk water into flour in small bowl until smooth. Add chicken broth, pepper and paprika. Whisk. Add to mushroom mixture. Heat and stir until boiling and thickened.

Add evaporated milk. Heat through. Makes 7 cups (1.75 L) soup.

1 cup (250 mL) soup: 129 Calories; 10 g Protein; 3 g Total Fat; 16 g Carbohydrate; 630 mg Sodium; 1 g Dietary Fibre

Pictured below.

Top: Cream Of Mushroom Soup, above
Bottom: Crab Bisque, page 149

Fresh Pea Soup

Gram made this after Sunday School—summer and winter. Garden-fresh colour, with a hard-to-beat fresh garden flavour. Garnish with fresh parsley.

Chopped onion	1/2 cup	125 mL
Hard margarine (or butter)	2 tbsp.	30 mL
All-purpose flour	1/4 cup	60 mL
Chicken stock (see Note)	4 cups	1 L
Fresh (or frozen) peas	2 1/2 cups	625 mL

Sauté onion in margarine in medium saucepan until soft and clear. Do not brown.

Add flour. Mix in. Stir in chicken stock until boiling and thickened.

Add peas. Simmer for 5 minutes. Run through blender. Return to saucepan until ready to serve. Makes a generous 4 cups (1 L).

1 cup (250 mL) soup: 234 Calories; 15 g Protein; 8.8 g Total Fat; 23 g Carbohydrate; 1574 mg Sodium; 5 g Dietary Fibre

Pictured above.

Note: Use homemade stock or three 10 oz. (284 mL) cans chicken broth plus water, to make 4 cups (1 L).

Oyster Soup

A family favourite from the Maritimes. Oysters were expensive so we only had this on rare occasions. Garnish with fresh parsley.

Milk	4 cups	1 L
Soda cracker crumbs	1/2 cup	125 mL
Salt	1 tsp.	5 mL
Pepper	1/4 tsp.	1 mL
Small fresh (or frozen or canned) oysters (about 24), with juice, cut up	2 cups	500 mL
Hard margarine (or butter)	1 tbsp.	15 mL

Combine first 4 ingredients in large saucepan. Heat until just boiling.

Add oysters with juice and margarine. Bring to a boil. Simmer for about 5 minutes until edges of oysters curl. Makes about 4 1/2 cups (1.1 L) soup.

1 cup (250 mL) soup: 242 Calories; 17 g Protein; 9.2 g Total Fat; 22 g Carbohydrate; 982 mg Sodium; trace Dietary Fibre

Pictured on this page.

Shrimp & Mushroom Soup

A delicious combination of shrimp and mushrooms. Makes a great starter soup for a sit-down dinner. Garnish with shrimp.

Hard margarine (or butter)	1 tbsp.	15 mL
Finely chopped onion	1/3 cup	75 mL
Chopped fresh mushrooms	2 cups	500 mL
All-purpose flour	1/4 cup	60 mL
Salt	1/2 tsp.	2 mL
Dry mustard	1/2 tsp.	2 mL
Garlic salt	1/4 tsp.	1 mL
Pepper	1/8 tsp.	0.5 mL
Skim evaporated milk	13 1/2 oz.	385 mL
Milk	1 1/3 cups	325 mL
Water	1 cup	250 mL
Sherry (or alcohol-free sherry), optional	1 tbsp.	15 mL
Canned broken (or cocktail) shrimp, with liquid	2 x 4 oz.	2 x 113 g

Melt margarine in non-stick frying pan. Add onion and mushrooms. Sauté until onion is soft and moisture is evaporated.

Mix in next 5 ingredients.

Stir in both milks and water until boiling and thickened. Add sherry. Stir.

Add shrimp with liquid. Heat through. Makes about 5 cups (1.25 L) soup.

1 cup (250 mL) soup: 206 Calories; 20 g Protein; 4.4 g Total Fat; 21 g Carbohydrate; 577 mg Sodium; 1 g Dietary Fibre

Pictured on this page.

Top: Oyster Soup, this page
Bottom: Shrimp & Mushroom Soup, this page

Squares

The most thumbed section of many old cookbooks is the one featuring squares. Because they are faster to make and often fancier than cookies, squares remain the preferred sweet to make for a special occasion. Brownies (page 154), Mystery Squares (page 154), Nut Smacks (page 156) and Chinese Chews (page 157) are oldies but goodies, and will probably continue to be favourites for years to come. When hosting a luncheon or having friends over for tea, squares are always welcome because of their small size and irresistible richness. They are also a good alternative to large, heavy desserts and offer the perfect sweet finale to any meal.

1. Brownies, page 154
2. Tropical Squares, page 154
3. Mystery Squares, page 154
4. Peanut Butter Squares, page 159

Tropical Squares

A pineapple and coconut topping. More moist the second day.

BOTTOM LAYER

All-purpose flour	1 cup	250 mL
Granulated sugar	1 tbsp.	15 mL
Hard margarine (or butter), softened	1/4 cup	60 mL
Baking powder	1/4 tsp.	1 mL
Large egg, fork-beaten	1	1

TOP LAYER

Large eggs, fork-beaten	2	2
Medium or flake coconut	2 cups	500 mL
Granulated sugar	1 cup	250 mL
Canned crushed pineapple, drained	14 oz.	398 mL
Hard margarine (or butter), melted	1 tbsp.	15 mL
Lemon juice	1 tsp.	5 mL

Bottom Layer: Mix first 4 ingredients in small bowl.

Add egg. Mix lightly. Press in ungreased 9 x 9 inch (22 x 22 cm) pan.

Top Layer: Combine all 6 ingredients in small bowl. Mix well. Spoon and spread over bottom layer. Bake in 350°F (175°C) oven for about 40 minutes. Cool. Cuts into 36 squares.

1 square: 97 Calories; 1 g Protein; 5.5 g Total Fat; 11 g Carbohydrate; 27 mg Sodium; trace Dietary Fibre

Pictured on pages 152/153.

Brownies

An old family recipe. Great with or without icing.

Hard margarine (or butter)	1/2 cup	125 mL
Unsweetened chocolate baking squares, cut up	2 x 1 oz.	2 x 28 g
Brown sugar, packed	1 1/2 cups	375 mL
Large eggs, fork-beaten	2	2
Vanilla	1 tbsp.	15 mL
All-purpose flour	1 cup	250 mL
Chopped walnuts	3/4 cup	175 mL

CHOCOLATE ICING

Hard margarine (or butter), softened	3 tbsp.	50 mL
Icing (confectioner's) sugar	1 1/3 cups	325 mL
Cocoa	1/3 cup	75 mL
Hot prepared coffee	1 1/2 tbsp.	25 mL

Melt margarine and chocolate in medium saucepan over low, stirring often. Remove from heat.

Stir in brown sugar. Add eggs and vanilla. Stir vigorously.

Add flour and walnuts. Stir just to moisten. Turn into greased 9 x 9 inch (22 x 22 cm) pan. Bake in 350°F (175°C) oven for about 25 minutes until wooden pick inserted in centre comes out clean. Do not overbake. Cool.

Chocolate Icing: Beat all 4 ingredients together in small bowl until smooth. Add more icing sugar or prepared coffee if needed to make proper spreading consistency. Spread over cooled brownies in pan. Cuts into 36 squares.

1 iced square: 130 Calories; 1 g Protein; 6.5 g Total Fat; 18 g Carbohydrate; 50 mg Sodium; 1 g Dietary Fibre

Pictured on page 152.

Mystery Squares

A shortbread base with a chewy coconut filling. Good with or without icing.

BOTTOM LAYER

All-purpose flour	1 cup	250 mL
Hard margarine (or butter), softened	1/2 cup	125 mL
Granulated sugar	2 tbsp.	30 mL

SECOND LAYER

Large eggs, fork-beaten	2	2
Brown sugar, packed	1 cup	250 mL
Vanilla	1/2 tsp.	2 mL
Salt	1/8 tsp.	0.5 mL
Medium coconut	1/2 cup	125 mL
All-purpose flour	2 tbsp.	30 mL
Baking powder	1 tsp.	5 mL

WHITE ICING

Icing (confectioner's) sugar	1 1/2 cups	375 mL
Hard margarine (or butter), softened	3 tbsp.	50 mL
Vanilla	1/2 tsp.	2 mL
Milk	2 tsp.	10 mL

Bottom Layer: Mix flour, margarine and sugar in small bowl until crumbly. Press in ungreased 9 x 9 inch (22 x 22 cm) pan. Bake in 350°F (175°C) oven for 10 minutes.

Second Layer: Combine eggs, brown sugar, vanilla and salt in medium bowl. Beat well. Stir in coconut, flour and baking powder. Pour over bottom layer. Bake for about 25 minutes until browned. Cool.

White Icing: Beat all 4 ingredients in small bowl, adding more icing sugar or milk for proper spreading consistency. Spread over cooled squares in pan. Cuts into 36 squares.

1 iced square: 108 Calories; 1 g Protein; 4.9 g Total Fat; 16 g Carbohydrate; 60 mg Sodium; trace Dietary Fibre

Pictured on page 153.

New Magic Squares

Chocolate base with a nutty topping.

Hard margarine (or butter)	1/3 cup	75 mL
Chocolate wafer crumbs	1 1/2 cups	375 mL
Flake coconut	1 cup	250 mL
Sliced almonds (or walnuts or pecans), toasted in 350°F (175°C) oven for 5 to 8 minutes	2/3 cup	150 mL
Semi-sweet chocolate chips	2/3 cup	150 mL
Sweetened condensed milk	11 oz.	300 mL
Sliced almonds, toasted in 350°F (175°C) oven for 5 to 8 minutes (optional)	1/4 cup	60 mL

Melt margarine in small saucepan. Stir in wafer crumbs. Press in 9 x 9 inch (22 x 22 cm) foil-lined pan. Bake in 350°F (175°C) oven for 10 minutes.

Sprinkle with coconut, almonds and chocolate chips. Press down firmly.

Drizzle condensed milk over top.

Sprinkle with almonds. Bake in 350°F (175°C) oven for 25 to 30 minutes. Cool. Cuts into 36 squares.

1 square: 104 Calories; 2 g Protein; 6.9 g Total Fat; 10 g Carbohydrate; 39 mg Sodium; 1 g Dietary Fibre

Pictured below.

Matrimonial Squares

Favourite date squares that are not nearly as messy to eat as some others. These crumbs hold together well.

OATMEAL LAYERS

All-purpose flour	1 1/4 cups	300 mL
Quick-cooking rolled oats (not instant)	1 1/2 cups	375 mL
Brown sugar, packed	1 cup	250 mL
Baking soda	1 tsp.	5 mL
Salt	1/2 tsp.	2 mL
Hard margarine (or butter), softened	1 cup	250 mL

DATE FILLING

Chopped dates	1 1/2 cups	375 mL
Granulated sugar	1/2 cup	125 mL
Water	2/3 cup	150 mL

Oatmeal Layers: Measure flour, rolled oats, brown sugar, baking soda, salt and margarine into large bowl. Cut in margarine until crumbly. Press a generous 1/2 of crumbs in greased 9 x 9 inch (22 x 22 cm) pan.

Date Filling: Combine dates, sugar and water in small saucepan. Bring to a boil. Simmer until mushy. If mixture becomes too dry before dates have softened, add more water. If you find you have too much water, simmer until some is evaporated. Spread over bottom layer of crumbs. Sprinkle second 1/2 of crumbs over top. Press down with your hand. Bake in 350°F (175°C) oven for 30 minutes until golden brown. Cool. Cuts into 36 squares.

1 square: 131 Calories; 1 g Protein; 5.7 g Total Fat; 20 g Carbohydrate; 142 mg Sodium; 1 g Dietary Fibre

Pictured below.

Left: New Magic Squares, above
Right: Matrimonial Squares, this page

Nut Smacks, below

Brazil Bars

A nutty, buttery bar. Almost a shortbread.

Butter, softened	6 tbsp.	100 mL
Brown sugar, packed	3/4 cup	175 mL
Large egg	1	1
Vanilla	1/2 tsp.	2 mL
All-purpose flour	1 1/2 cups	375 mL
Salt	1/4 tsp.	1 mL
Sliced or chopped Brazil nuts	3/4 cup	175 mL

Cream butter and brown sugar together in medium bowl. Beat in egg and vanilla.

Add flour, salt and Brazil nuts. Stir just to moisten. Press in greased 9 x 9 inch (22 x 22 cm) pan. Bake in 350°F (175°C) oven for 20 to 25 minutes until edges are starting to brown. Cool. Cuts into 36 bars.

1 bar: 73 Calories; 1 g Protein; 3.7 g Total Fat; 9 g Carbohydrate; 45 mg Sodium; trace Dietary Fibre

Pictured on pages 156/157.

Nut Smacks

Butterscotch flavour, rich with nuts and brown sugar.
An old family favourite.

BOTTOM LAYER

Brown sugar, packed	1/2 cup	125 mL
Egg yolks (large)	2	2
Vanilla	1 tsp.	5 mL
Hard margarine (or butter), softened	1/2 cup	125 mL
Salt	1/4 tsp.	1 mL
All-purpose flour	1 1/2 cups	375 mL
Baking powder	1 tsp.	5 mL

SECOND LAYER

Egg whites (large), room temperature	2	2
Brown sugar, packed	1 cup	250 mL
Chopped walnuts	1 cup	250 mL

Bottom Layer: Combine all 7 ingredients in large bowl. Mix until crumbly. Press firmly in ungreased 9 x 9 inch (22 x 22 cm) pan.

Second Layer: Beat egg whites in medium bowl until frothy. Add brown sugar 1/3 at a time, beating until stiff. Fold in walnuts. Spoon over bottom layer, spreading evenly. Bake in 350°F (175°C) oven for about 25 minutes until golden. Cool. Covering pan allows meringue to soften for easier cutting. Cuts into 36 squares.

1 square: 109 Calories; 1 g Protein; 5.3 g Total Fat; 14 g Carbohydrate; 58 mg Sodium; trace Dietary Fibre

Pictured above.

Top: Chip Bars, page 157
Bottom: Brazil Bars, above

Chip Bars

The flavour of toffee. These do a disappearing act fast.
Bars are easier to cut when nuts are chopped.

BOTTOM LAYER		
Hard margarine (or butter), softened	1/2 cup	125 mL
Brown sugar, packed	3/4 cup	175 mL
All-purpose flour	1 1/2 cups	375 mL
SECOND LAYER		
Butterscotch chips	2 cups	500 mL
Corn syrup	1/2 cup	125 mL
Cooking oil	2 tbsp.	30 mL
Peanuts, whole or chopped	2 cups	500 mL

Bottom Layer: Mix margarine, brown sugar and flour well in small bowl. Press in ungreased 9 x 13 inch (22 x 33 cm) pan. Bake in 375°F (190°C) oven for about 10 minutes.

Second Layer: Combine butterscotch chips, corn syrup and cooking oil in small saucepan. Heat over low, stirring constantly, until butterscotch chips are melted.

Add peanuts. Stir. Spoon over bottom layer. Bake in 375°F (190°C) oven for about 6 minutes. Cool. Cuts into 54 bars.

1 bar: 116 Calories; 2 g Protein; 5.5 g Total Fat; 16 g Carbohydrate; 29 mg Sodium; 1 g Dietary Fibre

Pictured on pages 156/157.

Chinese Chews, below

Chinese Chews

I remember Grandad making these after Gram died.
They are moist, so they last quite awhile.

Granulated sugar	1 cup	250 mL
Chopped dates	1 cup	250 mL
Baking powder	1 tsp.	5 mL
Salt	1/4 tsp.	1 mL
Chopped walnuts	1/2 cup	125 mL
All-purpose flour	3/4 cup	175 mL
Large eggs	2	2
Icing (confectioner's) sugar, for garnish	2 tbsp.	30 mL

Mix first 6 ingredients in medium bowl.

Beat eggs in small bowl until light in colour and thickened. Pour over flour mixture. Stir until well moistened. Scrape batter into greased 9 x 9 inch (22 x 22 cm) pan. Bake in 350°F (175°C) oven for about 25 minutes until wooden pick inserted in centre comes out clean. Cool.

Cut while still warm. Cool and sift icing sugar over top. Cuts into 36 squares.

1 square: 57 Calories; 1 g Protein; 1.5 g Total Fat; 12 g Carbohydrate; 23 mg Sodium; 1 g Dietary Fibre

Pictured above and on front cover.

Caramel Chocolate Squares

Rich chocolate flavour covers a shortbread base.

Hard margarine (or butter), softened	1/2 cup	125 mL
All-purpose flour	1 1/4 cups	300 mL
Brown sugar, packed	1/3 cup	75 mL
Light cream cheese, softened	4 oz.	125 g
Large egg	1	1
Caramel ice cream topping	3/4 cup	175 mL
Vanilla	1 tsp.	5 mL
Chopped walnuts (or pecans)	1/2 cup	125 mL
Milk chocolate chips	1 cup	250 mL

Mix margarine, flour and brown sugar in small bowl until crumbly. Reserve 2/3 cup (150 mL). Press remainder in ungreased 9 x 9 inch (22 x 22 cm) pan.

Beat cream cheese and egg in medium bowl. Add caramel topping and vanilla. Beat. Stir in reserved crumb mixture.

Add walnuts. Stir. Spoon over crust. Bake in 375°F (190°C) oven for 30 to 35 minutes.

Sprinkle with chocolate chips. Let stand until melted. Spread over all. Cool. Cuts into 36 squares.

1 square: 104 Calories; 2 g Protein; 5.9 g Total Fat; 12 g Carbohydrate; 71 mg Sodium; trace Dietary Fibre

Pictured on page 159 and on front cover.

Chocolate Goodies

Rich chocolate taste. Soft and gooey.

Hard margarine (or butter), softened	1/2 cup	125 mL
Brown sugar, packed	1 cup	250 mL
Large egg	1	1
Vanilla	1 tsp.	5 mL
All-purpose flour	1 1/4 cups	300 mL
Quick-cooking rolled oats (not instant)	1 1/2 cups	375 mL
Baking soda	1/2 tsp.	2 mL
Salt	1/2 tsp.	2 mL
Sweetened condensed milk	2/3 cup	150 mL
Semi-sweet chocolate chips	1 cup	250 mL
Hard margarine (or butter)	2 tbsp.	30 mL
Vanilla	1 tsp.	5 mL
Salt	1/4 tsp.	1 mL

Cream first amount of margarine and brown sugar together in large bowl. Beat in egg and first amount of vanilla.

Add flour, rolled oats, baking soda and first amount of salt. Mix. Press 2/3 of oat mixture in greased 9 x 9 inch (22 x 22 cm) pan.

Heat and stir remaining 5 ingredients in small saucepan until chocolate chips are melted. Spread over bottom layer. Drop remaining rolled oat mixture in little dabs over top. Spread as best you can. Don't be concerned if a few spaces aren't covered. Bake in 350°F (175°C) oven for 20 to 25 minutes. Cool. Cuts into 36 squares.

1 square: 127 Calories; 2 g Protein; 5.8 g Total Fat; 18 g Carbohydrate; 127 mg Sodium; 1 g Dietary Fibre

Pictured on page 159.

Chocolate Mince Squares

Moist, mildly spiced. Good texture.

Hard margarine (or butter), softened	1/2 cup	125 mL
Granulated sugar	1 cup	250 mL
Large eggs	2	2
Mincemeat	1 cup	250 mL
Chopped pecans (or walnuts)	1/2 cup	125 mL
Vanilla	1 1/2 tsp.	7 mL
All-purpose flour	1 1/4 cups	300 mL
Cocoa	1/4 cup	60 mL
Salt	1/2 tsp.	2 mL
CARAMEL ICING		
Brown sugar, packed	1/2 cup	125 mL
Milk	3 tbsp.	50 mL
Hard margarine (or butter)	1/4 cup	60 mL
Icing (confectioner's) sugar	1 1/2 cups	375 mL

Cream margarine and sugar together well in large bowl. Beat in eggs, 1 at a time. Add mincemeat, pecans and vanilla. Stir.

Add flour, cocoa and salt. Mix well. Spread in greased 9 x 9 inch (22 x 22 cm) pan. Bake in 350°F (175°C) oven for 30 to 35 minutes. Cool.

Caramel Icing: Heat and stir brown sugar, milk and margarine in small saucepan until boiling. Boil for 2 minutes. Remove from heat. Cool.

Add icing sugar. Beat until smooth. Add a bit more milk or icing sugar if needed to make proper spreading consistency. Makes about 7/8 cup (200 mL) caramel icing. Spread over cooled squares in pan. Cuts into 36 squares.

1 iced square: 141 Calories; 1 g Protein; 5.8 g Total Fat; 22 g Carbohydrate; 107 mg Sodium; 1 g Dietary Fibre

Pictured on page 159.

Peanut Butter Squares

Yummy taste. Soft in consistency. Thin like a candy bar.

Hard margarine (or butter)	1/2 cup	125 mL
Smooth peanut butter	1/2 cup	125 mL
Icing (confectioner's) sugar	1 1/4 cups	300 mL
Graham cracker crumbs	1 cup	250 mL
Milk chocolate chips	1 cup	250 mL

Melt margarine and peanut butter in small
saucepan, stirring constantly, until smooth.
Remove from heat.

Add icing sugar and graham crumbs.
Mix well. Press in greased 9 x 9 inch
(22 x 22 cm) pan.

Sprinkle with chocolate chips. Heat in
200°F (95°C) oven for about 5 minutes
to soften. Spread evenly over top. Cool.
Cuts into 36 squares.

*1 square: 96 Calories; 2 g Protein; 6.2 g Total Fat; 10 g Carbohydrate;
75 mg Sodium; trace Dietary Fibre*

Pictured on page 153.

Top: Chocolate Mince Squares, page 158
Bottom left: Chocolate Goodies, page 158
Bottom right: Caramel Chocolate Squares, page 158

Pumpkin Cheesecake Squares, below

Frosted Pumpkin Squares, below

Pumpkin Cheesecake Squares

A moist, spiced-just-right treat.

All-purpose flour	1 cup	250 mL
Brown sugar, packed	1/3 cup	75 mL
Hard margarine (or butter), softened	6 tbsp.	100 mL
Finely chopped pecans	1/2 cup	125 mL
FILLING		
Light cream cheese, softened	8 oz.	250 g
Granulated sugar	3/4 cup	175 mL
Canned pumpkin, without spices	1/2 cup	125 mL
Ground cinnamon	1 1/2 tsp.	7 mL
Ground allspice	1 tsp.	5 mL
Vanilla	1 tsp.	5 mL
Large eggs	2	2

Measure flour, brown sugar and margarine into small bowl. Mix in margarine until crumbly.

Stir in pecans. Reserve 3/4 cup (175 mL) for topping. Press remaining crumbs in ungreased 8 x 8 inch (20 x 20 cm) pan. Bake in 350°F (175°C) oven for 15 minutes. Cool slightly.

Filling: Beat cream cheese and sugar in small bowl. Add pumpkin, cinnamon, allspice and vanilla. Beat. Add eggs, 1 at a time, beating just to blend after each addition. Spread over crust. Sprinkle with reserved crumbs. Bake for 30 to 35 minutes. Cool. Cuts into 36 squares.

1 square: 88 Calories; 2 g Protein; 4.6 g Total Fat; 10 g Carbohydrate; 94 mg Sodium; trace Dietary Fibre

Pictured above.

Frosted Pumpkin Squares

A cake-type square. Cut in larger pieces for dessert.

Large eggs, fork-beaten	4	4
Granulated sugar	2 cups	500 mL
Canned pumpkin, without spices	1 cup	250 mL
Cooking oil	2/3 cup	150 mL
Ground cinnamon	2 tsp.	10 mL
Salt	1/2 tsp.	2 mL
All-purpose flour	2 cups	500 mL
Baking powder	1 tsp.	5 mL
Baking soda	1 tsp.	5 mL
Raisins	1 cup	250 mL
FROSTING		
Light cream cheese, softened	4 oz.	125 g
Hard margarine (or butter)	6 tbsp.	100 mL
Icing (confectioner's) sugar	2 1/2 cups	625 mL
Vanilla	1 tsp.	5 mL
Milk, if needed	2 tsp.	10 mL

Combine eggs, sugar and pumpkin in large bowl. Beat well. Add cooking oil, cinnamon and salt. Beat to mix.

Add flour, baking powder and baking soda. Stir. Add raisins. Stir. Turn into greased and floured 10 x 15 inch (25 x 38 cm) jelly roll pan. Bake in 350°F (175°C) oven for 20 to 25 minutes until wooden pick inserted in centre comes out clean.

Frosting: Beat first 4 ingredients on low just to moisten. Beat on medium to fluff up. Add milk, 1 tsp. (5 mL) at a time, to thin frosting. Spread while squares are still slightly warm. Cuts into 72 squares.

1 square: 94 Calories; 1 g Protein; 3.5 g Total Fat; 15 g Carbohydrate; 70 mg Sodium; trace Dietary Fibre

Pictured above.

Vegetables

In the late nineteenth and early twentieth centuries, boiling, baking and frying vegetables were the preferred methods of cooking. Seasoning at this time was not yet a common practice. By the First World War, however, most cookbooks suggested the use of butter, salt, pepper or white sauce over vegetables. It wasn't until the mid-twentieth century that vegetable casseroles became popular. Canned vegetables came into use during the nineteenth century, and frozen and dehydrated vegetables, including instant potatoes, in the twentieth century. During the 1940s and 1950s, baking soda was often added to the cooking water of green vegetables such as green beans, asparagus, broccoli and spinach to keep them bright green, until it was discovered that the vitamin C was destroyed. Today we have become more creative than ever in how we prepare and serve vegetables.

Beets And Onions

Good way to enjoy beets. They cook worry-free in the oven.

Peeled and grated raw beet (food processor works well)	4 1/2 cups	1.1 L
Very finely chopped onion	1/4 cup	60 mL
Salt	1/2 tsp.	2 mL
Pepper, sprinkle		
Hard margarine (or butter), melted (optional)	1 tbsp.	15 mL

Combine beet and onion in ungreased 1 1/2 quart (1.5 L) casserole. Sprinkle with salt and pepper. Cover. Bake in 350°F (175°C) oven for about 1 hour.

Drizzle with margarine. Makes 5 cups (1.25 L) vegetables.

1/2 cup (125 mL) vegetables: 41 Calories; 1 g Protein; 1.3 g Total Fat; 7 g Carbohydrate; 196 mg Sodium; trace Dietary Fibre

Pictured on page 162.

Tomato Dumplings

For something different, try this classic.

Canned tomatoes, with juice	28 oz.	796 mL
Granulated sugar	1 tsp.	5 mL
Finely chopped onion	1/4 cup	60 mL
Finely chopped celery	2 tbsp.	30 mL
Water	1/2 cup	125 mL
Salt	1/2 tsp.	2 mL
All-purpose flour	1 cup	250 mL
Baking powder	2 tsp.	10 mL
Granulated sugar	1 tsp.	5 mL
Salt	1/2 tsp.	2 mL
Shortening	1 tbsp.	15 mL
Milk	1/2 cup	125 mL

Combine first 6 ingredients in large pot or Dutch oven. Bring to a boil.

Combine flour, baking powder, and second amounts of sugar and salt in medium bowl. Cut in shortening until crumbly. Add milk. Stir to mix. Drop by spoonfuls over boiling tomatoes. Cover. Boil for 15 minutes. Serves 6.

1 serving: 145 Calories; 4 g Protein; 2.9 g Total Fat; 26 g Carbohydrate; 691 mg Sodium; 2 g Dietary Fibre

Pictured on page 162.

Bubble And Squeak

An old recipe from the British Isles.
Cabbage adds to appearance and to texture.

Mashed potatoes	4 cups	1 L
Cooked cabbage, chopped	4 cups	1 L
Salt	1 tsp.	5 mL
Pepper	1/4 tsp.	1 mL
Hard margarine (or butter)	2 tbsp.	30 mL

Mix first 4 ingredients in large bowl. Shape into patties.

Melt margarine in non-stick frying pan. Brown patties on both sides. Makes 8 large or 16 medium patties.

1 large patty: 160 Calories; 3 g Protein; 3.3 g Total Fat; 31 g Carbohydrate; 394 mg Sodium; 3 g Dietary Fibre

Pictured on page 162.

Variation: This may be browned in 1 big patty, turned out onto plate, then eased back into pan to brown other side. May also be scramble-fried instead of made into patties.

Zucchini Casserole

Golden brown crumbly topping over melted cheese.
Green and red show up from the vegetables. Doubles easily.

Zucchini, with peel, quartered lengthwise and sliced	2 cups	500 mL
Salt, sprinkle		
Medium onion, sliced	1	1
Hard margarine (or butter)	1 tsp.	5 mL
Large tomato, sliced	1	1
Salt, sprinkle		
Pepper, sprinkle		
Dried sweet basil, sprinkle		
Zucchini, with peel, quartered lengthwise and sliced	2 cups	500 mL
Salt, sprinkle		
Process cheese slices	6	6
TOPPING		
Hard margarine (or butter)	2 tbsp.	30 mL
Dry bread crumbs	1/2 cup	125 mL

Layer first amount of zucchini in greased 1 quart (1 L) casserole. Sprinkle with salt.

Sauté onion in margarine in non-stick frying pan until soft. Scatter over zucchini.

Add layer of tomato slices, overlapping if necessary. Sprinkle with salt, pepper and basil. Scatter second amount of zucchini over top. Sprinkle with salt. Lay cheese slices over top.

Topping: Melt margarine in small saucepan. Stir in bread crumbs. Sprinkle over cheese. Bake, uncovered, in 350°F (175°C) oven for about 40 minutes. Serves 4.

1 serving: 275 Calories; 11 g Protein; 17.7 g Total Fat; 20 g Carbohydrate; 642 mg Sodium; 4 g Dietary Fibre

Pictured on page 162.

Turnip Bake

A really delicious dish. Garnish with fresh tomato slices.

Yellow turnip, cut up	3 lbs.	1.4 kg
Water, to cover		
Large eggs, fork-beaten	2	2
Brown sugar, packed	1 tbsp.	15 mL
Salt	1/2 tsp.	2 mL
Pepper	1/8 tsp.	0.5 mL
All-purpose flour	2 tbsp.	30 mL
Baking powder	1 tsp.	5 mL
TOPPING		
Hard margarine (or butter)	2 tbsp.	30 mL
Soda cracker crumbs	1/2 cup	125 mL

Cook turnip in water in large saucepan until very soft. Drain well. Mash.

Combine next 6 ingredients in small bowl. Mix. Add to turnip. Beat well. Turn into ungreased 2 quart (2 L) casserole.

Topping: Melt margarine in small saucepan. Stir in cracker crumbs. Sprinkle over top. Bake, uncovered, in 350°F (175°C) oven for 30 to 35 minutes until set. Makes 5 cups (1.25 L) turnip.

1/2 cup (125 mL) turnip: 97 Calories; 3 g Protein; 4 g Total Fat; 13 g Carbohydrate; 301 mg Sodium; 2 g Dietary Fibre

Pictured on page 164.

Elegant Squash

With carrot and a seasoned crumb topping.

Grated carrot	1 cup	250 mL
Finely chopped onion	1/2 cup	125 mL
Cooking oil	1 tsp.	5 mL
Condensed cream of chicken soup	10 oz.	284 mL
Light sour cream	1 cup	250 mL
Cooked and mashed yellow squash (such as butternut)	2 cups	500 mL
Salt	1 tsp.	5 mL
Pepper	1/4 tsp.	1 mL
Brown sugar, packed	1 tbsp.	15 mL
Large eggs, fork-beaten	2	2
TOPPING		
Hard margarine (or butter)	2 tbsp.	30 mL
Dry bread crumbs	1/2 cup	125 mL
Poultry seasoning	1/4 tsp.	1 mL
Parsley flakes	1/2 tsp.	2 mL

Sauté carrot and onion in cooking oil in non-stick frying pan until soft.

Add next 7 ingredients. Stir well. Turn into ungreased 1 1/2 quart (1.5 L) casserole.

Topping: Melt margarine in small saucepan. Add bread crumbs, poultry seasoning and parsley. Stir. Sprinkle over top. Bake, uncovered, in 350°F (175°C) oven for about 1 hour until set. Serves 6.

1 serving: 238 Calories; 7 g Protein; 13.1 g Total Fat; 25 g Carbohydrate; 1011 mg Sodium; 3 g Dietary Fibre

Pictured on page 162.

1. Elegant Squash, above
2. Tomato Dumplings, page 161
3. Zucchini Casserole, this page
4. Bubble and Squeak, page 161
5. Beets And Onions, page 161

Top: Baked Onions, below
Bottom: Turnip Bake, page 163

Corn Scallop

Makes a nice vegetable dish. More special than many.

Skim evaporated milk	1/2 cup	125 mL
All-purpose flour	2 tbsp.	30 mL
Chopped green pepper	2 tbsp.	30 mL
Finely chopped onion	1/4 cup	60 mL
Soda cracker crumbs	1/4 cup	60 mL
Parsley flakes	1/2 tsp.	2 mL
Salt	1/2 tsp.	2 mL
Pepper	1/4 tsp.	1 mL
Ground marjoram, just a pinch		
Canned cream-style corn	2 x 10 oz.	2 x 284 mL
Grated medium Cheddar cheese	3/4 cup	175 mL
TOPPING		
Hard margarine (or butter)	2 tbsp.	30 mL
Dry bread crumbs	1/2 cup	125 mL
Onion powder	1/8 tsp.	0.5 mL
Grated medium Cheddar cheese	1/3 cup	75 mL

Whisk evaporated milk into flour in medium bowl until smooth. Add next 9 ingredients. Mix well. Turn into ungreased 1 quart (1 L) casserole.

Topping: Melt margarine in small saucepan. Stir in bread crumbs, onion powder and cheese. Sprinkle over top. Bake, uncovered, in 350°F (175°C) oven for about 45 minutes until bubbling. Serves 6.

1 serving: 279 Calories; 11 g Protein; 12.5 g Total Fat; 34 g Carbohydrate; 833 mg Sodium; 2 g Dietary Fibre

Pictured on page 165.

Baked Onions

A nice onion flavour. Not overbearing because the rice is cooked with the onion.

Hard margarine (or butter)	2 tbsp.	30 mL
Chopped onion	6 cups	1.5 L
Uncooked long grain white rice	1/2 cup	125 mL
Salt	1/4 tsp.	1 mL
Skim evaporated milk	2/3 cup	150 mL
Grated Muenster cheese	1 cup	250 mL

Melt margarine in non-stick frying pan. Add onion, rice and salt. You may need to do this in batches. Sauté until onion is soft. Turn into large bowl.

Add evaporated milk and cheese. Stir well. Turn into greased 1 1/2 quart (1.5 L) casserole. Cover. Bake in 350°F (175°C) oven for 55 minutes. Remove cover. Bake for 5 minutes until browned. Makes about 5 cups (1.25 L).

1/2 cup (125 mL) onion: 153 Calories; 6 g Protein; 6.2 g Total Fat; 19 g Carbohydrate; 195 mg Sodium; 2 g Dietary Fibre

Pictured above.

Glazed Onions

Makes an excellent side dish with a roast or pork chops.

Sliced onion (4 large)	6 cups	1.5 L
Water	1 cup	250 mL
Hard margarine (or butter)	2 tbsp.	30 mL
Granulated sugar	3 tbsp.	50 mL

Cook onion in water in covered non-stick frying pan for about 20 minutes. Drain.

Add margarine and sugar. Heat and stir until margarine is melted. Cook, uncovered, for 10 to 15 minutes, stirring often, until golden brown and water is evaporated. Makes 2 cups (500 mL).

1/2 cup (125 mL) onion: 117 Calories; 1 g Protein; 6 g Total Fat; 16 g Carbohydrate; 71 mg Sodium; 1 g Dietary Fibre

Pictured on page 165.

Stuffing Balls

Especially handy for freezing ahead.
Simply heat as few or as many as needed.

Hard margarine (or butter)	2 tbsp.	30 mL
Chopped onion	3/4 cup	175 mL
Chopped celery	1/2 cup	125 mL
Large eggs, fork-beaten	2	2
Frozen kernel corn	1 cup	250 mL
Milk	1 cup	250 mL
Dry bread crumbs	3 cups	750 mL
Poultry seasoning	1 1/2 tsp.	7 mL
Parsley flakes	1 1/2 tsp.	7 mL
Salt	3/4 tsp.	4 mL
Pepper	1/4 tsp.	1 mL
Hard margarine (or butter), melted	1/4 cup	60 mL

Melt first amount of margarine in non-stick frying pan. Add onion and celery. Sauté until soft.

Combine next 8 ingredients in large bowl. Add onion and celery. Mix well. Shape into 14 balls using 1/4 cup (60 mL) for each one. Add water if needed to hold together. Arrange in small greased roaster or baking dish large enough to hold in single layer.

Drizzle second amount of margarine over top. Cover. Bake in 350°F (175°C) oven for about 35 minutes. Makes about 14 stuffing balls.

1 stuffing ball: 174 Calories; 5 g Protein; 7.1 g Total Fat; 23 g Carbohydrate; 407 mg Sodium; 1 g Dietary Fibre

Pictured below.

Wild Rice Stuffing

A good stuffing for Cornish hens, chicken or whole salmon.

Wild rice	1/2 cup	125 mL
Brown rice	1/2 cup	125 mL
Water	3 cups	750 mL
Chicken bouillon powder	1 tbsp.	15 mL
Hard margarine (or butter)	2 tbsp.	30 mL
Chopped onion	1 cup	250 mL
Chopped fresh mushrooms	3 cups	750 mL
Chopped celery	1/4 cup	60 mL
Parsley flakes	1 tsp.	5 mL
Dried thyme	1/4 tsp.	1 mL
Ground marjoram	1/4 tsp.	1 mL
Chopped pecans	1/2 cup	125 mL

Combine first 4 ingredients in large saucepan. Cook for about 45 minutes until rice is tender and water is absorbed.

Melt margarine in non-stick frying pan. Add onion, mushrooms and celery. Sauté until soft.

Stir in parsley, thyme, marjoram and pecans. Add to rice mixture. Stir well. Makes 4 cups (1 L) stuffing.

1/2 cup (125 mL) stuffing: 180 Calories; 4 g Protein; 9 g Total Fat; 22 g Carbohydrate; 285 mg Sodium; 2 g Dietary Fibre

Pictured below.

Left: Glazed Onions, page 164
Top centre: Corn Scallop, page 164
Right: Wild Rice Stuffing, above
Bottom centre: Stuffing Balls, this page

Final Thoughts

My life is filled with fond memories of sharing time with my family in that most important part of the house—the kitchen. Preparing meals, sitting at the table, even stacking the dishwasher has been an opportunity for us to gather together every day.

For many people, though, these are experiences of the past. As a society, we no longer cook the way we once did, and eating together as a family has become, more often than not, an occasional event. That's a trend I would like to see change, and I think we may have the opportunity to do just that.

Two influences are responsible for the way we now eat: a hectic family life and the convenience of fast food. In the last 25 years we've seen extended work hours, longer commutes and added after-school activities make more demands on our free time. Naturally, the fast-food industry has jumped in to fill the need.

But convenience has overshadowed nutrition, and we're starting to see the results: bad eating habits and new, serious health concerns that affect all ages. And what have we been teaching our children? Well, we've shown them how to eat quickly and to treat mealtimes as if they're an inconvenience to be rushed through. We've also taught them that any food will do when we're pressed for time. Pausing to enjoy a proper meal and re-connect as a family has almost disappeared from many lives.

Still, the appeal of processed foods appears to be fading and a new appreciation for good, old-fashioned home cooking is emerging. After 25 years as a cookbook author, I am happy to see people demanding more primary ingredients such as fresh vegetables, whole grains and seasonal fruit. Not only does this create a wonderful opportunity to improve our eating habits, but it can also benefit our family life as we gather in the kitchen, even if just for one meal. The entire process—setting the table, cooking, eating and cleaning up—could easily become an everyday family routine again.

Even busy households can find the time for a home-cooked meal, because so many recipes are now designed to be prepared and cooked in less time than it takes to deliver a pizza. To help, many stores offer pre-cut, pre-washed fruits and vegetables, as well as marinated cuts of meat and fish.

So if this is the trend of tomorrow—more people looking for cooking ideas that are quick, easy, healthy and family-friendly—then I'm happy to help you get there. Because that's what I would really like to see in the future—all of us gathering in the kitchen, creating cherished memories.

Jean Paré

Bibliography

Anderson, Jean. *American Century Cookbook.* New York: Clark & Potter, 1997.

Canada's Food Guide Handbook. Ottawa: The Minister of National Health and Welfare, Revised Edition, 1983.

Dale, Rodney & Weaver, Rebecca. *Machines in the Home.* Toronto: Oxford University Press, 1992.

Ferguson, Carol. *A Century of Canadian Home Cooking.* Scarborough: Prentice-Hall Canada, 1992.

Panati, Charles. *Panati's Extraordinary Origins of Everyday Things.* New York City: Harper & Row, 1987 (Revised in 1989).

Stewart, Katie. *The Joy of Eating.* Owings Mills: Stemmer House Publishers, 1977.

The Development of Canada's Food Guide to Healthy Eating: Notes on Consumer Research. Ottawa: Health and Welfare Canada, June 11, 1993.

The Horizon Cookbook and Illustrated History of Eating and Drinking Through the Ages. New York: American Heritage, 1968.

USDA's Food Guide: Background and Development. Hyattsville: Publication Number 1514.

Using the Food Guide. Ottawa: The Minister of National Health and Welfare, 1992.

Wallace, Lilly Haxworth. *The Lily Wallace New American Cookbook.* New York City: Books Inc., 1946.

Wright, Lawrence. *Home Fires Burning: The History of Domestic Heating and Cooking.* London: Routledge & Kegan Paul Ltd., 1968.

Measurement Tables

Throughout this book measurements are given in Conventional and Metric measure. To compensate for differences between the two measurements due to rounding, a full metric measure is not always used. The cup used is the standard 8 fluid ounce. Temperature is given in degrees Fahrenheit and Celsius. Baking pan measurements are in inches and centimetres as well as quarts and litres. An exact metric conversion is given on this page as well as the working equivalent (Standard Measure).

Oven Temperatures

Fahrenheit (°F)	Celsius (°C)
175°	80°
200°	95°
225°	110°
250°	120°
275°	140°
300°	150°
325°	160°
350°	175°
375°	190°
400°	205°
425°	220°
450°	230°
475°	240°
500°	260°

Pans

Conventional Inches	Metric Centimetres
8x8 inch	20x20 cm
9x9 inch	22x22 cm
9x13 inch	22x33 cm
10x15 inch	25x38 cm
11x17 inch	28x43 cm
8x2 inch round	20x5 cm
9x2 inch round	22x5 cm
10x4 1/2 inch tube	25x11 cm
8x4x3 inch loaf	20x10x7.5 cm
9x5x3 inch loaf	22x12.5x7.5 cm

Spoons

Conventional Measure	Metric Exact Conversion Millilitre (mL)	Metric Standard Measure Millilitre (mL)
1/8 teaspoon (tsp.)	0.6 mL	0.5 mL
1/4 teaspoon (tsp.)	1.2 mL	1 mL
1/2 teaspoon (tsp.)	2.4 mL	2 mL
1 teaspoon (tsp.)	4.7 mL	5 mL
2 teaspoons (tsp.)	9.4 mL	10 mL
1 tablespoon (tbsp.)	14.2 mL	15 mL

Cups

	Metric Exact Conversion	Metric Standard Measure
1/4 cup (4 tbsp.)	56.8 mL	60 mL
1/3 cup (5 1/3 tbsp.)	75.6 mL	75 mL
1/2 cup (8 tbsp.)	113.7 mL	125 mL
2/3 cup (10 2/3 tbsp.)	151.2 mL	150 mL
3/4 cup (12 tbsp.)	170.5 mL	175 mL
1 cup (16 tbsp.)	227.3 mL	250 mL
4 1/2 cups	1022.9 mL	1000 mL (1 L)

Dry Measurements

Conventional Measure Ounces (oz.)	Metric Exact Conversion Grams (g)	Metric Standard Measure Grams (g)
1 oz.	28.3 g	28 g
2 oz.	56.7 g	57 g
3 oz.	85.0 g	85 g
4 oz.	113.4 g	125 g
5 oz.	141.7 g	140 g
6 oz.	170.1 g	170 g
7 oz.	198.4 g	200 g
8 oz.	226.8 g	250 g
16 oz.	453.6 g	500 g
32 oz.	907.2 g	1000 g (1 kg)

Casseroles (Canada & Britain)

Standard Size Casserole	Exact Metric Measure
1 qt. (5 cups)	1.13 L
1 1/2 qts. (7 1/2 cups)	1.69 L
2 qts. (10 cups)	2.25 L
2 1/2 qts. (12 1/2 cups)	2.81 L
3 qts. (15 cups)	3.38 L
4 qts. (20 cups)	4.5 L
5 qts. (25 cups)	5.63 L

Casseroles (United States)

Standard Size Casserole	Exact Metric Measure
1 qt. (4 cups)	900 mL
1 1/2 qts. (6 cups)	1.35 L
2 qts. (8 cups)	1.8 L
2 1/2 qts. (10 cups)	2.25 L
3 qts. (12 cups)	2.7 L
4 qts. (16 cups)	3.6 L
5 qts. (20 cups)	4.5 L

Index

A

Angel Cake, Mock 67
Appetizers
    Apple Brie Pizza 29
    Cheese Bites 18
    Cheese Tarts 19
    Chili Con Queso 22
    Cranberry Meatballs 25
    Cuke Spread 'R Dip 26
    Fluffy Salmon Spread 27
    Garlic Dip 26
    Ginger-Sauced Meatballs 24
    Guacamole Mold 22
    Jalapeño Pie 23
    Laurier Lake "Shrimp" 25
    Mushroom Canapés 20
    Mushroom Surprise 20
    Mushroom Toasties 20
    Mushroom Turnovers 19
    Mustard Ham Balls 24
    Parmesan Appies 28
    Pickled Onion Surprise 20
    Relish Cheese Ball 27
    Salami Rolls 28
    Sesame Wings 23
    Soy Fire Dip 26
    Spinach Balls 27
    Stuffed Mushrooms 28
    Teriyaki Chicken Wings 22
    Zucchini Treats 25
Apple Brie Pizza 29
Apple Cheese Muffins 48
Apple Pork Chops 134
Apple Scallop 57
Apricot Bran Muffins 49

Apricot Date Loaf 51
Apricot Shake 42
Armenian Pilaf 119
Asparagus, Saucy 57
Avocado Cucumber Soup 149
Avocado Mold 142

B

Bacon And Pea Salad 138
Bake, Dairy Beef 34
Bake, Ham Cauliflower 132
Bake, Quick Ham 132
Bake, Turnip 163
Baked Chops And Stuffing 134
Baked Fish Fillets 110
Baked Onions 164
Baked Pancake 60
Banana Graham Muffins 48
Banana Pie, Blue 122
Barbecued Steak 34
Barm Brack 51
Beacon Shrimp Omelet 55
Bean Salad 137
Beef
    Barbecued Steak 34
    Boiled Roast 37
    Broiled Steak 34
    Chili Modern 34
    Cranberry Meatballs 25
    Crispy Minute Steak 35
    Dairy Beef Bake 34
    Ginger-Sauced Meatballs 24
    Layered Meatloaf 38
    Lazy Ravioli 39
    Mellow Stew 35
    Mexicali Special 39
    Noodle Casserole 32
    Pacific Beef Stir-Fry 38
    Roast And Gravy 36
    Salami Rolls 28
    Shepherd's Pie 35
    Shipwreck 31
    Short Rib Magic 31
    Slow Stew 37
    Swiss Steak Casserole 31
    Stir-Fry Salad 57
    Three Layer Pasta And Beef 32
Beets And Onions 161

Berry Spectacular 100
Beverages
    Apricot Shake 42
    Cranberry Perc 43
    Fruit Shake 43
    Hot Mocha Drink 44
    Orangeade 42
    Party Punch 42
    Peach Shake 42
    Pear Shake 42
    Pink Sunrise Punch 42
    Rhubarb Punch 44
Biscuits, Tuna 55
Bisque, Crab 149
Blackberry Chicken 130
Blackberry Glaze 130
Blackberry Ribs 130
Blue Banana Pie 122
Blueberry Dessert, Creamy 104
Boiled Raisin Cake 64
Boiled Roast 37
Bran Buns 45
Bran Muffins, Apricot 49
Brandied Chicken 86
Brazil Bars 156
Breaded Pork Cutlets 134
Breads & Quick Breads
    Apple Cheese Muffins 48
    Apricot Bran Muffins 49
    Apricot Date Loaf 51
    Banana Graham Muffins 48
    Barm Brack 51
    Bran Buns 45
    Brown Bread 45
    Chelsea Buns 47
    Coconut Muffins 50
    French Puffins 51
    Lemon Muffins 49
    Marshmallow Puffs 60

Month Of Muffins 50
Pineapple Muffins 49
Swedish Tea Ring 58
Sweet Swirl Rolls 58
White Bread 47
Whole Wheat Bread 47
Brie Pizza, Apple 29
Broccoli Rice Chicken 83
Broccoli Salad 137
Broccoli Slaw 137
Broiled Steak 34
Brown Betty 106
Brown Bread 45
Brown Sugar Cookies 98
Brown Sugar Fudge 79
Brown Sugar Pound Cake 72
Brown Sugar Sauce 105
Browner, Gravy 37

Brownies 154
Brunch Cake, Cheese 59
Bubble And Squeak 161
Buns, see Breads & Quick Breads
Butter Date Pie 124
Butter, Old-Time 92

C

Caesar-Dressed Salad 141
Cakes
Berry Spectacular 100
Boiled Raisin 64
Brown Sugar Pound 72
Cheese Brunch 59
Chocolate Date 66
Coffee-Group 68
Dainty Queen 69
Dark Chocolate 66
Friendship 72
Fruitcake 63
Lazy Daisy 74
Lemon Rum 65
Mock Angel 67
Old Hermit 73
Orange 62
Piña Colada 64
Pineapple Nut Coffee 65
Red Velvet 70
Sour Cream 65
Sweet Cream Sponge 73
Syrup 74
Tomato Soup 68
Canapés, Mushroom 20
Candy & Snacks
Brown Sugar Fudge 79
Chili Popcorn 80
Chocolate Crisps 76
Date Loaf Candy 76
Dipped Truffles 78
Double-Decker Fudge 78
Honey Caramels 76
Peanut Crisps 76
Polynesian Popcorn 80
Russian Toffee 75
Ryley's Toffee 76
Spicy Cheddar Popcorn 80
Sponge Toffee 75
Sugar Nuts 79
Truffles 78
Vinegar Candy 78
White Truffles 78
Caramel Chocolate Squares 158
Caramel Icing 158
Caramels, Honey 76
Carrot Pie 128
Carrot Pudding 106
Casserole Lasagne 116
Casseroles
Chicken 82
Noodle 32
Salmon 111
Swiss Steak 31

Zucchini 163
Cauliflower Bake, Ham 132
Cheddar Popcorn, Spicy 80
Cheese Ball, Relish 27
Cheese Bites 18
Cheese Brunch Cake 59
Cheese Muffins, Apple 48
Cheese Pie, Lemon 124
Cheese Tarts 19
Cheesecake Squares, Pumpkin 160
Cheesecake, Turtle 100
Cheesy Manicotti 119
Chelsea Buns 47
Cherry Cola Salad 142
Cherry Cream Pie 122

Chicken
Blackberry 130
Brandied 86
Broccoli Rice 83
Continental 90
Easy 84
Elegant Chicken Phyllo 90
Glazed 88
Ham And Chicken En Croûte 90
Ham And Chicken Loaf 133
Margo's Rosemary 85
Mustard 87
Reverse Cordon Bleu 87
Sesame Wings 23
Teriyaki Chicken Wings 22
Whimsical 86
Chicken And Chutney 85
Chicken Breasts Supreme 88
Chicken Casserole 82
Chicken Chow Mein 84
Chicken Divan 81
Chicken Express 83
Chicken Fried Rice 82
Chicken In Gravy 85
Chicken Strata 54
Chicken With Ginger 88
Chili Con Queso 22
Chili Modern 34

Chili Popcorn .80
Chinese Chews 157
Chip Bars 157
Choco Peanut Dessert Topping 104
Chocolate Cake, Dark 66
Chocolate Crisps 76
Chocolate Crumb Crust 124
Chocolate Date Cake 66
Chocolate Goodies 158
Chocolate Graham Crumb Crust 127
Chocolate Icing 154
Chocolate Mince Squares 158
Chocolate Mocha Icing 66
Chocolate Oatmeal Cookies 94
Chocolate Orange Icing 62
Chocolate Raspberry Dessert 99
Chocolate Squares, Caramel 158
Chops And Stuffing, Baked 134
Chops, Apple Pork 134
Chow Chow Maritime 92
Chow Mein, Chicken 84
Chutney, Chicken And 85
Circus Cookies 95
Cobbler, Fruit 106
Cobbler, Rhubarb 102
Coconut Muffins 50
Coconut Topping 68, 74
Coffee Cake, Pineapple Nut 65
Coffee-Group Cake 68
Cola Salad, Cherry 142
Coleslaw Dressing 145
Compote, Curried Fruit 91
Condiments
    Chow Chow Maritime 92
    Curried Fruit Compote 91
    Old-Time Butter 92
    Pickled Peaches 92
    Spiced Plums 91
Continental Chicken 90
Cooked Salad Dressing 145
Cookies
    Brown Sugar 98
    Chocolate Oatmeal 94
    Circus 95
    Hermits 97
    Nutri .97
    Oatmeal 95
    Oatmeal Crisps 95
    Oatmeal Macaroons 94

    Pan Shortbread 98
    Snappy Gingersnaps 96
    Soft Molasses Drops 96
    Wartime 96
Cool Lime Soufflé 102
Cordon Bleu, Reverse 87
Corn Scallop 164
Crab Bisque 149
Cranberry Jelly Salad 143
Cranberry Meatballs 25
Cranberry Perc 43
Cream Cheese Pastry 19
Cream Of Garlic Soup 148
Cream Of Mushroom Soup 150
Cream Pie, Cherry 122
Cream, Strawberries And 104
Creamy Blueberry Dessert 104
Crispy Minute Steak 35
Crumb Crust, Chocolate 124
Crumb Crust, Chocolate Graham 127
Crust, Graham Cracker 121
Crust, Pizza 29
Cucumber Soup, Avocado 149
Cuke Spread 'R Dip 26
Curried Fruit Compote 91
Cutlets, Breaded Pork 134

D

Dainty Queen Cakes 69
Dairy Beef Bake 34
Dark Chocolate Cake 66
Date Cake, Chocolate 66
Date Filling 155
Date Loaf, Apricot 51
Date Loaf Candy 76
Date Pie, Butter 124
Date Pudding, Quick 103
Dill Sauce 111
Dilled Onions 138
Dipped Truffles 78
Dips
    Chili Con Queso 22
    Cuke Spread 'R 26
    Fluffy 145
    Garlic 26

    Hazelnut 103
    Soy Fire 26
Double-Decker Fudge 78
Dressings, see Salad Dressings
Dumplings, Tomato 161

E

Easy Chicken 84
Egg Salad Mold 142
Elegant Chicken Phyllo 90
Elegant Squash 163

F

Fiddlehead Salad 141
Fillets, Baked Fish 110
Fillings
    Cheese 58, 59, 119
    Date 155
    Mushroom 19
    Tuna 55
    Turkey 55
Finnan Haddie 109
Fish And Sauce 109
Fish & Seafood
    Baked Fish Fillets 110
    Beacon Shrimp Omelet 55
    Crab Bisque 149
    Finnan Haddie 109
    Fluffy Salmon Spread 27
    Laurier Lake "Shrimp" 25
    Lobster Newburg 112
    Niçoise Pasta Salad 56
    Oyster Soup 151
    Salmon Casserole 111
    Salmon Loaf 111

Salmon Pasta Dish 110
Shrimp And Mushroom Soup 151
Tuna Biscuits 55
Fish Sticks 108
Fluffy Dip 145
Fluffy Salmon Spread 27
Four Cheese Lasagne 114
French Puffins 51
Fresh Pea Soup 150
Fresh Raspberry Pie, Glazed 123
Fried Rice, Chicken 82
Friendship Cake 72
Frosted Pumpkin Squares 160
Frozen Peanut Butter Pie 124

Fruit Cobbler 106
Fruit Compote, Curried 91
Fruit In Jelly 107
Fruit Shake 43
Fruitcake 63
Fudge, Brown Sugar 79
Fudge, Double-Decker 78

G

Garbanzo Soup 146
Garden Pasta 115
Garlic Dip 26
Garlic Soup, Cream Of 148
Ginger, Chicken With 88
Ginger Pudding, Steamed 105
Ginger-Sauced Meatballs 24
Gingersnaps, Snappy 96
Glaze, Blackberry 130
Glaze, Lemon 65
Glazed Chicken 88
Glazed Fresh Raspberry Pie 123
Glazed Onions 164
Graham Cracker Crust 121
Graham Cracker Crust, Chocolate 127
Graham Muffins, Banana 48
Granola Bars 60
Gravy Browner 37
Gravy, Chicken In 85
Gravy, Roast And 36

Guacamole Mold 22

H

Ham And Chicken En Croûte 90
Ham And Chicken Loaf 133
Ham Bake, Quick 132
Ham Balls, Mustard 24
Ham Cauliflower Bake 132
Ham Loaf 133
Hazelnut Dip 103
Hermit Cake, Old 73
Hermits .97
Honey Caramels 76
Hot Mocha Drink 44

I, J, K

Icings
    Caramel 158
    Chocolate 154
    Chocolate Mocha 66
    Chocolate Orange 62
    Pineapple 64
    Vanilla 70
    White 154
Impossible Pie 129
Jalapeño Pie 23
Jelly, Fruit In 107
Jelly Salads, see Molded Salads
Kahlúa Pie 127

L

Lasagne, Casserole 116
Lasagne, Four Cheese 114
Laurier Lake "Shrimp" 25
Layered Meatloaf 38
Lazy Daisy Cake 74
Lazy Ravioli 39
Lemon Cheese Pie 124
Lemon Glaze 65
Lemon Muffins 49
Lemon Rum Cake 65
Lentil Spinach Soup 146
Lettuce Salad, Orange 140
Lime Soufflé, Cool 102
Loaf, Apricot Date 51
Loaf, Ham 133
Loaf, Ham And Chicken 133
Loaf, Salmon 111
Lobster Newburg 112

M

Macaroni And Cheese 54
Macaroons, Oatmeal 94
Manicotti, Cheesy 119
Maple-Flavoured Syrup 60
Margo's Rosemary Chicken 85
Marmalade Tarts 127
Marshmallow Puffs 60
Matrimonial Squares 155
Meat Sauce 119
Meatballs, Cranberry 25
Meatballs, Ginger-Sauced 24
Meatloaf, Layered 38
Meringue 125, 128
Mellow Stew 35
Mexicali Special 39
Mince Pie, Mock 125
Mince Squares, Chocolate 158
Minute Steak, Crispy 35
Mocha Drink, Hot 44
Mocha Icing, Chocolate 66
Mock Angel Cake 67
Mock Mince Pie 125
Molasses Drops, Soft 96
Molded Salads
    Avocado 142
    Cranberry Jelly 143
    Egg Salad 142
    Guacamole 22

Month Of Muffins 50
Muffins
    Apple Cheese 48
    Apricot Bran 49
    Banana Graham 48
    Coconut 50
    French Puffins 51
    Lemon 49
    Month of 50
    Pineapple 49
Mushroom Canapés 20
Mushroom Filling 19
Mushroom Salad, Spinach 139

Mushroom Salad, Tomato 139
Mushroom Sauce 109
Mushroom Soup, Cream of 150
Mushroom Soup, Shrimp And 151
Mushroom Surprise 20
Mushroom Toasties 20
Mushroom Turnovers 19
Mushrooms, Pasta And 113
Mushrooms, Stuffed 28
Mustard Chicken 87
Mustard Ham Balls 24
Mystery Squares 154

N

New Magic Squares 155
Niçoise Pasta Salad 56
Noodle Casserole 32
Noodle Slaw 138
Noodles, One-Pot 115
Noodles With Herbs 115
Nothing Dessert 107
Nut Coffee Cake, Pineapple 65
Nut Smacks 156
Nutri Cookies 97
Nuts, Sugar 79

O

Oatmeal Cookies 95
Oatmeal Cookies, Chocolate 94
Oatmeal Crisps 95
Oatmeal Macaroons 94
Oatmeal Pie 123
Old Hermit Cake 73
Old-Time Butter 92
Omelet, Beacon Shrimp 55
One-Pot Noodles 115
Onion Soup 147
Onion Surprise, Pickled 20
Onions, Baked 164
Onions, Beets And 161
Onions, Dilled 138
Onions, Glazed 164
Orange Cake 62

Orange Icing, Chocolate 62
Orange Lettuce Salad 140
Orangeade 42
Oriental, Pasta Salad 136
Oyster Soup 151

P

Pacific Beef Stir-Fry 38
Pan Shortbread 98
Pancake, Baked 60
Parmesan Appies 28
Parsley Pesto Pasta 113
Party Punch 42
Pasta
    Armenian Pilaf 119
    Casserole Lasagne 116
    Cheesy Manicotti 119
    Chicken Casserole 82
    Dairy Beef Bake 34
    Four Cheese Lasagne 114
    Garden 115
    Layered Meatloaf 38
    Lazy Ravioli 39
    Macaroni And Cheese 54
    Mexicali Special 39
    Niçoise Pasta Salad 56
    Noodles With Herbs 115
    One-Pot Noodles 115
    Parsley Pesto 113
    Peanut-Sauced 114
    Pesto-Sauced Salad 136
    Salmon Pasta Dish 110
    Three Layer Pasta And Beef 32
Pasta And Mushrooms 113
Pasta Salad Oriental 136
Pastry, Cream Cheese 19
Pea Salad, Bacon And 138
Pea Soup, Fresh 150
Peach Shake 42
Peaches, Pickled 92
Peanut Butter Pie, Frozen 124
Peanut Butter Squares 159
Peanut Crisps 76
Peanut Dessert Topping, Choco 104
Peanut-Sauced Pasta 114
Pear Shake 42
Pecan Dressing 145
Perogies 118
Pesto Dressing 136

Pesto Pasta, Parsley 113
Pesto-Sauced Salad 136
Phyllo, Elegant Chicken 90
Pickled Onion Surprise 20
Pickled Peaches 92
Pies
    Blue Banana 122
    Butter Date 124
    Carrot 128
    Cherry Cream 122
    Frozen Peanut Butter 124
    Glazed Fresh Raspberry 123
    Impossible 129
    Jalapeño 23
    Kahlúa 127
    Lemon Cheese 124
    Mock Mince 125
    Oatmeal 123
    Shepherd's 35
    Strawberry 126
    Toffee 121
    Vinegar 128
    Working Man's 122
Pilaf, Armenian 119
Piña Colada Cake 64

Pineapple Icing 64
Pineapple Muffins 49
Pineapple Nut Coffee Cake 65
Pink Sunrise Punch 42
Pizza, Apple Brie 29
Pizza Crust 29
Plums, Spiced 91
Polynesian Popcorn 80
Popcorn
    Chili .80
    Polynesian 80
    Spicy Cheddar 80
Poppy Seed Salad 141
Pork
    Apple Pork Chops 134
    Baked Chops And Stuffing 134
    Blackberry Ribs 130
    Breaded Pork Cutlets 134

Ginger-Sauced Meatballs 24
Ham And Chicken En Croûte 90
Ham And Chicken Loaf 133
Ham Cauliflower Bake 132
Ham Loaf 133
Mustard Ham Balls 24
Quick Ham Bake 132
Reverse Cordon Bleu 87
Super Sauerkraut Supper 132
Sweet And Sour 131
Sweet And Sour Ribs 130
Potato Raita 140
Potato Soup 148
Pound Cake, Brown Sugar 72
Puddings
Carrot 106
Quick Date 103
Steamed Ginger 105
Tapioca 103
Pumpkin Cheesecake Squares 160
Pumpkin Soup 148
Pumpkin Squares, Frosted 160
Punches
Party .42
Pink Sunrise 42
Rhubarb 44

Q

Queen Cakes, Dainty 69
Quick Breads, see Breads & Quick Breads
Quick Date Pudding 103
Quick Ham Bake 132

R

Raisin Cake, Boiled 64
Raita, Potato 140
Raspberry Dessert, Chocolate 99
Raspberry Pie, Glazed Fresh 123
Raspberry Sauce 99
Ravioli, Lazy 39
Red Pepper Sauce 118
Red Velvet Cake 70

Relish Cheese Ball 27
Relish Dressing, Tomato 145
Reverse Cordon Bleu 87
Rhubarb Cobbler 102
Rhubarb Punch 44
Ribs
Blackberry 130
Short Rib Magic 31
Sweet And Sour 130
Rice Chicken, Broccoli 83
Rice, Chicken Fried 82
Rice Stuffing, Wild 165
Roast And Gravy 36
Roast, Boiled 37
Rolls, Sweet Swirl 58
Rosemary Chicken, Margo's 85
Rum Cake, Lemon 65
Russian Toffee 75
Ryley's Toffee 76

S

Salad Dressings
Coleslaw 145
Cooked Salad 145
Pecan 145
Pesto 136
Sunny 145
Tomato Relish 145
Salads
Avocado Mold 142
Bacon And Pea 138
Bean 137
Broccoli 137
Broccoli Slaw 137
Caesar-Dressed 141
Cherry Cola 142
Cranberry Jelly 143
Dilled Onions 138
Egg Salad Mold 142
Fiddlehead 141
Niçoise Pasta 56
Noodle Slaw 138
Orange Lettuce 140
Pasta Salad Oriental 136
Pesto-Sauced 136
Poppy Seed 141
Potato Raita 140
Spinach Mushroom 139

Springtime 141
Stir-Fry 57
Sweet Wheat 140
Tomato Mushroom 139
Salami Rolls 28
Salmon Casserole 111
Salmon Loaf 111
Salmon Pasta Dish 110
Salmon Spread, Fluffy 27
Sandwiches, Turkey 55
Sauces
Brown Sugar 105
Dill .111
Meat 119
Mushroom 109
Peanut 114
Raspberry 99
Red Pepper 118
Seafood 55
Smoky Sweet And Sour Sauce 130
Sweet And Sour 131

Saucy Asparagus 57
Sauerkraut Supper, Super 132
Scallop, Apple 57
Scallop, Corn 164
Seafood Sauce 55
Sesame Wings 23
Shakes
Apricot 42
Fruit .43
Peach 42
Pear .42
Shepherd's Pie 35
Shipwreck 31
Short Rib Magic 31
Shortbread, Pan 98
Shrimp And Mushroom Soup 151
"Shrimp," Laurier Lake 25
Shrimp Omelet, Beacon 55
Slaw, Broccoli 137
Slaw, Noodle 138
Slow Stew 37
Smoky Sweet And Sour Sauce 130

Snappy Gingersnaps 96
Soft Molasses Drops 96
Soufflé, Cool Lime 102
Soups
    Avocado Cucumber 149
    Crab Bisque 149
    Cream Of Garlic 148
    Cream Of Mushroom 150
    Fresh Pea 150
    Garbanzo 146
    Lentil Spinach 146
    Onion .147
    Oyster .151
    Potato .148
    Pumpkin 148
    Shrimp And Mushroom 151
Sour Cream Cake 65
Soy Fire Dip 26
Spiced Plums 91
Spicy Cheddar Popcorn 80
Spinach Balls 27
Spinach Mushroom Salad 139
Spinach Soup, Lentil 146
Sponge Cake, Sweet Cream 73
Sponge Toffee 75
Spread, Fluffy Salmon 27
Springtime Salad 141
Squares
    Brazil Bars 156
    Brownies 154
    Caramel Chocolate 158
    Chinese Chews 157
    Chip Bars 157
    Chocolate Goodies 158
    Chocolate Mince 158
    Frosted Pumpkin 160
    Matrimonial 155
    Mystery 154
    New Magic 155
    Nut Smacks 156
    Peanut Butter 159
    Pumpkin Cheesecake 160
    Tropical 154

Squash, Elegant 163
Steak
    Barbecued 34
    Broiled 34
    Crispy Minute 35
    Swiss Steak Casserole 31
Steamed Ginger Pudding 105
Stew, Mellow 35
Stew, Slow 37
Stir-Fry, Pacific Beef 38
Stir-Fry Salad 57
Strata, Chicken 54
Strata, Turkey 54
Strawberries And Cream 103
Strawberry Pie 126
Stuffed Mushrooms 28
Stuffing, Baked Chops And 134
Stuffing Balls 165
Stuffing, Wild Rice 165
Sugar Nuts 79
Sunny Dressing 145
Super Sauerkraut Supper 132
Swedish Tea Ring 58
Sweet And Sour Pork 131
Sweet And Sour Ribs 130
Sweet Cream Sponge Cake 73
Sweet Swirl Rolls 58
Sweet Wheat Salad 140
Swiss Steak Casserole 31
Syrup Cake 74
Syrup, Maple-Flavoured 60

T

Taffy Topping 74
Tapioca Pudding 103
Tarts, Cheese 19
Tarts, Marmalade 127
Tea Ring, Swedish 58
Teriyaki Chicken Wings 22
Three Layer Pasta And Beef 32
Toffee
    Russian 75
    Ryley's 76
    Sponge 75
Toffee Pie 121
Tomato Dumplings 161
Tomato Mushroom Salad 139
Tomato Relish Dressing 145

Tomato Soup Cake 68
Topping, Coconut 68, 74
Topping, Taffy 74
Tropical Squares 154
Truffles 78
Truffles, Dipped 78
Truffles, White 78
Tuna Biscuits 55
Turkey Sandwiches 55
Turkey Strata 54
Turnip Bake 163
Turnovers, Mushroom 19
Turtle Cheesecake 100

V

Vanilla Icing 70
Vinegar Candy 78
Vinegar Pie 128

W

Wartime Cookies 96
Wheat Salad, Sweet 140
Whimsical Chicken 86
White Bread 47
White Icing 154
White Truffles 78
Whole Wheat Bread 47
Wild Rice Stuffing 165
Wings, Sesame 23
Wings, Teriyaki Chicken 22
Working Man's Pie 122

Z

Zucchini Casserole 163
Zucchini Treats 25

"...that's what I would really like to see in the future—all of us gathering in the kitchen, creating cherished memories."

Jean Paré